Like John Owen, Steve Griffiths is a
deep love for Christ and for his word, and who is passionately
concerned to make the teaching of the Bible relevant to his inner-
city congregation in the twenty-first century. Further, he also shares
Owen's respect for the historic testimony of the Christian church
and acknowledges the need for believers today to wrestle with and
be guided by the cumulative insights and perspectives of the church
of the past. In this book, the reader will find an example of just such
wrestling, as Griffiths comes to grips with the teaching of that giant
of the church, John Owen, on the crucial issue of sin. In a therapeutic
and self-obsessed age such as ours, the church needs to hear again
the Pauline teaching on sin and grace which Owen expounded so
brilliantly. I trust that Dr Griffith's book, the work of a minister and
of a theologian, will help to bring this about.

Carl R Trueman
Associate Professor of Church History
and Historical Theology,
Westminster Theological Seminary,
Philadelphia.

John Owen, prince of Puritan theologians, continues to be the subject
of continued interest and research, and Steve Griffith's work is a
welcome addition to material on Owen. He rightly sees Owen's sense
of sin and its seriousness as fundamental to his theology, and is
concerned to expound Owen's doctrine as it relates to sin in the
individual, in society and in the church. Only thus can we see the
richness of God's grace in providing a sufficient redemption in Jesus
Christ. By studying Owen in his own terms, rather than in his relation
to other theologians, Griffiths has given an honest portrait of both
the greatness of the man and the greatness of his message.

Iain D. Campbell
Free Church of Scotland

To Clare and Rebekah,
both of whom have been my teachers in the faith.

This book is dedicated
to the memory of my dear sister Jackie,
who now knows in full what we know only in part.

Redeem the Time

*The problem of sin
in the writings of John Owen*

Steve Griffiths

Mentor

ISBN 185792 655 2

Published in 2001
by Christian Focus Publications,
Geanies House, Fearn, Ross-shire
IV20 1TW, Great Britain

Cover design by Owen Daily

Contents

FOREWORD *by Dr. Sinclair B. Ferguson*.......5

INTRODUCTION.......7

1. OWEN'S THEOLOGICAL FRAMEWORK.......17
Federal Theology.......18
The Nature of Man.......29
The Nature of Sin.......44
Conclusion.......53

2. SIN AND THE INDIVIDUAL.......57
Sin in the Mind.......59
Sin in the Affections.......78
Sin in the Will.......82
The Destruction of the Image.......86
The Body and the Outworking of Sin.......89
The Influence of Satan.......91
Conclusion.......93

3. SIN AND SOCIETY.......95
The Idea of 'Nation' and Nationalism.......100
Sin and the Monarchy.......103
The Millennial Hope.......108
The Re-admittance of the Jews to England.......116
Owen and Republicanism.......121
Owen after the Restoration.......130
God's Providence.......136
Conclusion.......142

4. SIN AND THE CHURCH.......145

Election and Covenant.......146

The Justification for Separation.......153

Arminianism.......164

Socinianism.......174

Quakerism.......178

Roman Catholicism.......184

Conclusion.......193

5. SIN AND THE NEED FOR HOLINESS.......195

Corporate Holiness.......195

Spiritual Mindedness.......206

The Nature and Practice of Mortification.......209

Union with Christ.......218

Conclusion.......224

CONCLUSION.......227

BIBLIOGRAPHY.......237

NOTES.......249

SCRIPTURE INDEX.......303

PERSONS INDEX.......307

FOREWORD

When J C Ryle (Bishop of Liverpool in the late nineteenth century) published his now famous book entitled *Holiness*, he introduced his theme – to the surprise of many – with a vigorous chapter on sin. His opening words concisely stated his reasons: 'He that wishes to attain right views about Christian holiness must begin by examining the vast and solemn subject of sin. He must dig down very low if he would build high.'

This paradox – if we are to experience the grace that leads to godliness we must discover the depths and hidden layers of the presence and subtle power of sin – is one that is apparently difficult for us twenty-first century Christians to grasp. We are more used to being taught that we must cease to think in such categories, to eschew all 'worm theology' which demeans our humanity and our dignity (when in fact it is only thus that we take our humanity and dignity seriously). Today we are more accustomed to being encouraged to develop a better self image and an increased sense of self-worth. Yet, clearly, Ryle's paradox was lifted straight out of the Bible: only the sin conscious become grace conscious; only by grace do we become godly. Only when we sense how much we have been forgiven do we begin to love much in return (Luke 7:47). There is a necessary, logical, spiritual cycle here which we dismiss at our peril.

Ryle had learned this principle from David and from Paul, and he had discovered the most profound exposition and application of it in the great seventeenth-century Oxford pastoral theologian John Owen.

Dr. Stephen Griffiths, the author of this fine work, is also, like Ryle, an Anglican minister and has come on a similar pilgrimage. For his interest in the doctrine of sin is not merely academic and technical, but deeply personal and pastoral. Having grasped Ryle's paradox for himself, he has turned to the study of the writings of Owen, Ryle's teacher, and now presents us with the fruit of his studies.

So here we have the privilege of the best of several worlds: a study of a monumentally important Christian doctrine which simultaneously leads us into the life of one of the most significant reformed theologians at one of the most critical times in the history of the English church, and then provides us with the bonus of theology that is pastorally relevant in our contemporary world.

To read John Owen is to enter a rare world. Whenever I return to one of his works I find myself asking, 'Why do I spend time reading lesser literature?' I believe all lovers of John Owen and his writings, like myself, will salute Dr. Griffiths for sharing with us the results of his arduous studies. And all 'serious readers' (to use Owen's own way of describing you!) will appreciate the deep impact of concentrated thought on such a central theme in biblical theology. In a day when pastoralia is often very untheological, and theology very unpastoral, the rediscovery of Owen's theology has proved to be a great blessing to many. Into that blessing I hope you will now allow Dr. Griffiths to lead you.

Sinclair B Ferguson
St. George's-Tron Church
Glasgow

INTRODUCTION

The increasing awareness of the importance of John Owen's writings is a welcome development in recent years.[1] His influence on seventeenth-century theology, ecclesiology and politics was so immense that any true analysis of that period ignores him at its own peril. As each generation rediscovers him afresh, so that acknowledgement of his importance is bound to grow. There is certainly no denying his importance to the development of the English Reformed tradition. Owen was a leading theological light, respected, by ally and enemy alike, for the depth and clarity of his theological and pastoral capabilities. Whilst there were many who did not agree with him they could never ignore him, for his influence in both Church and State was pivotal, as a short biographical outline will reveal.[2]

John Owen was born at Stadham[3] in Oxfordshire in 1616, the son of a Puritan clergyman, and received an education at Queen's College, Oxford. Soon after receiving the degree of MA in 1635, Owen was ordained deacon. He spent some time as a private tutor before publishing his first work, *A Display of Arminianism,* in 1642 and taking up the living of Fordham in Essex. The following year, he married a Miss Mary Rooke, with whom he had eleven children. There is only scant information available about these children, despite the valiant efforts of Owen's biographer, Peter Toon. To date, the only information has been about the baptism of their first son, John,[4] the marriage partner of daughter Mary,[5] and the burial information of Judith[6] and melon-loving Mathew![7] In *God's Statesman*, Toon also draws attention to a reference in a contemporary letter that two of the children died during the Oxford plague of 1655.[8] For the first time, extra information about the children can be given in this book; other personal details as well as the names of four more children – Mary, Elizah, Thomas and Elizabeth.[9]

Owen had made many influential contacts during his time at Oxford and it was not long before he was thrust into the public

arena through an invitation to preach before Parliament at the end
of the first civil war in April 1646.[10] His ensuing move to St.
Peter's, Coggeshall saw the beginnings of his Congregationalist
tendencies[11] and it was during this time that his theological
masterpiece on the atonement was published: *Salus Electorum,
Sanguis Jesu; or The Death of Death in the Death of Christ*.[12]

Owen was introduced to Oliver Cromwell following a sermon
preached to Parliament in April 1649 and he was invited to become
one of his chaplains. This inevitably increased his spiritual
involvement in political life and he was appointed preacher to the
Council of State before taking up the post of Dean at Christ Church,
Oxford and, thereafter, of Vice-Chancellor. Following a public
division between himself and Cromwell, which will be chronicled
later in this work, Owen left the position in 1657 and this marked
the beginning of his disappearance from public life. He did take
an active role in the Savoy Assembly in 1658 but the following
year he was accused of plotting the overthrow of Richard
Cromwell; an accusation he strenuously denied four years later,
claiming that he 'never had a hand...unto any political alteration'.[13]
As the Restoration movement strengthened, Owen increasingly
forsook the public arena and concentrated on his literary and
pastoral tasks, primarily in Oxford and London.

However, far from this being a retirement, it marked the
beginning of a new phase of ministry that was no less controversial
than his activities in previous years. At this time, Owen was offered
– but did not take up – an invitation to the First Congregational
Church in Boston[14] and the Presidency of Harvard College.[15]
Furthermore, and as a result of his 1662 publication
Animadversions on a Treatise Entitled 'Fiat Lux',[16] Lord
Clarendon[17] offered Owen a preferment in the restored Church of
England but he turned this down. Indeed, Owen's nonconformity
was, if anything, strengthening with the publication of *A Discourse
concerning Liturgies, and Their Imposition*.[18] His nonconformity
eventually led to his prosecution in 1665 for holding meetings in
his Stadham home. Following the easing of restrictions in 1672
under the Declaration of Indulgence, his congregation united with
that of the deceased Joseph Caryl,[19] one of his closest companions

throughout the previous two decades, in Leadenhall Street, London.

Owen's literary output continued unabated in the years leading up to his death. It was during this period that he wrote some works that were destined to play a major part in the legacy of Owen to future generations, most notably his *Pneumatologia or, Discourse Concerning the Holy Spirit* [20] and his magnificent *Exposition of the Epistle to the Hebrews*.[21] Owen believed the latter to be the culmination of his life's work. In his funeral oration for Owen, David Clarkson[22] commented that 'His excellent *Comment upon the Hebrews* gain'd him a name and esteem, not only at home, but in foreign countries. When he had finished it...he said, Now his work was done, it was time for him to die.' Owen continued to write and act as pastor to his congregations, despite his failing health, until his death on 24 August 1683 at home in Ealing.[23] In his funeral address, Clarkson said that Owen was 'a great light...one of eminency for holiness and learning and pastoral abilities.'

But in what theological category can we put Owen? By what label can we describe his theology? Standing firmly in the Reformed Orthodox tradition, Owen was a recognised leader in the Puritan movement. Much has been written by way of examining the nature and defining features of the Puritans and Puritanism. I do not propose to do the same in this work. Yet to label Owen a Puritan creates as many problems as it solves, since the very notion of a Puritan is difficult to define and common denominators amongst the Puritan community are hard to find.[24] As Tyacke has commented, 'To some extent, Puritanism has always existed in the eye of the beholder.'[25] This is especially the case with the seventeenth century, a time when many within the established church aligned themselves with the Puritans, not through any allegiance to their teaching but purely in an effort to avoid the Catholicism that was purportedly endorsed by Archbishop Laud.[26] In this sense, all 'anti-Arminians' came to be known as 'Puritans' despite the fact that they might not endorse orthodox Calvinism specifically or 'Puritan' thought in general.[27] Nevertheless, 'Puritanism' is an accepted term amongst scholars and is one that must be considered.

As Collinson suggests, words ending in -ism were rarely used in Tudor and Stuart times to describe abstract principles,[28] so it is perhaps more apt to define Puritanism by the Puritans themselves rather than *vice versa*. This book accepts the idea that the Puritan era is to be taken as the century between the Acts of Uniformity: 1559-1662. Acknowledging, amongst others, the works of Knappen,[29] Trinterud[30] and Porter[31] in this vital task of definition, I accept the idea that the focus of Puritanism is on two specific areas: ecclesiology and spirituality. The Puritan movement can be defined ecclesiologically as symbolising the efforts of those 'hotter sort of Protestants'[32] who believed in the continuance of 'one National Church in England' whilst also desiring that the Church 'be reformed after the model of Geneva'.[33] Trinterud concurs with this view when he states that 'Defined as simply as possible, Puritanism was the Protestant form of dissatisfaction with the official religion of England...'[34] The reform of the Church was certainly a key issue for the Reformed tradition of the seventeenth century, both within and outside the established church, and is a major component of any definition of Puritanism. However, in contradistinction to this, William Perkins[35] has historically been listed amongst the Puritans despite rejecting it as a 'vile' term himself[36] and, ironically, never having published a word concerning the modification of Church government, despite his fringe involvement in a Cambridge Presbyterian movement.[37] Thus, when applied theologically or as a religious term, Puritanism incorporates a wider field of interest than that expressed by ecclesiastical interests alone. The term is also taken to denote the ideals of a holy community with a profound moral earnestness in life: 'Puritanism was something more than a system of doctrine. It was above all...a life, a real, earnest, practical life.'[38] Certainly the Puritans were separated from non-Puritans through the distinctive religious psychology by which they were characterised and even caricatured.[39] Whatever perspective is taken on the Puritan tradition, Owen falls within it. But it remains a non-specific term, arguably too loose to serve any real purpose.

Similarly, the term 'Calvinist' will not suffice as a description of Owen. Certainly Owen believed that his own thought was set firmly within the Calvinist tradition. He was happy to be included 'among Protestants, as being *Reformatists*, or as they call us, *Calvinists*'[40] and much of what he wrote was acceptable to both 'moderate' and 'high' Calvinists alike. But to label Owen a 'Calvinist', with the connotations of a twentieth-century understanding, is again too limiting, since the theology he endorsed was constructed out of a tradition amongst which Calvin was but one figure. Owen had the masterful ability to cast his net wide in search of God's truth and his influences are a reflection of that. It is noticeable, for instance, that Aquinas is quoted more often than Calvin in Owen's works. Augustine's writings are perhaps the richest source of all. And alongside these, Owen draws deeply on the wells of historical theology to illustrate and inform his own ideas; Greek philosophers, biblical and patristic writers, Reformation theologians, contemporary colleagues, even Catholic theologians are credited where Owen believes credit to be due. In the light of this, perhaps it would be more accurate, then, to think of Owen as 'Reformed' since that is a term more able to carry the wide implications of Owen's thought.

The recent emergence of Owenian research has already been noted. At last, Owen seems to be getting the attention and respect he deserves as a key seventeenth-century figure. In defence of adding to that research, three points need to be made which will anticipate the objectives of the ensuing book.

First, the doctrine of sin was foundational to Owen's writings. Not just Owen, either: few, if any, substantial Reformed works were published without reference to, or containing analysis of, sin, as we shall see throughout this work. Whilst it is certainly true that all Owenian scholars have, to some degree, touched on his understanding of sin, there has not been any work to date that focuses in detail on this topic. This is a somewhat surprising omission, given the centrality of the idea of fallen humanity in Owen's theological scheme. Gleason came closest in his publication, *John Calvin and John Owen on Mortification*. Sadly however, he missed the opportunity by becoming embroiled in the anachronistic and unhelpful 'Calvin and the Calvinists' debate that will be detailed below. Packer took a pastoral rather than theological approach in *Among God's Giants*. Nevertheless, the need for a focused consideration is still there. This present work, then, aims to meet a very real need in deepening our understanding of Owen and locating him within his context.

Secondly, this work will make some attempt to prevent the fossilisation of Owenian research before it has had a chance to flourish. To clarify: it seems that recent work on Owen has primarily been carried out within the context of the 'Calvin and the Calvinists' debate. This is a vital issue which arose through Basil Hall's 1966 essay, 'Calvin against the Calvinists'[41] and which has since been developed by a number of scholars, not least in the 1979 publication of R.T. Kendall's thesis, *Calvin and English Calvinism to 1649*.[42] That book developed the controversial idea that the English Reformed tradition had moved so far away from the teachings of Calvin, through the influence of Beza, that, in reality, the Arminians were closer to Calvin's thought than they. The work came in for much criticism, primarily by Paul Helm in his article 'Calvin, English Calvinism and the Logic of Doctrinal Development'[43] and by W. Stanford Reid in his article 'A Review of Kendall "Calvin and English Calvinism to 1649"'.[44] As a result of these critiques, Kendall's thesis has been largely discredited, an opinion which the current thesis upholds. Whilst this has been an exceptionally important debate to have, it is worrying to see that most of the ensuing work on Owen has deviated little *in context* from that argument. Whatever aspect of Owen's theology has been examined, it has usually been done so with regard to his continuity or otherwise with the teachings of Calvin. One effect of this is that Owen has rarely been considered, other than by Toon, Packer and Trueman, as a theologian in his specific historical context. The aim of this book, then, is to do just that; to consider Owen's writings on sin within the historical setting in which he wrote and pastored. That is not to say that the 'Calvin and the Calvinists' debate will be ignored but only that it is not pivotal to the argument of this book.

Third, this work aims to pick up the left-handed gauntlet thrown down by Toon in *God's Statesman*:

It must be admitted that despite the many new facts about his career and connexions which have come to light in this study, Owen as a man, as a human being, still remains an elusive character. After reading the *Reliquiae* or Dr. Nuttall's biography, one feels that one knows Owen's contemporary, Richard Baxter, as a real, living person, but the same cannot be said of Owen after reading this or previous 'Memoirs.'[45]

Toon is right, of course. To date, no one has yet managed to reveal Owen *the man*. In an attempt to meet this challenge, new questions have had to be asked of Owen and a new premise has had to be sought in approaching his writings, namely: what was of *fundamental* importance to Owen and what was his *primary* motivation in ministry? The answer is blindingly simple. Owen was a pastor. Of fundamental importance to him was the spiritual growth of those amongst whom he ministered. His primary motivation was the growth in holiness of his flock. Everything else stems from that truth. He was not *primarily* concerned with unswerving faithfulness, or otherwise, to Calvin, Aristotle or Augustine. He was not *fundamentally* concerned with loyalty to any one theological tradition. Owen's first loyalty was to no man. God was his judge and he was acutely aware that he would be judged on his performance as a minister of the gospel.

Taking that as the premise for this book, we are able to meet with Owen *the man* and explore his doctrine of sin in the context of his pastoral ministry. So, in the course of the following pages, we will relate to Owen as dedicated pastor, father, gardener, keen (though presumably moderate) ale drinker, university disciplinarian, polemical wit, political agitator, radical adviser, formidable opponent, theological genius and much more. But, always, his doctrine of sin influenced, informed and dictated his activities and writings.

As his writings are examined we shall see that, throughout his life, Owen appeared to retain an essentially unchanging understanding of the nature and effect of sin; his theological and philosophical framework remained basically constant. However, the manner in which he approached the topic in practice was not so static. Owen's application of his theology was always worked out in the light of the circumstances in which he found himself. Owen tailored his understanding of sin to the needs and situation of the audience to which he wrote. Because of this, Owen can never be accused of turning out dry theology that has no practical use. On the contrary, his writings were imbued with a vitality that went to the very heart of the reality of sin as it is found within the created order and, crucially, in contemporary events and debates.

The intention of this book can be anticipated by a brief overview of the five chapters. In Chapter One, consideration is given to the theological framework that supported Owen's doctrine of sin. A working definition for Owen was that sin is an aberration from the image of God in the individual and Owen's philosophical and theological foundations for developing that idea are laid out there. Chapter Two then builds on this by considering the very nature of sin itself and exactly how it works in the individual. Chapter Three aims to examine a much broader, and perhaps more conceptual, aspect of Owen's teaching: that sin is not only a problem for each individual before God but that it also has corporate implications that reflect on the life of the nation. Chapter Four continues this theme of corporate sin but this time examines the manner in which it is present within the Church. Finally, Chapter Five examines Owen's teaching on the need for holiness both in the corporate bodies of State and Church and in each individual. The relationship between sin and holiness is analysed here. It is hoped that by approaching the topic in this way adequate detail will be given over to Owen's theological teaching but always in the light of the historical setting in which he is situated. As we embark on our study of Owen's approach to sin, our aim is to come to an appreciation of just how central this idea of fallen humanity was to every aspect of Owen's theological thought and activity.

The emphasis that Owen laid on sin was no morbid obsession. Rather, that which was at stake for Owen was a true doctrine of God and a vindication of His character in the light of a corrupted and broken created order. Owen's treatment of sin does not and cannot stand in isolation; it can only be considered in the light of his doctrine of God and what it means for the believer to reflect that image. Reformed teaching on such topics as predestination, election, assurance of salvation, pneumatology, christology and so on are inextricably bound up with the notion of sin. This work aims to explain and explore the correlation among these various doctrines as Owen treats them and to analyse their interdependence.

Owen believed sin to be a great problem. But he also believed in a great God who could counter the effects of the Fall. Outlined in the following pages is the manner in which Owen approached this epic relationship between the Creator and his beloved creatures.

1

OWEN'S THEOLOGICAL FRAMEWORK

No theology is developed in a vacuum. It is the result of men and women seeking after God in their own particular context and that context is, at the very least, both sociological and theological. John Owen was no exception to this. Any accurate assessment of his teaching on sin must necessarily begin with an analysis of that context. The purpose of this first chapter, then, is to explore the theological framework within which Owen developed his teaching on sin. The historical context, although implicit in this chapter, will become more apparent as we move through our work.

The seventeenth century was an exciting time to be engaged in academic pursuits. A storm of fresh and creative thinking was raging across the Continent and influencing English thought, in almost every discipline. Science was on the verge of enjoying significant triumphs. Philosophical and political disciplines were engaging in new thought about the nature and status of humanity. Related to all this was the rise of new interpretations of Scripture and the questioning of the function, even the validity, of ecclesiastical authority. In every way, the seventeenth century was a major transitional epoch from medievalism to the modern world.[1]

Whilst many hoped to challenge the claims of Christianity with the new learning,[2] still others perceived the advances of knowledge as no real threat to the ultimate truths of the Christian faith. Owen fell within this latter category for one simple reason. He believed that no new knowledge or depth of learning could alter the basic truth about humanity: that the individual enjoys, or was created to enjoy, a relationship with God.[3] Whatever else may be discovered about the nature of man, or even the nature of the cosmos, nothing can detract from this fundamental truth. Furthermore, the reality of sin was, for Owen, another fundamental truth. Humanity was destined for a life with God but sin prevents that.[4] Victory over sin is the ultimate quest for every individual. Owen was to devote his life and ministry to that quest.

The nature of that quest is, of course, open to interpretation. As we have already noted, Owen stood within the Reformed milieu and so his teaching on sin presupposed certain understandings prominent within this interpretative model of Christian doctrine. Foundational to his approach was the relationship between covenant and the image of God within humanity. An examination of Owen's treatment of this relationship is essential to contextualise his teaching on the nature of sin itself.

Federal Theology

The idea of a covenant relationship, the notion that the believer's relationship with God is founded on one or more mutual covenants or promises, is foundational to much Reformed theology. As we shall see below, this federal theology has been subject to a variety of interpretations, not least in seventeenth-century England. Despite these differences however, John Ball spoke for perhaps the entire tradition when he outlined the reasoning behind such an approach. Covenant between man and God is needed:

> First that the creature might know what to expect from the Creator, into what state soever cast. Secondly, that the same creature might always recognise and acknowledge what to retribute. Thirdly, such manner as dealing suites best withe the nature of the reasonable creature, and his subordination to the Almighty.[5]

This federal theology was understood by many to provide the key to the interpretation of Christian experience. Most importantly for our purposes, the concept of divine covenant, by which are linked to the provisions of God certain promises and threats corresponding to faithfulness or disobedience on the part of the individual,[6] provides the foundation for a Reformed doctrine of sin. This is certainly the case in Owen's treatment of sin in that he was unequivocal about the fact that these covenants made between man and God are agreements that form the basis of any subsequent relationship.[7]

By way of introduction, we would do well to note that Owen's federal reading of Scripture reflected not just the shape of the biblical material but also elements within contemporary society. The feudalism of medieval society was disintegrating at a rapid rate, not least in England where the existence of itinerants, travellers and vagabonds had become an increasing part of modern-day life.[8] The bonds of contract between master and servant were becoming increasingly obsolete, which, in part, was resulting in instability and a lack of social cohesion. The need for order and a sense of personal responsibility was considered paramount in preventing civilised society coming apart at the seams.[9] The Puritan response, in part, was to internalise that sense of discipline.

We must not underestimate Owen's concern for order in matters spiritual. Order was at the heart of his ecclesiology such that his desire was for '*the church* [to] *render the worship itself in its performance more decent, beautiful, and orderly*'[10] and for 'the gathering of the saints into complete church-order'.[11] The negation of order is one effect of sin on the mind as 'this hath befallen it by the loss of that fixed regularity which it was created in'.[12] Most vitally, order is at the very heart of God, revealed to us through the graces of Christ, and this sense of order is fundamental to federal theology:

> So are the graces of Christ; in the gospel they are distinctly and in order set forth, that sinners by faith may view them, and take from him according to their necessity. They are ordered for the use of the saints in the promises of the gospel...and on the account hereof is the covenant said to be 'ordered in all things' (2 Sam. 23:5).[13]

Owen reflected the desire of contemporary society for order and cohesion in all things. As much as federalism can be advanced as a valid theological system in itself, it is important not to underestimate the historical context in which it was developed.

The exact theological development of federal theology is a complex issue. It is not our purpose to examine the history of this in any real depth but only inasmuch as it relates to Owen's own thought. Nevertheless, a brief overview does pave the way for us to realise the remarkable way in which Owen was able to draw threads from differing traditions and hold them together in a coherent and logical system.

Initially, we are bound to recognise the fundamental difference between the federal theology of the English Reformed tradition in juxtaposition to that of Continental Reformers in the seventeenth century. Whilst federal theology was foundational to Continental Reformed theology, it was not linked in the same way to matters of conscience, as Muller states:

> In England more than on the continent the complex analysis of 'cases of conscience' became characteristic of Reformed piety. The English Puritans contributed a wealth of treatises and sermons on problems of individual conduct and piety, to the point that several seventeenth century thinkers observed with pride that the continent looked to England for definitive formulations of practical theology. In these works the Puritan moralists examined each problem, anxiety, and temptation confronting the Christian life as a case to be tried at the bar of God's saving will....Inward moral controversies might thereby become...evidences of personal communion with God's saving will under the covenant of grace.[14]

This differing emphasis in English federalism may perhaps be accounted for by the fact that it developed, to an extent, independently of Continental theology. Tyndale had expressed a primitive concept of federal theology as early as 1527:

> Our mind, intent, and affection or zeal, are blind, and all that we do of them, is condemned of God; and for that cause hath God made a testament between him and us, wherein is contained both what he would have us to do, and what he would have us ask of him.[15]

For Tyndale, God and humanity are integrally linked by a covenant relationship that has obligations on both parties. Tyndale's approach seems to suggest that the covenant relationship is a contractual one; that God's saving activity is dependent on the response of the individual. However, as Trueman suggests, the context of Tyndale's writings shows otherwise:

It is clear...that Tyndale's view of the covenant cannot be contractual. He rejects the idea that the works merit salvation in any intrinsic way. More importantly, he bases his conception of the covenant upon the prior establishment of the familial relationship between God and man. This relationship originates in the unilateral act of God in salvation, and is founded upon love, not commercial considerations... The covenant concept does not introduce the idea of works as a condition of salvation; rather, it is to provide a convenient framework within which to underline this ethical imperative: it is to make the sons of God obedient rather than the obedient the sons of God.[16]

The relationship between covenant and contract is one that has been much debated, especially concerning the Continental development of federal theology. Trinterud's identification of the apparent polarisation between Calvin and Olevianus on the one hand and Luther and Bullinger on the other[17] is a faulty reading of history, as Bierma has shown.[18] The notion that Genevan Reformers taught a unilateral and unconditional covenant relationship whilst the Rhineland Reformers taught a bilateral contractual relationship appears to be an untenable idea. The Continental Reformers were acting largely independent of Tyndale.[19] Greenhough suggests that, because of chronological and geographical considerations, the cross-fertilisation of thought amongst Reformers could have occurred between Luther and Tyndale and between Luther and Calvin but not between Tyndale and Calvin. Given these restrictions, however, they were developing a similar approach to federalism, namely that the covenant relationship incorporates both a unilateral and a bilateral dimension. To quote Bierma on this vital issue,

What scholars from Trinterud to Baker have failed to realize is that *all* the sixteenth-century Reformed theologians – Zwingli, Bullinger, Calvin, Olevianus, Musculus, Ursinus, Perkins etc. – recognized both a unilateral and a bilateral dimension to the covenant of grace.... The mainstream of Reformed theology... – including both the Zurich and the Genevan covenant traditions – flowed into the seventeenth century well between these two poles.[20]

Federal theology had become foundational for English Reformed thinking by the seventeenth century and Owen's own ministry. It seems plausible that this was the result of the amalgamation of both the independent development of the English tradition and a reflection of Continental thought. The strands of thought informing contemporary Reformed thinking were varied indeed. Concerning the specific influences on Owen's concept of federalism, more will be said below. Suffice it at this point to mention that the bilateral approach was fundamental to Owen's understanding of the doctrine.

The nature of this covenant relationship, then, is understood in the same manner throughout the Reformed movement of the sixteenth and seventeenth centuries. Where there is less agreement, however, is on the number of covenants made between man and God. Clearly there is much within Calvin's teaching to suggest that he was working within a covenantal framework.[21] Indeed, if that were not there, it would be difficult to account for the rise of a developed form of federal theology in the Calvinist tradition, initially through the *Summa Theologiæ* of Ursinus, within two decades of the French Reformer's death. Nevertheless, the covenant of works, which was a fundamental aspect of Owen's federalism, was absent from Calvin's teaching. The idea that God made a covenant with Adam that guaranteed eternal life in return for his work of obedience – a covenant which was broken through the Fall – was not something which Calvin elucidated. For him, there is only one covenant: the covenant of grace that stands for all time: 'God has never made any other covenant than that which he made formerly with Abraham, and at length confirmed by the hand of Moses.'[22]

It was in the Westminster Confession of Faith that the Reformed notion of federal theology was given official sanction in England.[23] The development of, and perhaps the departure from, the teachings of Calvin is clear in this document. The idea of two covenants was outlined, namely a covenant of works and a covenant of grace. It must be stressed, however, that the Westminster Confession of Faith was not the first to propose this idea. It had already been cited in 1594 by the Dutch supralapsarian Franz Gomarus in his

Oratio de foedere Dei, although he did not offer a systematised federalism.[24] Whilst Gomarus did not specifically speak of covenants of works and grace, it has been proposed that his *foedus gratiae* and *foedus supranaturale* are the same concepts in form if not in name.[25] Karl Barth, in *Church Dogmatics*, attributed the conception of the two-fold covenant understanding directly to Ursinus:

> The introduction of what later became the dominant twofold concept must be attributed to Ursinus...There is a *foedus naturae* which was contracted with man at creation and is therefore known to man by nature. It promises eternal life to those who obey, but threatens eternal punishment to those who disobey. In contrast there is a *foedus gratiae* which is not known to man by nature. This is the fulfilling of the Law accomplished by Christ, our restoration by His Spirit, the free promise of the gift of eternal life to those who believe Him. Nature and grace are both on the same historical level, and confront one another as the principles of individual covenants.[26]

Regardless of when and where the two-fold covenant concept originated, it is certainly the case that Westminster was the first time that it had been officially received in England. The covenant of works in this document was understood to be a covenant based on the divine law which had been revealed to Adam; a covenant which remains foundational to any relationship with God:

> The moral law is the declaration of the will of God to mankind, directing and binding every one to personal, perfect, and perpetual conformity, and obedience thereunto, in the frame and disposition of the whole man, soul, and body, and in performance of all those duties of holiness and righteousness which he oweth to God and man: promising life upon the fulfilling, and threatening death upon the breach of it.[27]

Whilst this two-fold notion of covenant was understood well by some, there were inherent dangers in the teaching as proposed by others. Baxter, for example, became guilty of neonomianism in the manner of his understanding;[28] the covenant of works was understood by him to be something that demands an inherent principle within humanity capable of achieving the ends that are proposed:

> Our Evangelical Righteousness is not without us in Christ, as our legall Righteousness is: but consisteth in our own actions of Faith and Gospel Obedience. Or thus: Though Christ performe the conditions of the Law, and satisfied for our non-performance; yet it is ourselves that must perform the conditions of the Gospel.[29]

This teaching was clearly at odds with Calvin, who understood the gracious acting of God in the individual to give the power of adherence to the covenant relationship.[30] But the question remains, however, whether the introduction of a covenant of works inevitably leads to the barbarising of covenant theology inherent in Baxter's approach, or whether there may be a way to harmonise Calvin's one-covenant idea with a more developed understanding.

Owen shows us that there is a better way. Certainly his teachings on federal theology far surpassed, in complexity, those of the Westminster Confession and revealed an extension to Calvin's approach. What Owen was able to do, however, was hold in tension the intent of Calvin with the development of Westminster. Unlike Calvin, Owen understood the logically primary covenant to be one of works. The key to his understanding of this was revealed more clearly on other occasions where he called it the covenant of creation, life or nature.[31] He believed that 'man in his creation, with respect unto the ends of God therein, was constituted under a covenant'.[32] In this covenant, Adam was 'encouraged unto obedience'[33] to God as the basis of that constitution and, indeed, as the basis of his entire relationship with God:

> 'Do this and live,' was that rule of it which the nature of God and man, with their mutual relation unto one another, did require. But we were made *meet* for this obedience, and enabled unto it, only by virtue of this *image of God* implanted in our natures. It was morally a power to live unto God in obedience, that we might come to the enjoyment of him in glory.[34]

But what is important here is that Owen recognised the grace of God at work within human nature enabling us to obedience. The covenant is not conditional or dependent upon any good work within the natural abilities of man but it is entirely dependent on the grace of God. By taking this approach to the subject, the intent of Calvin's covenant of grace was upheld and the error of Baxter's neonomianism was avoided. The initial covenant is one in which both works and grace are inextricably intertwined. As Bierma notes, 'The covenant is ratified with us not by our coming first to God in faith and obedience but by Christ first instilling in us an "eagerness" (*studium*) for reconciling ourselves to God and by Christ *creating* in us the faith and obedience that satisfy the stipulations of the covenant.'[35]

Yet as much as God's grace is at work in this covenant, it is undeniably the case that it is marked with the ordinance of worship and response to God on the part of man. Owen commented that

> The law of his obedience was attended with promises and threatenings, rewards and punishments, suited unto the goodness of God; for every law with rewards and recompenses annexed hath the nature of a covenant. And in this case, although the promises wherewith man was encouraged unto obedience, which was that of eternal life with God, did in strict justice exceed the worth of the obedience required, and so was a superadded effect of goodness and grace, yet was it suited unto the constitution of a covenant meet for man to serve God in unto his glory; and, on the other side, the punishment threatened unto disobedience, in death and an everlasting separation from God, was such as the righteousness and holiness of God, as his supreme governor, and Lord of him and the covenant, did require. Now, this covenant belonged unto the law of creation.[36]

It was Adam's failure to keep this covenant of works that brought guilt and condemnation upon the human race, since the first man is our federal head and we are co-joined with him in our relationship with God.[37] In the light of that failure by Adam, and its ensuing consequences for humanity, there was the need for a second covenant.

This second covenant is most properly called the covenant of grace. This, however, is not a covenant that is made directly with humanity in itself but with a Mediator on its behalf, namely Jesus Christ. It is an 'everlasting covenant'[38] in which 'God hath himself undertaken the whole'[39] inasmuch as the conditions attached to it devolve on the Mediator himself:

> Man by his fall, having made himself incapable of life by that covenant (of works), the Lord was pleased to make a second, commonly called the covenant of grace; whereby he freely offereth to sinners life and salvation by Jesus Christ, requiring of them faith in him, that they may be saved; and promising unto all those that are ordained unto life his Holy Spirit, to make them willing and able to believe.[40]

For Owen, this covenant of grace is itself founded upon a third covenant, that of redemption: an idea pivotal to his entire federal system. This is the result of a transaction in eternity between the Father and the Son;[41] a transaction which was itself a covenant: 'Christ's...mediation on our behalf...is that compact, covenant, convention, or agreement, that was between the Father and the Son, for the accomplishment of the work of our redemption by the mediation of Christ, to the praise of the glorious grace of God.'[42]

The covenant of redemption was a logical necessity in Owen's thought if the covenant of grace is to benefit the elect.[43] The atonement for sin made by Christ is dependent on this pre-existent covenant between the first two members of the Trinity. The promises annexed to this covenant are made by God to Christ in his capacity as Mediator, namely that he will be exalted and glorified as a reward for his atoning sacrifice. Owen suggested that it is only in the context of this covenant that meaning can be given to the death of Christ and the subsequent pardoning of sinners. The background to Owen's understanding of this will be examined more fully below.

Ferguson rightly recognises that Owen spoke of a further covenant that finds its basis in the events on Mount Sinai.[44] Whilst Owen accepted that man is unable to please God through the broken covenant of works,[45] the precepts of that covenant are renewed at

Sinai: 'The law thus declared and written by him was the same, I say, materially, and for the substance of it, with the law of our creation, or the original rule of our covenant obedience unto God.'[46]

The introduction of covenants after the covenant of works does not alter the nature of sin. It is only because man was unable to be saved under the first covenant that God introduced salvation by grace. Such a comment, however, seems to suggest that God somehow failed in the first covenant. But Owen's approach does not materially differentiate between the covenants. Certainly there is a logical differentiation but all of them are infused with the grace of God. Owen spoke of the differing covenants as 'renovations' of the first covenant of works.[47] Ferguson comments on this paradox thus: 'In one sense then, the people were under the covenant of grace, and yet in a dispensation governed by the principles of the covenant of works. To employ Owen's own expressions, there is "renovation" and "innovation" together.'[48]

Whether there be, in strict accordance with Calvin only one covenant, or in accordance with the Westminster Confession two covenants or whether, as with Owen, more are accepted, there need not be cause for division. Owen pointed the way forward in remaining true to both Calvin and Westminster in principle whilst developing the teachings of both in practice. What remained for Owen was the fundamental importance of this teaching to our understanding of the relationship between humanity and God, an understanding clarified by Thomas Whitefeild:

> From the nature of the Covenant which God hath made with his people; all true beleevers are within the compasse of this Covenant, and this Covenant is an everlasting Covenant, Jeremiah 32.40. By this Covenant God hath bound himselfe to put away their iniquities, and to remember their sinnes no more, Jeremiah 31.34. and this being a branch of the everlasting Covenant, all true beleevers to whom it belongs, shall enjoy the benefit of it.[49]

Since the believers' relationship is dependent upon the idea of covenant, sin is necessarily related to the law and, to that extent, federal theology was foundational for Owen's understanding of sin.

Given the extension of his thought from the Westminster Confession of Faith concerning federal theology, we are left with the question of exactly how and why Owen came by his ideas. Was his thought truly unique or is there a hidden source that needs to be uncovered in order more adequately to assess the validity of Owen's approach? In answering that question we discover that Owen was far from unique in his ideas and that he relied in no small degree directly on the formative work of his Continental contemporary, Johannes Cocceius.[50] Even though, as we have seen, the idea predates him, the term 'federal theology' is generally connected to his 1648 work *Summa doctrinae de foedere et testamento Dei* and it is in his writings that the concept found its first systematic exposition.

Perhaps it is not surprising that Owen should have been attracted to the writings of Cocceius; they shared a similar desire to confound the Socinians in print as well as a love for the Epistle to the Hebrews. But Owen's was more than a passing interest and what is apparent is that he had studied Cocceius' writings very carefully. In the records of his library auctioned after his death, we find that Owen possessed no fewer than five of Cocceius' works.[51] Furthermore, Owen followed Cocceius' teaching about the sacramental nature of the two trees in the Garden of Eden[52] and, most importantly for our purposes, had referred the reader to his writings on the Book of Job in *Vindiciæ Evangelicæ*.[53] It is the nature of that referral that is important for us, since it has to do with the relationship between the Father and the Son from all eternity. The issue under discussion for Owen at this juncture of his treatise was the obedience and submission of Christ to the Father: 'All along, in the carrying on of his work, he professes that this condition [of submission and obedience] was by his Father prescribed him, that he should be his servant, and yield him obedience in the work he had in hand.'[54] After this, he quotes from Job 33:23,24 and refers the reader to Cocceius on the topic.

The link between Owen's thought and that of Cocceius on federal theology is implicit in this. At the very heart of Cocceius' system was the eternal covenant made between the Father and the Son; what Owen called the covenant of redemption. Barth describes Cocceius' understanding of this as

> the unfolding of a pre-temporal occurence, an eternal and free
> contract (*pactum*) made between God the Father and God the Son,
> in which the Father represents the righteousness and the Son the
> mercy of God, the latter adopting the function of a Mediator and
> pledge in the place of men.[55]

This covenant was of course dependent on the submission of Christ
to the will of the Father, the very issue that Owen had stressed in
Vindiciæ Evangelicæ.

As was mentioned above, the covenant of redemption was a
logical necessity for Owen in the development of his federal
theology; there is a sense in which his whole system stands or
falls on the validity of this proposal. The debt that Owen owed to
Cocceius for the development of his theological framework, then,
is incalculable. We may note in passing that it is perhaps no
coincidence that Owen outlined his understanding of the covenant
of redemption in two primary works, his *Vindiciæ Evangelicæ*
and his *Epistle to the Hebrews*. Should we be surprised that his
drawing on the ideas of Cocceius is most clearly evident in the
two strands of theology that most closely bound them: their desire
to confute Socinianism (the reason for the penning of *Vindiciæ
Evangelicæ*) and their love of that biblical epistle?

The Nature of Man
Alongside federal theology, Owen set his treatment of sin within
the broader framework of man being made in the image of God.[56]
The truth of this assertion is not immediately obvious when reading
his works on sin, since Owen himself did not always draw an
explicit relationship between the two concepts. Nevertheless, the
relationship is always implicit at least and is vital to the correct
understanding of Owen's teaching. The link between sin,
sanctification and the image of God was clear for Owen; the
combat of sin in the life of the believer through sanctification is
nothing less than the restoration of the image of God in that
individual.[57]

Owen's system of analysing the notion of man being made in the image of God appears at first to work in reverse, both chronologically and theologically. Ferguson outlines his approach thus:

> For Owen, the essence of sanctification consists in the restoration of the broken image of God. It is a work of re-creation; and it is by the image being restored that we discover what that image originally was...we discover what man lost in the fall by learning what is restored to him in sanctification.[58]

In short, Owen did not look to Adam to discern what it means for the believer to be made in the image of God. Rather he looked to Christ and the Holy Spirit by whom comes sanctification and restoration. The ramifications of this are such that the approach itself in part determines the very outcome of his definition of man in the image of God. As we consider Owen's teaching on this, we shall see that his approach was similar to that of Calvin but is a direct reversal of that which both Augustine and Aquinas offer. His approach was fundamentally different since his reason for writing on this topic was not the same as theirs; Owen wrote for a clearly defined pastoral end and so his argument drew on ethical connotations to a far greater degree than either Augustine or Aquinas. Despite the difference of approach, however, we shall see that the outcome of his argument endorsed the ideas of both Augustine and Aquinas in that the image of God in man is a dynamic principle and that the image is located primarily in the rational faculties.

Owen was firmly convinced that the image of God in man serves one primary purpose, namely, enjoyment of life with God, with all the benefits and duties that that entails: 'That habitual grace and original righteousness wherewith he was invested was in a manner due unto him for the obtaining of that supernatural end whereunto he was created.'[59] Again, '[Adam's] soul was made meet and able to live to God, as his sovereign lord, chiefest good, and last end.'[60] Owen's teaching was dependent on this idea inasmuch as he believed that to be made in the image of God was primarily an ethical concept, not a psychological and physical concept, and is inextricably intertwined with the concept of covenant.

This teleological approach which underpinned Owen's biblical understanding was commonplace within Reformed theology. One example of this is from William Benn[61] in a posthumous publication called *Soul Prosperity*, which carried a Preface from Owen: 'Remember this, That the ruling, predominant, chief and principal end in labouring for the things of this world, should be in reference to the world to come...So in labouring after all the things of this life, we should desire them; not as stops, but as steps in our way to heaven.'[62]

The teleological approach endorsed by Owen and his Reformed contemporaries was fundamentally based on a commonplace pre-Enlightenment methodology for scriptural interpretation. We note, however, the influence of Aristotle in this regard. *The Nicomachean Ethics*, a work by Aristotle to which Owen referred, was founded on the premise of teleology:

> Now if there is an end (τελος) which as moral agents we seek for its own sake, and which is the cause of our seeking all the other ends...it is clear that this must be the good, that is the absolute good. May we not then argue from this that a knowledge of the good is a great advantage to us in the conduct of our lives? Are we not more likely to hit the mark if we have a target?[63]

Clearly Aristotle did not claim that there must be only one end to be desired for itself at the exclusion of everything else. Rather, the life of an individual ought to be governed by certain desires and interests which, in their totality and according to their priority, lead towards a final end. Aristotle equated the final end of which he speaks to 'happiness':

> Now happiness (ευδαιμονια) more than anything else appears to be just such an end, for we always choose it for its own sake and never for the sake of some other thing...nobody chooses happiness as a means of achieving...anything else whatsoever than just happiness...Happiness then, the end to which all our conscious acts are directed, is found to be something final and self-sufficient.[64]

Aristotle's conclusion is primarily ethical:

> We are now in a position to describe the happy man as 'one who
> realizes in action a goodness that is complete and that is adequately
> furnished with external goods, and that not for some limited period
> but throughout a fully rounded life spent in that way.'[65]

With regard to his anthropology in general, and his understanding
of sin in particular, Owen endorsed this teleological framework.
He understood humanity to have been created for, and ultimately
to be moving towards, a final end which is a life with God; a
complete restoration of the *imago Dei* that was marred in Adam:

> That Adam in the state of innocency, besides his natural life,
> whereby he was a living soul, had likewise a supernatural life
> with respect unto its end, whereby he lived unto God. This is
> called 'the life of God,' Ephesians 4:18, which men now in the
> state of nature are alienated from; – the life which God requires,
> and which hath God for its object and end.[66]

Again, 'This life was necessary unto him with respect unto the
state wherein and the end for which he was made. He was made to
live unto the living God.'[67]

Even after the Fall, humanity retained its teleological aim,
which was the basis for Owen's understanding of the process of
regeneration:

> Although it be a great work in itself, that wherein the renovation
> of the image of God in us doth consist, yet it is not wrought in any
> but with respect unto a farther end in this world; and this end is,
> that we may live unto God. We are made like unto God, that we
> may live unto God.[68]

This is not to suggest, however, that Owen merely transposed
Aristotle's arguments and created a biblical understanding in the
light of that. His was predominantly a scriptural approach to the
concept of the image of God in man and his findings from scripture
were merely illuminated by Aristotle's ideas. Owen paralleled

Aristotle's teaching, rather than reproduced it, by speaking of happiness as being found in that life with God. Aristotle provided the organisational principle whilst scripture provided the content, a synthesis which can be illustrated in the following passage from *A Vision of Unchangeable, Free Mercy*:

> The soul of man is of a vast, boundless comprehension; so that if all created good were centred into one enjoyment, and that bestowed upon one soul, because it must needs be finite and limited, as created, it would give no solid contentment to his affections, nor satisfaction to his desires. In the presence and fruition of God alone there is joy for evermore; at his right hand are rivers of pleasure, the well-springs of life and blessedness.[69]

This pursuit of happiness through obedience necessarily involves the combat of sin:

> *Without sincerity and diligence in a universality of obedience, there is no mortification of any one perplexing lust to be obtained*...Whilst there abides a treachery in the heart to indulge to any negligence in not pressing universally to all perfection in obedience, the soul is *weak*, as not giving faith its whole work; and *selfish*, as considering more the trouble of sin than the filth and guilt of it; and lives under a constant *provocation* of God.[70]

Further to this, Owen believed the final end to involve the eradication of sin: 'All that have an apprehension of a future state of happiness do agree in this matter, that it contains in it, or is accompanied with, *a deliverance and freedom from all that is evil*.'[71]

Teleological assumptions, then, were foundational for Owen's understanding of man being made in the image of God. The final end of humanity is happiness in a life with God, the restoration of the *imago Dei*, but sin and evil are barriers to this. His teleology embraced the concept of an 'inclusive end' which is obedience to God and the mortification of sin within the process of sanctification.

Owen outlined three methods by which the end of man was to

be fulfilled by way of the image of God within. First, that he might
'*make a representation of* [God's] *holiness and righteousness*
among his creatures.'[72] In order to enjoy life with God, humanity
needs first to know and acknowledge God. By creating man in his
image, God was placing a representation of himself within creation
in order to enhance the knowledge of his glory, wisdom and power
and thereby to encourage worship. Secondly, that it 'might be a
means of rendering actual glory unto him from all other parts of
the creation.'[73] Not only does God deserve worship and praise
from humans but from all creation also. The image of God in man
would be a way for creation to understand God and give glory to
him for his works of power. This, of course, is not to be understood
in any pantheistic sense; rather, Owen was treating humanity as
somehow the representative head of creation and, as humanity
worships God, there is a sense in which all creation is represented
in that act. Thirdly, that it might be 'a means to bring man unto
that *eternal enjoyment* of Himself.'[74] The image of God within
was deemed by God to be the source of holiness and obedience by
which the relationship between the individual and the Creator could
be sustained.

Before analysing exactly what Owen understood by the image
of God within man, it is necessary first to examine the approaches
of Augustine, Aquinas and Calvin to this topic; three theologians
who were immensely influential on Owen's developing theological
thought. We have already noted that the approaches offered by
Augustine and Aquinas differ from those of Calvin and Owen,
and neither of the Reformed theologians were uncritical of their
methodology, as we shall see. It is true that Owen did indeed treat
the idea of man being made in the image of God in trinitarian
terms.[75] However, his treatment of this topic was markedly
different from that of Augustine in *The Trinity*, and Owen, perhaps
in reference to Augustine, wrote of 'the vanity of all other glosses
and expositions.'[76] This is not to suggest, however, that Owen
rejected the Augustinian teaching. In an implicit sense, it formed
the basis for his own understanding, and the writings of Owen on
the image of God were an attempt to apply the conceptual thinking
of Augustine in a pastoral sense.

Augustine treated the notion of man in the image of God in *The City of God*[77] but most fully in *The Trinity*.[78] The context of Augustine's writing was somewhat different from Owen, most especially in the latter treatise, since he was concerned there to understand the mystery of the Trinity by studying man in the image of God. Augustine worked on the assumption that, since God is Trinity and man is made in his image, there must be a trinity of sorts in man. Augustine outlined a number of different trinities within the psychological make-up of man that can be considered the image of God, two of these ideas being of particular importance.

First, Augustine examined the nature of the mind and discerned there a trinity; mind itself, its own self-awareness and its love for itself.[79] The love of itself of which Augustine wrote is not a selfish or introverted type of love. Rather it must be understood as an appreciation of its own existence which serves as a motivating factor in a psychological sense. This trinity is analogous to the divine Trinity in that it mirrors the latter in terms of relationship and substance; each one is mutually exclusive yet they are inextricably bound in relationship with each other. There is mixture yet without confusion:

> But with these three, when mind knows and loves itself the trinity remains of mind, love, knowledge. Nor are they jumbled up together in any kind of mixture, though they are each one in itself and each whole in their total, whether each in the other two or the other two in each, in any case all in all...In a wonderful way therefore these three are inseparable from each other, and yet each one of them is substance, and all together they are one substance or being, while they are also posited with reference to one another.[80]

However, Augustine realised the inadequacy of his argument in that the notion of 'mind' is a non-relational idea (unlike 'love' and 'knowledge'). Thus he developed his idea a stage further by speaking of the trinity of mind in terms of memory, understanding and will.[81] By speaking of the mind in these terms, Augustine was re-iterating the ideas of mutuality and relationship as well as the idea of equality:

These three then...are not three lives but one life...one in that they are one life, one mind, one being...But they are three in that they have reference to each other. And if they were not equal, not only each to the other but also each to them all together, they would not of course contain each other. In fact though they are not only each contained by each, they are all contained by each as well.[82]

Having examined this idea, Augustine related it further to his epistemology by stating the two activities with which the mind is involved: knowledge (*scientia*) and wisdom (*sapientia*):

Action by which we make good use of temporal things differs from contemplation of eternal things, and this is ascribed to wisdom, the former to knowledge...If then this is the correct distinction between wisdom and knowledge, that wisdom is concerned with the rational cognizance of temporal things, it is not hard to decide which should be preferred and which subordinated to the other.[83]

Since wisdom is the contemplation of eternal objects, the mind is drawn either to itself or to God. Augustine concluded that the mind most fully reflects the image of God when it comprehends its own reliance and derivation from God; in comprehending itself it is ultimately led to a comprehension of God: 'This trinity is found in one quite simply undivided mind...only in that part which is concerned with the contemplation of eternal things can one find something that is not only a trinity but also the image of God.'[84]

This comprehension of God turns the mind to the Creator in an attitude of love, which is a dynamic principle. Thus Augustine's conclusion was that the image of God in man is not a static principle. Rather it is something that needs to be defined in terms of potentiality, as something to be achieved. This, of course, is the goal of the Christian life. Augustine's position as described above, alongside his teleological conclusion, is summed up in these words from *The City of God*:

And we indeed recognise in ourselves the image of God, that is, of the supreme Trinity, an image which, though it be not equal to God, or rather, though it be very far removed from Him – being neither co-eternal, nor, to say all in a word, consubstantial with Him – is yet nearer to Him in nature than any other of His works, and is destined to be yet restored, that it may bear a still closer resemblance. For we both are, and know that we are, and delight in our being, and our knowledge of it.[85]

Aquinas reflected the ideas of Augustine in *De veritate*[86] – a detailed exegesis of Augustine's treatment of the subject in *The Trinity* – and more fully in *Summa Theologiæ*.[87] Indeed, his section on the image of God in man in the latter work is primarily an exegetical appreciation of the teachings of Augustine. Aquinas' aim was to assert the idea that the image of God in man is to be found most fully in the rational faculties, most especially the mind.

Aquinas asserted that although the image of God is to be found in man it is not a perfect image.[88] Considering the grammatical implications of Scripture's assertion that humanity is made 'after' the image of God, Aquinas drew a distinction between Christ as exhibiting the perfect image and humanity in general as the image:

The Firstborn of all creation is God's perfect image, perfectly realising that of which he is the image, and so he is said to be 'the image' quite simply, and never to be 'after the image'. But man is both said to be 'the image', because of his likeness to the original, and 'after the image', because the likeness is imperfect...God's image is in his firstborn Son as a king's image is in his son, who shares his nature; whereas it is in man as in an alien nature, like the king's image on a silver coin.[89]

Following Augustine, Aquinas believed the image of God to be a possible assertion only in the light of the rationality and intelligence of the mind.[90] Furthermore, humanity is most completely in the image of God when it imitates God, namely, 'as it imitates God's understanding and loving of *himself*.'[91] Aquinas expounded this idea thus:

God's image can be considered in man at three stages: the first stage is man's natural aptitude for understanding and loving God, an aptitude which consists in the very nature of the mind, which is common to all men. The next stage is where man is actually or dispositively knowing and loving God, but still imperfectly; and here we have the image by conformity of grace. The third stage is where a man is actually knowing and loving God perfectly; and this is the image by likeness of glory.[92]

In consequence, there is a three-fold image in humanity, 'namely the image of *creation, of re-creation, and of likeness.* The first stage of image then is found in all men, the second only in the just, and the third only in the blessed.'[93] Thus Aquinas, after Augustine, related the image of God in man to a dynamic principle, namely love for God. This is something to be achieved by each individual and can in no terms be considered as a static concept.

Although Calvin stood in the same tradition, he did not accept the speculative approach of Augustine uncritically: 'There is no solidity in Augustine's speculation, that the soul is a mirror of the Trinity, inasmuch as it comprehends within itself, intellect, will, and memory.'[94] He did, however, concur with the view that the image of God in man is a dynamic principle rather than a static concept. For Calvin, the image of God demands 'not merely a knowledge that God is, but also, nay chiefly, a perception of His will towards us. It concerns us to know not only what He is in Himself but also in what character He is pleased to manifest Himself to us.'[95]

As for Owen, his own teachings reflected the concepts of both Augustine and Aquinas although he did not explicitly draw on them in his writings on the image of God in man. Rather, he took the tradition that they represented as given, and built on that to present the reader with an understanding of the topic that could promote personal holiness and Christian discipleship. In doing this, Owen's writings took on ethical connotations that reflected his pastoral and practical concerns.

Owen concurred with that which had gone before by locating the image of God primarily in the soul and most notably in the rational faculties of man: 'Man was created in a resemblance and likeness unto God in that immortal substance breathed into his nostrils, Genesis 2:7, in the excellent rational faculties thereof...'[96] Again, 'A universal rectitude of nature, consisting in light, power, and order, in his understanding, mind, and affections, was the principal part of this image of God wherein he was created.'[97]

This is not to suggest however that Owen dismissed the idea of the image being reflected in the body as well as the soul. There still remains a vestige of the image of God that was bestowed in the covenant of creation, which communicates itself in the whole of a person, body and soul:

> That our entire nature was originally created in the *image* of God I have proved...and it is by all acknowledged. Our whole souls, in the rectitude of all their faculties and powers, in order unto the whole life of God and his enjoyment, did bear his image. Nor was it confined to the soul only; the body also, not as to its shape, figure, or natural use, but as an *essential part* of our nature, was interested in the image of God by a participation of original righteousness. Hence the whole person was a meet principle for the communication of this image of God unto others, by the means of natural propagation, which is an act of the entire person; for a person created and abiding in the image of God, begetting another in his own image and likeness, had, by virtue of the covenant of creation, begotten him in the image also, – that is, had communicated unto him a nature upright and pure.[98]

This concurs with Calvin's understanding as outlined in his *Institutes*:

> Let it be understood, that the image of God which is beheld [in the physical body] or made conspicuous by these external marks, is spiritual... though the primary seat of the divine image was in the mind and the heart, or in the soul and its powers, there was no part of the body in which some rays of glory did not shine.[99]

By locating the image of God primarily in the rational faculties, Owen was not simply making a psychological statement but also re-iterating the idea of that image as being a dynamic principle. In *A Display of Arminianism*, Owen further elucidated the idea by stating the reason why this is a necessary part of humanity's make-up: 'Our nature was then inclined to good only, and adorned with all those qualifications that were necessary to make it acceptable unto God, and able to do what was required of us by the law, under the condition of everlasting happiness.'[100] Again, this is an idea reminiscent of the writings of Calvin:

> [Paul] shows that the new man is renewed after the image of him that created him (Col. 3:19). To this corresponds another passage, 'Put ye on the new man, who after God is created' (Eph. 4:24). We must now see what particulars Paul comprehends under this renovation. In the first place, he mentions knowledge; and, in the second, true righteousness and holiness. Hence we infer, that at the beginning the image of God was manifested by light of intellect, rectitude of heart, and the soundness of every part.[101]

The practical implications of Owen's understanding are further elucidated by another comment in *A Display of Arminianism*:

> We were created 'in the image of God,' Genesis 1:27, – in such a perfect uprightness as is opposite to all evil intentions, Ecclesiastes.7:29; to which image when we are again in some measure 'renewed' by the grace of Christ, Colossians 3:10, we see by the first-fruits that it consisted in 'righteousness and true holiness,' – in truth and perfect holiness, Ephesians 4:24...we have thought that the original righteousness wherein Adam was created had comprehended the integrity and perfection of the whole man; not only that whereby the body was obedient unto the soul, and all the affections subservient to the rule of reason for the performance of all natural actions, but also a light, uprightness, and holiness of grace in the mind and will, whereby he was enabled to yield obedience unto God for the attaining of that supernatural end whereunto he was created.[102]

From what has been suggested above, there seem to be three predominant themes that characterise Owen's understanding of this issue.

First and foremost, that the image of God in man is integrally linked to moral rectitude and holiness; a covenant understanding:

> With respect unto his *moral condition* and principle of obedience

unto God, it is expressed, Genesis 1:26, 27, 'And God said, Let us make man in our image, after our likeness...' He made him...perfect in his condition, every way complete, – fit, disposed, and able to and for the obedience required of him.[103]

Again, 'We may consider the *moral state* and condition of man...in reference unto his obedience to God and his enjoyment of him. This was the principal part of that image of God wherein he was created.'[104]

Owen justified this idea by using Ecclesiastes 7:29 as an exegetical tool for Genesis 1:26,27. Owen did this on a number of occasions[105] but one such example will suffice: 'Man was created in a resemblance and likeness unto God...especially in the integrity and uprightness of his person, Ecclesiastes 7:29, wherein he stood before God, in reference to the obedience required at his hands.'[106] The writer of Ecclesiastes states in this verse that 'God made man upright' (יָשָׁר) which, for Owen, carried clear moral connotations. It is in this sense that the original design for humanity exhibited a natural righteousness: 'Man was created in the image of God, in knowledge, righteousness, and holiness...[and] moral goodness, integrity, and uprightness, is equivalent unto righteousness.'[107] Owen expanded his idea thus:

> *First*, An *ability to discern* the mind and will of God with respect unto all the duty and obedience that God required of him...*Secondly*, A free, uncontrolled, unentangled *disposition* to every duty of the law of his creation, in order unto living unto God. *Thirdly*, An *ability* of *mind* and *will*, with a readiness of compliance in his affections, for a due regular *performance of all duties, and abstinence from all sin.*[108]

Second, Owen suggested that the incarnate Christ is a model and an example of what it means to be made in the image of God. This is, of course, entirely in keeping with his understanding of sin as a theocentric rather than an anthropocentric issue. By this is meant that the fundamental context of Owen's treatment of sin was set within his doctrine of God and not independent from that. Owen's anthropological teaching was never developed in isolation but is always in relation to man's responsibilities to God, primarily through federal theology. Owen believed that by turning to Christ as exemplar, the soul is conformed to the image of God: 'There proceedeth – from the real object of our faith, Christ, as the image of God – a transforming power, whereby the soul is changed into the same image, or is made conformable unto Christ; which is that whereunto we are predestinated.'[109] Again,

> [Every believer] hath the idea or image of Christ in his mind, in the eye of faith, as it is represented unto him in the glass of the Gospel.... And hereby the mind is transformed into the same image, made like unto Christ so represented unto us – which is the conformity we speak of.... One end of God in...implanting his glorious image upon [the human nature of Christ], was, that he might in him propose *an example* of what he would by the same grace renew us unto, and what we ought in a way of duty to labour after.[110]

It needs to be stressed, however, that the idea of the soul turning to Christ as exemplar was, for Owen, a principle of activity, not merely a passive inquiry. This is an idea which Owen proposed most fully in *The Person of Christ* [111] and he suggested two ways in which this occurs; first, concerning the internal holiness of the human nature of Christ and, second, his duties of obedience.

Owen believed internal conformity to the holiness of Christ to be a fundamental aspect of Christian discipleship: '*Conformity*...is required of us unto him. This is the great design and projection of all believers.'[112] Taking Romans 8:29 as his starting-point, Owen suggested that Christ is the prototype of the glory that is to be bestowed on all believers in the renovation of their nature. Since the image of God in the covenant of works has been lost, humanity has no comprehension of it outside of its representation in Christ revealed through the scriptures. Transformation into that image is achieved in two ways.

First, Owen stated that 'Unless we have a spiritual light to discern the glory and amiableness of [the character of Christ]...we speak in vain of any design for conformity unto him.'[113] To grow into conformity of these graces necessarily involves a zealous desire for them. Without such a passionate desire to exhibit the self-same characteristics, there can be no conformity to Christ and therefore no restoration of the image of God in the individual. This motivation inevitably requires an opposition to personal sin alongside a gradual growth in the duty of holiness.

Second, Owen suggested that

> The following the *example* of Christ [sic] in all duties towards God and men, in his whole conversation on the earth, is the second part...The field is large which here lies before us, and filled with numberless blessed instances... [therefore] one or two general instances [shall suffice].[114]

Owen mentions meekness, lowliness, loving kindness, patience and forbearance as characteristics of the example that Christ sets before the believer alongside his self-denial and readiness to suffer with patience. Concerning the restoration of the image of God in man, Owen concluded, 'his grace in them all is our only pattern in what is required of us.'[115]

Third, as has been indicated before, Owen suggested that the image of God within man could only be comprehended through its renewal:

> The infinite wisdom of God had this further design in it also, – namely, that [Christ] might be the pattern and example of the renovation of the image of God in us, and of the glory that doth ensue thereon...as we have been borne the 'image of the first Adam' in the depravation of our natures, so we should bear the 'image of the second' in their renovation.[116]

Again, this is an idea in which Owen echoed Calvin, who earlier had stated in his *Institutes* that

> Our definition of the image seems not to be complete until it appears more clearly what the faculties are in which man excels, and in which he is to be regarded as a mirror of the divine glory. This, however, cannot be better known than from the remedy provided for the corruption of nature...our deliverance begins with that renovation which we obtain from Christ, who is, therefore,

called the second Adam, because he restores us to true and substantial integrity.[117]

Owen understood this renovation of human nature to be a primary work of the Holy Spirit and we reiterate that there was in Owen's approach a logical reversal of the approach of Augustine and Aquinas. Whilst the latter looked primarily to Adam to discover the nature of the image, Owen (and Calvin before him) looked to Christ as the example and the work of the Holy Spirit in sanctification as the means of comprehension. Whilst there was little difference in the conclusions that each theologian reached, the divergence of content and methodology is noteworthy.

The Nature of Sin

In order to assess the effect of sin in the world and in the life of the individual, consideration needs to be given to Owen's understanding of the nature of sin itself. In so doing, we must first acknowledge the fact that Owen did not attempt to produce a new understanding of sin so much as pastorally apply the accepted Reformed teachings of the church on this issue:

> [The nature of sin] has been largely treated on, to the great benefit and edification of the church. In what we have now in design we therefore take them all for granted, and endeavour only farther to carry on the discovery of it in its actings and oppositions to the law and grace of God in believers.[118]

In outlining the nature of sin, Owen employed two seemingly paradoxical ideas: that of sin as a privation and sin as an active force. However, Owen held these two ideas together in masterful tension and thereby paved the way for a clear understanding of exactly how sin defaces the image of God in man.

Owen believed sin, in some sense, to be a privation. In his work *A Discourse On the Holy Spirit*, Owen summed up this idea in the statement that 'Men's disability to live to God is their sin.'[119] This is an idea that speaks of sin in a negative sense: a privation of the ability to live for God. This is further elaborated in the same discourse when Owen stated that

From what hath been discoursed, we may discover the nature of this spiritual death [i.e. the life of sin], under the power whereof all unregenerate persons do abide: for there are three things in it: 1. A *privation* of a principle of spiritual life enabling us to live unto God; 2. A *negation* of all spiritual, vital acts, – that is, of all acts and duties of holy obedience, acceptable unto God, and tending to the enjoyment of him; 3. A total *defect* and want of *power* for any such acts whatever.[120]

These three principles outlined by Owen provide access to his understanding of sin as privation.

First, sin is a privation of a principle of spiritual life: 'Those, therefore, who are thus dead have no principle or first power of living unto God, or for the first performance of any duty to be accepted with him, in order to the enjoyment of him, according to either covenant.'[121] The concept employed here is explicitly and crucially related to the idea of covenant. Sin interrupts the journey of the individual towards the final end, which is enjoyment of a life with God.

That Owen stood in the Augustinian tradition in this regard is undeniable. Augustine, remaining faithful to his Platonic interpretation of Scripture, had argued that all things created were good through the fact that the Creator God is, in essence, good Himself.[122] Thus if goodness is to be so defined, evil and sin must be understood to be the privation of this. This understanding of the nature of sin and evil is found in many of his writings, not least in *Enchiridion*: 'what are called vices in the soul are nothing but privations of natural good. And when they are not transferred elsewhere: when they cease to exist in the healthy soul, they cannot exist anywhere else.'[123] Again, 'For defection from that which supremely is, to that which has less of being – this is to begin to have an evil will.'[124] As Gilson states by way of commentary, 'An evil nature is one in which measure, form or order is vitiated, and it is only evil in exact proportion to the degree in which they are vitiated.'[125] Evil was thus understood by Augustine to be a privation of a good that the creature should possess. There is a failure to be what it should and this results in partial non-being, or what Owen termed 'no principle or first power of living unto God.'

The logical conclusion of such an idea may suggest that total depravation can only lead to extinction. The result of the diminishing good is 'evil' and total corruption must necessarily lead to complete non-being, as Augustine suggested: 'But if it should be thoroughly and completely consumed by corruption, there will then be no good left, because there will be no being.'[126] Owen accepted this idea but denied that sinful humanity is completely deprived of a sense of God:

> And because these faculties [of the soul] are the principle and subject of all actual obedience, it is granted that there is in man a natural, remote, *passive power* to yield obedience unto God, which yet can never actually put forth itself without the *effectual* working of the grace of God, not only enabling but working in them *to will and to do.*[127]

Thus the natural instinct to live unto God remains, preventing the complete regression into non-being, but only in a passive state, unable of itself to respond to God without the vivifying power of the Holy Spirit acting upon it. Again, this is an idea fully expounded by Augustine in *The City of God*:

> man did not fall away as to become absolutely nothing; but being turned towards himself, his being became more contracted than it was when he clave to Him who supremely is. Accordingly, to exist in himself, that is, to be his own satisfaction after abandoning God, is not quite to become a nonentity, but to approximate to that.[128]

Thus, for Owen as for Augustine, sin and evil do not exist of and for themselves but are, in reality a deficiency of existence. Just as darkness can be said to exist – but only as the absence of light, so sin can be said to exist – but only as the absence of love for God. This metaphor of darkness and light is one specifically employed by Augustine:

> Yet both of these are known to us...not by their positive actuality, but by their want of it...For when the eyesight surveys objects that strike the sense, it nowhere sees darkness but where it begins

not to see. And so no other sense but the ear can perceive silence, and yet it is only perceived by not hearing. Thus too, our mind perceives intelligible forms by understanding them; but when they are deficient, it knows them by not knowing them; for 'who can understand defects?'[129]

Secondly, Owen understood sin to be a negation of all spiritual, vital acts, – that is, of all acts and duties of holy obedience, acceptable unto God, and tending to the enjoyment of him.[130] In its most fundamental form, sin is disobedience; an idea which again accords with Augustine who stated that 'to do evil is nothing but to stray away from education [the knowledge of what is good]'.[131] Referring to Adam in particular, Owen stressed the point thus:

The sin of man consisted formally in *disobedience*; and it was the disobedience of him who was every way and in all things obliged unto obedience. For man – by all that he was, by all that he had received, by all that he expected or was further capable of, by the constitution of his own nature, by the nature and authority of God, with his relation thereunto -- was indispensably obliged unto universal obedience. His sin, therefore, was the disobedience of him who was absolutely obliged unto obedience by the very constitution of his being and necessary relation unto God. This was that which rendered it so exceeding sinful, and the consequents of it eternally miserable; and from this obligation his sin, in any one instance, was a total renunciation of all obedience unto God.[132]

Owen offered a clear definition of sin as a privation in this passage by drawing a parallel between the disobedience of Adam and his original constitution in relationship with God. The disobedience of Adam is a privation of the vital and spiritual acts which were essential to his original nature; he was created obedient and good and his wilful denial of that state was, in itself, a privation of his created nature. Sin is only to be considered a vice because it occurs in a nature whose destiny was to live in relationship and union with God, as Augustine stated: 'Wickedness can be a flaw or vice only where the nature previously was not vitiated'.[133]

Thirdly, Owen recognised sin to be a privation in that it is the total absence of power to live a life of spiritual obedience.[134] Owen went on to illustrate the idea thus: 'So the dead body of Lazarus was quickened and animated again by the introduction of his soul; but in itself it had not the least active disposition nor inclination thereunto. And no otherwise is it with a soul dead in trespasses and sins.'[135] Owen commented on the *potentia obedientialis* (power for obedience) which is a latent power within the individual that is able to receive the gift of grace and spiritual life from God but he referred to this as

> a remote power, in the nature of its faculties...but an immediate power, disposing and enabling it unto spiritual acts, it hath not. And the reason is, because natural corruption cleaves unto it as an invincible, unmoveable habit, constantly inducing unto evil, wherewith the least disposition unto spiritual good is not consistent.[136]

This idea is further clarified elsewhere in the same discourse: 'No principle of operation can subsist in an independence of God, nor apply itself unto operation without his concurrence...and our spiritual life, as in us, consists in the vital actings of this Spirit of his in us; for "without him we can do nothing," John 15:5.'[137] Again,

> The soul is not, in and by its essential properties, the quickening principle of [the spiritual life], but it is the principle that is quickened. And when the quickening principle of the spiritual life departs, it leaves the soul with all its natural properties entire as to their essence, though morally corrupted; but of all the power and abilities which it had by virtue of its union with a quickening principle of spiritual life, it is deprived.[138]

This idea is again in accord with Augustine about whom Evans comments:

> Everything Augustine has to say about evil must be read in the light of one central principle: that the effect of evil upon the mind is to make it impossible for the sinner to think clearly, and

especially to understand higher, spiritual truths and abstract ideas.[139]

Thus Owen understood sin to be, in one sense, a privation: a privation of the spiritual element of life which inspires the individual to be obedient to God.

However, the primary motif that Owen used in writing about sin is a far more 'positive' one; sin as a very real force active in the life of every individual. Owen consistently grounded the nature and effect of sin in personal experience and in highly experiential terminology. There is a sense in which Owen almost personified sin, speaking of it as if it had a real being with essential and accidental qualities. Owen wrote of the deceitfulness of sin[140] and referred to sin entangling the affections.[141] The idea of the 'mind being conquered'[142] was prevalent in his writings and he taught that sin is a deceiving power.[143]

The concluding supposition might be that Owen's philosophical assumption of sin as a privation does not work out in practical experience and that his pastoral application necessitated an abandonment of his philosophical principles. This most certainly is not the case. Owen's ability to hold together this seemingly paradoxical approach is evidenced through consideration of his description in *On Indwelling Sin* of sin as a law.[144] This idea, founded on Paul's autobiographical passage in Romans 7, suggested to Owen two themes relevant to sin as a law.

First, the law of sin has dominion in the life of the individual. Owen refuted the idea that sin has a *moral* dominion but it does nevertheless have a *real and effective* dominion:

> The law of sin hath not in itself a moral dominion, – it hath not a rightful dominion or authority over any man; but it hath that which is equivalent unto it...even in [believers] it is a law still; though not a law unto them, yet, as was said, it is a law in them.[145]

Owen understood sin to have dominion by the very fact that Scripture refers to it as a law; a law, almost by definition, exercises dominion over an individual. Thus sin demands obedience from the individual to its particularities.

Secondly, the law of sin has power, albeit weakened in the life of the believer:

> It is still a law, and that in them; so that all its actings are the actings of a law, – that is, it acts with power, though it have lost its complete power of ruling in them. Though it be *weakened*, yet its nature is not *changed*. It is a law still, and therefore powerful...[it] hath *an efficacy to provoke* those that are obnoxious unto it unto the things that it requireth.[146]

Owen suggested that the power of sin as a law resides in the fact that it offers rewards and punishments to the individual; the pleasures of sin are its own reward whilst it twists the reality of life in order to suggest punishment for non-obedience to its lawful dominion:

> It hath also punishments that it threatens men with who labour to cast off its yoke. Whatever evil, trouble, or danger in the world, attends gospel obedience, – whatever hardship or violence is to be offered to the sensual part of our natures in a strict course of mortification, – sin makes use of, as if they were punishments attending the neglect of its commands.[147]

Owen stated that the power of sin as a law is immense and governs the thoughts of many individuals; so much so that they are led to reject the gospel of Christ:

> Unless a man be prepared to reject the reasonings that will offer themselves from the one and the other of these, there is no standing before the *power* of the law. The world falls before them every day. With what deceit and violence they are urged and imposed on the minds of men...Look on the generality of men, and you shall find them wholly by these means at sin's disposal. Do the profits and pleasures of sin lie before them? – nothing can withhold them from reaching after them. Do difficulties and inconveniences attend the duties of the gospel? – they will have nothing to do with them; and so are wholly given up to the rule and dominion of this law.[148]

Herein lies the power and dominion of sin as a law; not that it is anything other than a privation but through its impact on the psychological categories of the individual – the mind, will and affections: 'It is not an outward, written, commanding, directing law, but an inbred, working, impelling, urging law. A law *proposed* unto us is not to be compared, for efficacy, to a law *inbred* in us.'[149]

Owen did not jettison his philosophical acceptance of sin as a privation in applying this teaching in a pastoral setting. Rather, what he suggested is that the positive power of sin is not something innate to itself (which it cannot be since it has no positive nature). The power and dominion of sin is 'activated' through the response of the soul to its privation:

> The flesh, which is the seat and throne of this law, yea, which indeed is this law, is in some sense the man himself, as grace also is the new man. Now, from this consideration of it, that it is an indwelling law inclining and moving to sin, as an inward habit or principle, it hath sundry advantages increasing its strength and furthering its power.[150]

Again,

> Sometimes men, by hearkening to their temptations, do stir up, excite, and provoke their lusts; and no wonder if then they find them present and active...This law of sin 'dwelleth' in us; – that is, it adheres as a depraved principle, unto our minds in darkness and vanity, unto our affections in sensuality, unto our wills in a loathing of and aversation [sic] of that which is good; and by some, more, or all of these, is continually putting itself upon us, in inclinations, motions, or suggestions of evil, when we would be most gladly quit of it.[151]

For Owen, then, sin is a privation. It is regression towards non-being, nothingness. In and of itself it has no essence or being. It is only given that being, that dominion, that power, when the categories of the soul – the mind, the will and the affections – respond to the suggestions of sin and allow it form and authority.

The *nature* of sin does not change but the *efficacy* of it does:

> I say, then, that this spiritual darkness hath a power over the minds
> of men to alienate them from God; that is, this which the Scripture
> so calleth is not a mere *privation*, with an impotency in the faculty
> ensuing thereon, but a depraved *habit*, which powerfully, and, as
> unto them in whom it is, unavoidably, influenceth their wills and
> affections into an opposition unto spiritual things, the effects
> whereof the world is visibly filled withal at this day.[152]

Again, this is an Augustinian concept. In *The City of God*,
Augustine suggested that by accepting vice and evil, the soul is
harming itself. The soul is by nature good, since God has created
it but in its acceptance of the suggestions of sin it makes itself an
enemy of God:

> In Scripture they are called God's enemies who oppose His rule,
> not by nature, but by vice; having no power to hurt Him, but only
> themselves. For they are His enemies, not through their power to
> hurt, but by their will to oppose Him...Therefore the vice which
> makes those who are called His enemies resist Him, is an evil not
> to God, but to themselves. And to them it is an evil, solely because
> it corrupts the good of their nature. It is not nature, therefore, but
> vice, which is contrary to God...For how do [vices] hurt them but
> by depriving them of integrity, beauty, welfare, virtue, and, in
> short, whatever natural good vice is wont to diminish or destroy?[153]

In her book, *Augustine on Evil*, Evans sums up Augustine's
position, which Owen adopted, excellently:

> Evil changed men so radically that they became mortal...It is to
> be feared because it distorts God's good creatures, letting loose
> in the world damaged beings who are actively malevolent,
> exercising their wills for evil with a terrible energy, making the
> negative appear positive by the force of their desire. We must,
> therefore, fear, not an abstraction, but the terrible 'angelic
> darkness', darkness personified, the brightest creatures bereft of
> light and intent on destruction. In the wills of rational beings who
> have turned from the good there is power and substance, that which
> makes the 'nothing' of evil a 'something'.[154]

Thus whilst teaching sin as privation, Owen acknowledged its very real power and dominion when in harness with the categories of the soul. It follows that his teaching was not so much concerned with the defeat of sin itself but with the internal battle faced by every individual. The enemy within, the active power that corrupts and depraves, that separates humanity from God, is not so much sin but the marred mind, will and affections after the Fall. The problem of sin – both philosophically and pastorally – is primarily concerned with the restoration of the *imago Dei*, the destruction of which has unleashed sin into the soul and the world as a positive force. Not only does this cause immense harm to the individual but also to those institutions and gatherings that are comprised of individuals. Therein lies the motivation for Owen in developing and teaching such an all-encompassing treatment of sin:

> Do you find [sin] dwelling in you, always present with you, exciting itself, or putting forth its poison with facility and easiness at all times, in all your duties, 'when you would do good?' [sic]. What humiliation, what self-abasement, what intenseness in prayer, what diligence, what watchfulness, doth this call for at your hands! What spiritual wisdom do you stand in need of! What supplies of grace, what assistance of the Holy Ghost, will be hence also discovered! I fear we have few of us a diligence proportionable to our danger.[155]

Conclusion

Central to the argument of this book is the fact that Owen's portrayal of sin was not static: that Owen himself was influenced to no small degree by the social, religious and political movements of his day. However, although his portrayal of sin altered throughout the forty years of his literary and pastoral career, the framework within which he developed his teaching did not change. Owen remained essentially faithful to the Reformed doctrines that have been outlined above. What we are about to uncover in the following chapters is not a new teaching on sin. It was never Owen's desire to produce that. What he was attempting to achieve was the application of the received Reformed doctrine on this topic, in sometimes quite radical ways, to the specific situations he encountered. But how valid was Owen's theological framework?

Concerning the developed federal theology that Owen propounded, he does indeed lay himself open to criticism. This is most especially evident with regard to his reliance on the notion of a covenant of redemption. Since he was endorsing the teaching of Cocceius, is Owen open to the same charges of inconsistency and extra-biblical interpretation that Barth lays at the feet of the Continental theologian?[156] Barth suggests that to propose a covenant of redemption in these terms is to misinterpret the nature of the Godhead; that the Father and the Son can in no way be considered as two legal subjects who are at liberty to enter into a contract together. Such an idea destroys the concept of unity within the Godhead and is suggestive of a dualism that concedes the possibility of a clash of wills between the members of the Trinity. Furthermore, Barth suggests that any covenant made must involve all the parties concerned and that the covenant of redemption does not include one crucial party, namely humanity.

However, Barth may have done well to read Owen on this matter before criticising Cocceius in this way, for Owen was acutely aware of the difficulties that the idea of such a covenant created. He was anxious to defend the unity of the Godhead whilst still crediting each member with a distinct personality:

> It is true, the will of God the Father, Son and Holy Ghost, is but one. It is a natural property, and where there is but one nature there is but one will: but in respect of their distinct personal actings, this will is appropriated to them respectively, so that the will of the Father and the will of the Son may be considered [distinctly] in this business... Notwithstanding the unity of essence that is between the Father and the Son, yet is the work distinctly carried on by them.[157]

Owen was at pains to defend the unity of the Godhead yet at the same time express the particularity of each of the members. That he could find no linguistic formula that achieved clarity in this matter is hardly surprising, for which theologian has ever plumbed the depths of the mystery of the Triune Godhead? What is beyond doubt, however, is that even when adhering to a federal system that was reliant upon a covenant of redemption, Owen was able to maintain biblical orthodoxy.

What becomes clear in our analysis of Owen's theological framework is the profound ability he had to remain faithful to his tradition whilst adapting it for his purposes in a contemporary setting. Owen had the clarity of thought to be able to intertwine seemingly polarised schemes of thought and create a logical, coherent system. His reversal of Augustine and Aquinas' approach to the image of God in man is not a denial of their teaching; merely a transposition of the same into an ethical and pastorally sympathetic approach. His ability to hold in tension the ideas of sin as a privation as well as a very real power that exercises dominion over the soul is masterful. The depth of his loyalty to the Reformed tradition is not open to question. Owen had a deep and profound understanding of the nuances of Reformed thinking. Even when it might appear that he had strayed from its orthodoxy, as in his development of the Westminster Confession's understanding of federal theology, it was never a denial of its doctrines; only a clarification of its understanding. Furthermore, his adherence to the writings of Augustine, most especially as interpreted by Calvin, has been made clear.

Owen was very much part of a historic tradition. Situated firmly within his own cultural setting, and writing theology specifically for that setting, he was never tempted to jettison the foundations of antiquity in an attempt to titillate and impress. To do so would be an abrogation of scriptural principles and would negate Owen's ministry. Owen had a message to tell about the nature and effect of sin. It was not a new message. But it was one that demanded new applications in a new era, as we shall now discover.

2

SIN AND THE INDIVIDUAL

The Reformed pastors of the sixteenth century rose to the challenge of a new style of religious leadership. Systematic approaches to pastoring the faithful were pursued; systems which incorporated a variety of approaches but always with the intent of saving souls from the clutches of sin. Perkins, in outlining the duty of pastors, commented that

> They must privately conferre, visit, admonish and rebuke and principally they must preach...and the end they must aime at must be to winne soules...And the rather must all Christian Ministers seriously intend the saving of souls, inasmuch as Antichrist doth so earnestly seek the destruction of soules, by winning them to his synagogue.[1]

As the sixteenth century progressed, however, there was a reversal of priorities within the pastoral office. Initially, the task had been perceived primarily in missionary terms i.e. winning souls from the deceit of Antichrist.[2] Only after that was the task to build up the faith of believers. However, by the middle of the seventeenth century, that order had been inverted, as becomes clear from Owen's comment in *The Duty of a Pastor*:

> *Our work* is the same with the apostles; the *method* directly contrary. The apostles had a work committed to them, and this was their method: – *The first work* committed to the apostles was the convincing and converting sinners to Christ among Jews and Gentiles, – to preach the gospel, to convert infidels; – this they accounted their chief work...And then, *their second work* was to teach those disciples to do and observe whatever Christ commanded them, and to bring them into church order...Now the same work is committed unto the pastors of churches; but in a

contrary method. The first object of our ministry is the church –
to build up and edify the church. But what then? Is the other part
of the work taken away, that they should not preach to convert
souls. [sic] God forbid.[3]

This is an idea with which Baxter concurred:

The work of the ordinary ministry...being only to gather and govern
the churches, their work lay in explaining and applying the word
of God and delivering his sacraments, and now containeth these
particulars following: 1. To preach the gospel for the conversion
of the unbelieving and ungodly world.[4]

This, then, is the specific contemporary context in which Owen
developed his teaching on sin: first, to build up and edify believers
and only after that for the purposes of mission and evangelism.
The state of the individual believer before the Judgement Throne
of God was of paramount importance for Owen. The effect of sin
on society as a whole and on the church is subordinate to this
inasmuch as it is only the sinful corruption of individuals which
invades and corrupts these institutions.

It is therefore right at this point to consider Owen's teaching
about the effect of sin on the individual. We have noted his
conviction that sin is, at its most basic, the breaking of the covenant
relationship and the disruption of the image of God in man. In
order to ground this theory in practical application, it is now
necessary to consider Owen's perception of the psychological and
physical make-up of the individual and how sin acts upon each
part. Consideration will then be given to two aspects of Owen's
teaching which are derivative of this, namely his understanding
of the function of the body in the process of sin and the role played
by Satan.

Owen accepted a bi-partite division between body and soul. It
is, however, his psychological categories, broadly identified as
the activity of the soul, which are of most interest to our present
study. Owen identified the psychological categories as being mind,
affections and will. He was not, of course, unique in holding this
view. The threefold categories had been a standard medieval

position and were accepted teaching within the Reformed tradition.[5] However, it is interesting to note that Calvin did differ slightly in his own approach. In his *Institutes*, he commented that 'the soul consists of two parts, the intellect and the will'.[6] Nevertheless, he was aware of the further distinction of the affections and did not discount it:

> Others distinguish thus: They say that sense inclines to pleasure in the same way as the intellect to good; that hence the appetite of sense becomes concupiscence and lust, while the affection of the intellect becomes will. For the term appetite, which they prefer, I use that of will, as being more common.[7]

The vital difference between Calvin's context and that of Owen is that Calvin was attempting to achieve simplicity in order to make a further theological point.[8] Owen, conversely, was examining the psychological categories more specifically and so brevity was not a concern for him in this regard. There is, then, no need to regard Owen's teachings as a development of Calvin's thought, or a moving away from it. Rather, a different context demanded a different approach that remained loyal to Calvin in its fundamentals.

Whilst mind, affections and will are inextricably intertwined as components of the soul, they each perform a different function and thus each category entertains sin in a way unique to itself. The impact of the Fall had a radical affect on humanity; the image of God has been marred, even lost; a fact that is evidenced most clearly in these faculties of the soul. To analyse Owen's approach in this regard, it is necessary for us to consider the effect of sin on each category separately.

Sin in the Mind

As with both the will and the affections, Owen's teaching concerning the nature and function of the mind needs to be considered with two distinct terms of reference: pre-Fall and post-Fall. Common to both, however, is Owen's belief that the function of the mind is that of the leading faculty in human nature, giving direction and purpose to the activities of the will and the affections:

'[The duty of the mind is] to keep the soul unto a constant, holy consideration of God and His grace...by [enquiring] what is good or evil and [judging] ethically what shall be done or refused.'[9]

The primary function of the mind is the exercise of its powers of reason. Since the defining feature of Adam being made in the image of God was his covenant relationship with God – the covenant of works – the mind was originally meant, through the gracious principle of God within, to enable and resource Adam's compliance with the same:

> This in Adam was the image of God, or an habitual conformity unto God, his mind and will, wherein the holiness and righteousness of God himself was represented, Genesis 1:26,27. In this image he was created, or it was concreated with him, as a perfection due to his nature in the condition wherein he was made. This gave him an habitual disposition unto all duties of that obedience that was required of him; it was the rectitude of all the faculties of his soul with respect unto his supernatural end, Ecclesiastes 7:29.[10]

Inherent in the relationship between God and the individual is the idea that the mind of God communicates with the mind of man through reason: 'According to these distinct faculties and powers of our souls [*natural light, rational consideration, faith*], God is pleased to reveal or make known himself, his mind or will.'[11] We reiterate the point that fundamental to Owen's argument was the belief that knowledge of God cannot be attained by means of reason alone. Rather, cognitive activity merely lays the foundations for the indwelling Spirit to perform a work of grace in the life of the believer.[12]

Owen developed this idea using Aristotelian and Thomist concepts. According to both Aristotle and Aquinas,[13] perfect knowledge consists in comprehending an object by using the essence of the object itself as the principle of demonstration. This is an idea that Aquinas developed with regard to our knowledge of God, when he stated that there are certain truths about God that totally surpass man's ability...Since, indeed, the principle of all knowledge that the reason perceives about some thing is the understanding of the very substance of that being...Now, sensible things cannot lead the human intellect to the point of seeing in them the nature of the divine substance; for sensible things are affects that fall short of the power of their cause.[14]

But, with regard to faith, Aquinas was able to state that

in many ways, [it] perceives the invisible things of God in a way higher than that of natural reason as it reaches towards God from creatures. Hence it is said in Ecclesiasticus 3:23: 'Many things beyond human understanding have been revealed unto thee.'[15]

Since God is a spiritual substance, the same therefore is required to comprehend him.

Contextualised within the broader tradition but most especially following Aquinas, Owen understood the rational faculty of the soul to be the arena for the initial promptings of the Holy Spirit towards saving faith. The result of this activity of the Spirit in the mind is manifold. The believer discovers a sense of the power and reality of spiritual matters and this strengthens faith. The experience of faith in the mind of the believer leads to a deepening understanding of the wisdom and authority of God. This, of course, is a work of the Holy Spirit and cannot be understood or comprehended in purely rational terms. Cognitive understanding of God, enabled by the Holy Spirit, is not an end in itself but only a means towards enjoying a right relationship with God.

In all his deliberations on the function and nature of the mind, Owen combined his Aristotelian and Thomist approach with an adherence to the teachings of Augustine, which borrow freely from neo-Platonism. Augustine himself had stressed the priority of the mind as a psychological category in his dialogue *On Free Will*, stating that

Whatever it is that puts man above the beasts, mind or spirit (perhaps it is best called by both names, for we find both in the divine Scriptures), whatever it is called, if it dominates and rules the other parts of which man is composed, then a man is most perfectly ordered.[16]

Owen also accepted the Augustinian notion that reason cannot be divorced from the illuminating power of God in the heart of the individual. Augustine understood reason to be, in some sense, the fulfilment of human nature[17] in that it constitutes man as being made in the image of God and enables him to participate in the Divine nature: 'For Reason who speaks with you promises to let you see God with your mind as the sun is seen with the eye.'[18]

Albeit in a different context, Calvin too wrote of reason as a means by which the mind gains knowledge of God:

> Then the mere knowledge of a God sufficiently proves that souls which rise higher than the world must be immortal, it being impossible that any evanescent vigour could reach the very fountain of life...the swiftness with which the human mind glances from heaven to earth, scans the secrets of nature...with intellect and memory digests each in its proper order...clearly shows that there lurks in man a something separated from the body. We have intellect by which we are able to conceive of the invisible God and angels – a thing of which body is altogether incapable. We have ideas of rectitude, justice, and honesty – ideas which the bodily senses cannot reach. The seat of these ideas must therefore be a spirit.[19]

As well as incorporating historic teaching into his writings, Owen contended with contemporary debate in this matter. He developed his own ideas, in part, in opposition to the writings of the Cambridge Platonists. These were a small group of men linked to the University in that town whose influence was considerable amongst their peers. The primary leaders – Whichcote,[20] Smith,[21] Cudworth,[22] More[23] and Culverwell[24] – were well known for the remarkable depth and clarity of their learning. They were respected too for their manner of living. The rule by which they lived out their Christian faith was one of universal charity towards those of other theological persuasions. Mild manners and genteel spirits were the hallmarks of their lives, as this section from Whichcote's *Aphorisms* (No. 956) reveals:

Religion doth possess and affect the *whole* man; in the understanding, it is knowledge; in the life, it is obedience; in the affections, it is delight in God; in our carriage and behaviour, it is modesty, calmness, gentleness, candor, ingenuity; in our dealings, it is uprightness, integrity, correspondence with the rule of righteousness.[25]

Owen was undoubtedly well acquainted with the teachings of this group of clergymen. When his books were auctioned after his death, many works by the Cambridge Platonists were in his collection.[26] Ownership of books does not necessarily imply that they have been read, but it is a reasonable assumption, given the scarcity and cost of books in Owen's time and the development of his argument in related matters, that he was indeed aware of the train of thought within these treatises. Furthermore, Owen was discerning about those aspects of their arguments and ideas he recognised as acceptable and those which were deemed to be opposed to orthodox Christian truth. For example, in his 1654 treatise, *The Doctrine of the Saints' Perseverance*, Owen wrote with respect about the ideas of Nathaniel Culverwell. Indeed, he went so far as to rank him with Beza, Perkins, Dodd, Sibbes and Cotton amongst others, stating that it is amongst men like these, Culverwell included, 'whose fame upon this very account, of the eminent and effectual breathing of a spirit of holiness in their writings, is gone out into all the nations about us, and their remembrance is blessed at home and abroad.'[27] However, only seven years earlier, in *The Death of Death in the Death of Christ*, he had been particularly scathing of the writings of Henry More, whose thoughts on the atonement of Christ Owen described as 'empty janglings'. Indeed, Owen described More as a man 'who is skilful only at fencing with his own shadow!'[28]

The notion that was proposed by the Cambridge Platonists, with the exception of Nathaniel Culverwell who maintained a much more orthodox Calvinist approach in emphasising the weakness of the human mind, was that 'rational knowledge of supersensible reality is attainable.'[29] For these men, the supremacy of reason was foundational for their teaching. Like Owen, they recognised reason (νους) to be a faculty of the soul; indeed, they were in agreement that it is the highest faculty since it is by reason that the soul communicates with God. But they were to go further than Owen would consider appropriate by stating that reason 'is the very voice of God.'[30] The implication of this view, for the Cambridge Platonists, was that faith was the mind's assent to the evidence about spiritual matters that reason presents to it. There is an innate ability in man, through natural revelation in the world, to comprehend God. The purpose of the Scriptures is no more than to reinforce the truths that are naturally accessible to the mind of man through reason.[31] It is not surprising, perhaps, that the ideas of the Cambridge Platonists were criticised by Calvinist theologians for their Arminian tendencies, the latter being a natural consequence of neo-Platonist teaching on the emanation of goodness into the created order.[32]

This was diametrically opposed to Owen's understanding of the nature of the mind, post-Fall. For him, all men remain in a state of spiritual blindness without the effective operation of the Holy Spirit in their souls, having no ability to do or be otherwise. Owen was quick to condemn the writings of the Cambridge Platonists in this regard: 'Some at present talk much about the power of the *intellectual faculties* of our souls, as though they were neither debased, corrupted, impaired, nor depraved...Indeed, some of them write as if they had never deigned once to consult the Scriptures.'[33]

Owen's final comment is rhetoric, however, since the Cambridge Platonists were highly learned in the Scriptures. Indeed, despite their intensely philosophical leanings they would claim, quite rightly, that Scripture was foundational to their ideas[34] and that philosophical writings were only drawn upon to illustrate and reinforce the truth of their ideas or the moral implications of the same. To that extent, then, the Cambridge men claimed to have based their teaching about reason on the Scriptures and, in the light of the early Genesis chapters, they did recognise an impairing of the faculties of the mind by the Fall. Reason had been affected through that event but only as 'an old MS., with some broken periods, some letters worn out; it was a picture which had lost its gloss and beauty, the oriency of its colours, the elegancy of its lineaments, the comeliness of its proportions – it was like Leah, blear-eyed.'[35]

However, the notion of 'impairment' fell far short of Owen's own notion of depravity of the mind and was in no way acceptable to him. For Owen, the mind has been completely corrupted by sin; irreversibly so without the effectual work of the Holy Spirit in the process of regeneration and sanctification.[36] Any idea that there is an innate power within the mind to comprehend spiritual reality was anathema to Owen.

For Owen, the Fall radically altered the way in which the mind works; whilst the function remained the same in essence, the ability of the believer to fulfil that function was destroyed.

> There was the same cogitative or imaginative faculty in us in the state of innocency as there remains under the power of sin; but then all the actings of it were orderly and regular, – the mind was able to direct them all unto the end for which we were made...But now, being turned off from him, the mind...engageth in all manner of *confusion*; and they all end in *vanity* and disappointment.[37]

The effect of the Fall on humanity, then, was to invert the psychological priority within each individual; that which had formerly been an intellectual being, with the reason informing the will, became a voluntarist being with the corrupted will and affections now driving and informing the mind. Owen adopted this as his foundational approach for comprehending the effect of the Fall on the mind:

> The mind and reason were in perfect subjection and subordination to God and his will...The mind's subjection to God was the spring of the orderly and harmonious motion of the soul and all the wheels in it. That being disturbed by sin, the rest of the faculties move cross and contrary one to another.[38]

Owen held to Calvin's distinction[39] – which he in turn attributed to Augustine – between spiritual gifts and natural gifts; that the spiritual gifts have become depraved through the Fall, whereas the natural gifts have only been corrupted. Since the function of the mind is to facilitate man's response to God in a covenant relationship – and is therefore a primarily spiritual category – the Fall has rendered the individual incapable of responding to God in an appropriate manner. Thus the need for the renewal of the mind by the Holy Spirit was paramount in Owen's doctrine of salvation:

> Whereas the mind of man, or the minds of all men, are by *nature depraved, corrupt, carnal*, and *enmity against God*, they cannot themselves, or by virtue of any innate ability of their own, understand or assent unto spiritual things in a spiritual manner...*there is and must be wrought in us, by the power of the Holy Spirit, faith supernatural and divine, whereby we are enabled so to do, or rather whereby we do so.*[40]

Given the importance of the mind for Owen, it was perhaps inevitable that he should see it as the primary point of entry for sin:

> Where the mind is tainted, the prevalency [of sin] must be great; for the mind or understanding is the leading faculty of the soul, and what that fixes on, the will and the affections rush after, being capable of no consideration but what that presents unto them.[41]

Owen quoted Matthew 6:23 to confirm this view: 'If then the light in you is darkness, how great is the darkness!' The power of sin in the mind finds its outworking in a number of ways.

The deadening of the mind towards God is achieved primarily through the deceit of sin as stated in Hebrews 3:13.[42] Owen believed every human lust to be deceitful but not in its essential nature; it only becomes deceitful through the law of sin that acts upon it. Owen likened the lusts of the mind to that of water from a contaminated spring: 'where there is poison in every stream, the fountain must needs be corrupt.'[43]

Owen understood the nature of deceit itself to consist in presenting the soul with lies or half-truths. Only the desirable aspects of an action are presented[44] and reality is thereby obscured.[45] Thus the mind is deceived into making false judgements about that which is proposed. The process of deceit is slow in order that its design may not be apprehended all at once. Owen recognised a natural link between deceit and temptation. Indeed, the two terms could be understood as interchangeable: sin, the source of temptation, lies in deceit. Owen clarified this by stating that 'in the business of sin, to be effectually tempted, and to be beguiled or deceived, are the same.'[46]

As we might expect, the notion of temptation is a complex one in Owen's writings. There is a form of temptation that leads to sin but there is another form of temptation that comes from God. This latter form is in no way meant to lead the individual into sin. In *Of Temptation*, Owen suggested three ways in which God tempts people. First, by asking great things of them in order that they may grow into holiness and a greater strength of character, such as was the case of Abraham's instruction to sacrifice Isaac.[47] Secondly, by allowing the affliction of great sufferings in order to try their faith, as has been the case with Christian martyrdom. Thirdly, in accordance with Deuteronomy 8:3, by his secret provision in times of need in order to discover whether the believer will acknowledge the grace of God or not.[48]

The type of temptation with which we are currently concerned, however, is not that which comes from God but the 'temptation in its special nature, as it denotes an *active efficiency towards sinning*.'[49] Owen wrote at great length on this topic, outlining temptation's source and effect as well as the method of combating this evil. Quoting James 1:14,15, Owen outlined five steps in the process of sin through temptation: deception, enticement and conception, development and then achievement.[50] It is in the first of these, deception, that the activity of sin is wrought on the mind, diverting its attentions away from a true contemplation of God. Sin does this in two ways.

First, sin 'doth it by a horrible *abuse of gospel grace*.'[51] Owen believed the purpose of grace to be the enabling of holy living. However, the outworking of sin upon the mind 'separates between the doctrine of grace and the use and end of it.'[52] Thus sin induces the believer to dwell upon the theory and idea of grace rather than allowing it to influence the style and standard of living. Such behaviour results in a false assurance of forgiveness that allows for continuing sin: 'From the doctrine of the assured pardon of sin, it insinuates a regardlessness of sin.'[53] Such deceit was condemned by Paul in Romans 6:1-2 and by Jude (verse 4) and Owen followed their teaching thus:

> This is the trial and touchstone of gospel light: – If it keep the heart sensible of sin, humble, lowly, and broken on that account, – if it teach us to water a free pardon with tears, to detest forgiven sin, to watch diligently for the ruin of that which we are yet assured shall never ruin us, – it is divine, from above, of the Spirit of grace.[54]

Temptation plays upon this cheapened understanding of grace by denying the need for tenacious living and disregarding the seriousness of sin 'whereby the deceitfulness of sin draws off the mind from a due attendance unto that sense of its vileness which alone is able to keep it in that humble, self-abased frame that is acceptable with God'.[55]

Secondly, sin 'takes advantage to work by its deceit, in this matter of drawing off the mind from a due sense of it, from the state and condition of men in the world'.[56] Drawing on Jeremiah 2:2, Owen suggested that the believer is more spiritually aware in the early days of faith and that initial belief encompasses a stronger sense of sinfulness than that which accompanies spiritual maturity.[57] This is not because such maturity understands the function of sin better than the newly converted; rather, weariness and a neglect of spiritual duty often accompany spiritual maturity. Thus 'if...the mind do not affect the heart with sorrow and grief [concerning its sin], the whole will be cast out, and the soul be in danger of being hardened.'[58]

Owen perceived sin also to work deceit in the mind by leading the believer to the neglect of meditation and prayer. Owen likened this activity of sin to the parable of the Wedding Feast recorded in Luke 14:16-19: 'All those who excused themselves from coming into the marriage-feast of the gospel, did it on account of their being engaged in their lawful callings...By this plea were the minds of men drawn off from that frame of heavenliness which is required to our walking with God.'[59]

Thus sin at work in the mind minimises the significance of spiritual duties and the need for obedience. The mind becomes apathetic to all things godly and distracted from things spiritual. Owen did not suggest that the mind of the believer ceases from glorifying God but such worship might become generalised in its form. There comes into the heart of the believer a feeling of self-satisfaction and contentment with the *status quo* that is unbecoming of the Christian and dishonouring to God.[60] Using Amos 5:21-25 as his example, Owen commented on the

> many duties of worship and obedience performed by a woeful generation of hypocrites, formalists, and profane persons, without either life or light in themselves, or acceptation with God, their minds being wholly estranged from a due attendance unto what they do by the power and deceitfulness of sin.[61]

The victory of sin in this regard thus produces spiritual sloth and, to complement his use of Amos 5, Owen called upon many other scriptural references in his warning against this particular outworking of sin in the mind.[62] Owen understood spiritual sloth to have four characteristics. First, inadvertency, in which he states that 'a secret regardlessness is apt to creep upon the soul'. Secondly, an 'unwillingness to be stirred up unto its duty'. Thirdly, 'weak and ineffectual attempts to recover it unto its duty' and fourth, 'heartlessness upon the apprehensions of difficulties and discouragements.'[63]

Owen outlined four ways in which sin so works within the individual. Initially, sin 'makes advantage of its weariness unto the flesh.'[64] Reflecting on the words of Jesus in Matthew 26:41 that 'the spirit is willing but the flesh is weak', Owen suggested that weariness of the flesh results in an unwillingness to pray. Such an attitude that is born out of physical tiredness eventually becomes endemic in one's spirituality:

> And it may come at length unto that height which is mentioned, Malachi 1:13, 'Ye have said, Behold, what a weariness is it! and ye have sniffed at it, saith the Lord of hosts'...And this the

deceitfulness of sin makes use of to draw the heart by insensible
degrees from a constant attendance unto it.[65]

Such an attitude leads to the second way in which sin is at work in
this matter, namely that 'the deceitfulness of sin makes use of
corrupt reasonings, taken from the pressing and urging *occasions
of life*.'[66] Owen was aware of the pressures of everyday life but
was insistent that excess time spent on regular duties is nothing
less than 'robbing God of that which is due to him and our own
souls'.[67]

Thirdly, and resulting from what has gone before, sin may 'draw
[the mind] off from its attendance unto this duty, by a tender of
compensation to be made in and by other duties'. The way in
which these other duties may seem to act in compensation for the
need of prayer is likened to Saul's sin in 1 Samuel 13:9f.[68] Finally,
sin works by promising the soul that it may become diligent once
more when time and energy permit. However, the damage is done
and the time and moment is irrevocably lost.[69] Such an attitude
inevitably conflicted harshly with Owen's Puritan sense of self-
discipline and moral conscience. Prayer must necessarily be a daily
activity, regular in attendance and a priority not lightly set aside.

Thus it is that temptation must first reason with the mind if it is
to have a later effect on the affections and will. Such reasoning, over
a period of time, lessens the abhorrence toward sin in the believer:

> By long *solicitations*, causing the mind frequently to converse
> with the evil solicited unto, it begets extenuating thoughts of it...It
> may be when first it began to press upon the soul, the soul was
> amazed at the ugly appearance of what it aimed at, and cried,
> 'Am I a dog?' If this indignation be not daily heightened, but the
> soul, by conversing with the evil begins to grow, as it were, familiar
> with it...then...lust hath then enticed and entangled.[70]

Owen understood the power of temptation to '*darken the mind*,
that a man shall not be able to make a right judgment of things, so
as he did before he entered into it. As in the men of the world, the
god of this world blinds their minds that they should not see the
glory of Christ in the gospel.'[71] By succumbing to temptation,

believers can become so obsessed with an object that the mind is distracted from the very thing that can provide relief; the mind is drawn away from God and 'shall walk on in darkness and have no light.'[72] And so temptation works in the mind by confusing the inclinations of the heart. The entanglement of the affections results in the inability of the mind to make rational judgements: 'Give me a man engaged in hope, love, fear, in reference to any particulars wherein he ought not, and I shall quickly show you wherein he is darkened and blinded.'[73]

Owen's teaching on the effect of sin on the mind needs to be set within the wider context of the theological debate of his day, not just regarding the Cambridge Platonists. There is certainly a polemical intent in a great deal that he has to say on this topic. As we shall see below, Owen was reacting in part to the excesses of his radical contemporaries, most notably the Quakers and the Antinomians. Owen clearly believed the cognitive senses to be primary in the development of a right understanding of God. Thus any religious activity that does not rely, to some extent, upon right understanding, was thought by Owen to be an arena through which the deceit of sin can work itself in the life of the believer. In this regard, Owen's teaching focused upon three primary issues: the need for God-centred rationality in faith, the development of a self-critical analytical mode of thinking and the necessity of structured prayer and meditation.

First, concerning the need for God-centred rationality. Owen's attitude so described is clear in his literary treatment of the Quakers, who deprecated the use of understanding and human learning.[74] The testimony of one William Dewsbury, recounted by William Braithwaite, will suffice to show the extent to which such learning was abandoned within their movement:

> His spiritual travail was long and hard, beginning when he was a boy of thirteen. 'I heard,' he says, 'much speaking of God and professing Him in words from the letter of the Scripture, but I met with none that could tell me what God had done for their souls.' At length all his 'Fig-leaf coverings were rent,' the Lord 'manifested His power' to him, and brought 'the immortal seed to birth' within him, and he bears this personal testimony: 'I came

to my knowledge of eternal life not by the letter of the scripture, nor from hearing men speak of God, but by the Inspiration of the Spirit of Jesus Christ who is worthy to open the seals.'[75]

Such reliance amongst the Quaker movement upon the Spirit's action within at the expense of a developed cognitive appreciation of God was a cause of sardonic attack by Owen:

> Our Quakers, who have for a long season hovered up and down like a swarm of flies, with a confused noise and humming, begin now to settle in the opinions lately by them declared for. But what their thoughts will fall in to be concerning the Holy Ghost, when they shall be contented to speak intelligibly, and according to the usage of other men, or the pattern of Scripture the great rule of speaking or treating about spiritual things, I know not, and am uncertain whether they do so themselves or no. Whether he may be the light within them, or an infallible afflatus, is uncertain. In the meantime, what is revealed unto us in the Scripture to be believed concerning the Holy Ghost, his Deity and personality, may be seen.[76]

His attitude towards the Quakers is partly obscured by his wit but Owen elsewhere lamented them as being 'poor deluded souls' whose faith was nothing more than 'an ulcer,'[77] and in whose 'present madness [have] renewed [the Montanist] follies.'[78] His position is made clearer still when he writes 'Satan in these days assaults the sacred truth of the Word of God, in its authority, purity, integrity, or perfection, especially in the poor, deluded, fanatical souls amongst us, commonly called Quakers.'[79]

Owen recognised that the deceit of sin performs its work too in those who do accept cognitive understanding but abrogate scriptural principles. Owen's most strenuous attacks in this regard were against the Antinomians, whose teachings in England can be dated back to 1615 with the preaching of John Eaton[80] of Wickham Market, Suffolk. Eaton was criticised by Peter Gunter in 1615 of preaching 'libertinism'; that after justification, God no longer saw the sin of the believer. Eaton's posthumously published book, *The Honey-Combe of Free Justification by Christ alone*

(1642) brought the Antinomian debate into the public arena. He had written the treatise as a polemic against the insistence of the Reformed Orthodox tradition on using the law as a rule of life for the believer.[81] Moreover, Eaton believed his ideas concerning free justification to be little more that a reiteration of the thoughts of Luther, found especially in his *Commentary on Galatians*. In accord with Luther, Eaton believed the law to have little place in the life of the believer; it being merely an instrument by which the sinner is brought to Christ. Thereafter, the believer no longer requires the law. Archbishop Abbot, describing Eaton as 'simple and ignorant', deprived him of his living in 1619.

Notwithstanding, some aspects of Eaton's theology were acceptable to some Puritans in the Calvinist tradition. Indeed, the emphasis of his christology, which speaks of Christ suffering the curse and wrath of God against sinners, is echoed in Owen's own writings.[82] However, Eaton developed his teaching further than either Owen or his contemporaries could accept. Perhaps due to an incoherent differentiation between justification and sanctification, Eaton believed that God only sees the imputed righteousness of Christ and not the sin of the believer.[83] This led to the charge of teaching moral and ethical licentiousness. Further, Eaton was perhaps unwise in his use of theological language in describing the state of the believer before God; claims of union with Christ and private revelation that 'opens unto us the very closets of heaven' did nothing to help his cause.[84]

Antipathy towards Antinomian theology was intense amongst Reformed theologians as this quotation from Annesley[85] illustrates:

> If they have (indeed) found out a cage of such unclean Birds, as chatter with their foul mouths; Let us continue in sin, that grace may abound...if they be acquainted with any such Anti-nomians, as will not receive the Law of God for the rule of their actions; we will help to drive them out of these Coasts, or (if they please) out of the World.[86]

This is a view with which Samuel Young concurred: 'But there is no end of Naming the black, horrid and blasphemous Notions and Expressions in [Antinomianism].'[87]

For Owen and his Reformed contemporaries, the debate with Antinomianism was not a theological nicety; it was an issue of immense pastoral concern that attacked a true doctrine of God. The pastoral nature of this confrontation is amply illustrated by this story recounted by Thomas Gataker:[88]

> I remember, while I abode at Lincolns Inne, to have visited a religious Lady, sister to a reverend Divine of special note in those daies: whom I found somewhat perplexed; the ground thereof arising from some conference that had newly passed between her and a grave Divine of great repute, but in somethings warping a little way [towards Antinomianism]...who questioning her... began to chide her, and told her that she went needlessly about the bush, when she had a neerer and readier way to hand...God will save sinners. But I am a sinner. Therefore God will save me...I told her...she might with as good ground thus reason; God will damn sinners. I am a sinner. Therefore God will damn me...[Antinomians] are given up to strong delusions, that believ [sic] some kind of lies, I know not what to say or think of those, that teach men to believ such lies as these are.[89]

Owen believed Antinomianism to be deceit of the worst kind. Not only was there an acceptance in their doctrine of eternal justification, a concept which Owen utterly rejected,[90] but their teachings seemed to him to deny the importance of the atonement and the regenerative work of the Holy Spirit, and thereby compromise a true doctrine of God:

> [Antinomianism is] most derogatory unto the law of God, which affirms [the law] to be divested of its power to oblige unto perfect obedience, so as that what is not so shall (as it were in spite of the law) be accepted as if it were so, unto the end for which the law requires it.[91]

Secondly, concerning the need for a self-critical mode of thinking. Puritan spirituality was inextricably linked with moral self-examination, which was concerned in large part with the effect of sin on the mind.[92] Owen advocated the usefulness of critiquing one's ability and progress in withstanding the fiery darts of temptation as a method of assessing one's relationship with God.[93] He believed such a self-understanding concerning one's spiritual duty to be of primary importance, for, without this, sin works freely in the mind: 'When a man is *weakened*, made *negligent* or *formal* in duty...let him know, that though he may not be acquainted with the particular distemper wherein it consists, yet in something or other he is entered into temptation.'[94] Such carelessness in duty is impossible to reconcile with the nature of Christian discipleship and difficult to repair in the life of the believer, such is the power of sin in the mind. The outward performance of Christian behaviour is continued but, as with the Church in Sardis,[95] the interior life of faith is dead.

Owen further suggested that such self-criticism needs to take into account the individual temperament of the believer which itself harbours a tendency towards particular sins:

> As men have peculiar natural tempers...so men have *peculiar lusts* or corruptions, which, either by their natural constitution or education, and other prejudices, have got deep rooting and strength in them. This, also, is to be found out by him who would not enter into temptation.[96]

By such self-knowledge the believer is better able to withstand the encroachment of sin upon the mind. Temptation will be recognised at an early stage, thus increasing the ability of the believer to deny it access and power in behavioural and thought patterns. Owen elucidated thus: 'Be acquainted, then, with thine own heart: though it be deep, search it; though it be dark, inquire into it; though it give all its distempers other names than what are their due, believe it not.'[97]

Thirdly, and as a result of this self-critical mode of thinking, was the realisation for Owen that no individual has any innate power to combat the workings of sin in the mind. The chief weapon that is to be employed, therefore, is prayer for self-preservation by the work of the Holy Spirit in the soul.[98] Owen placed considerable emphasis on prayer as an instrument for combat against sin in the mind. Indeed, he considered it to be the primary focus for the avoidance of temptation: 'He that would be little in temptation, let him be much in prayer. This calls in the suitable help and succour that is laid up in Christ for us, Hebrews 4:16. This casteth our souls into a frame of opposition to every temptation.'[99] Again,

> Store the heart with a sense of the love of God in Christ, with the eternal design of his grace, with a taste of the blood of Christ, and his love in the shedding of it; get a relish of the privileges we have thereby, – our adoption, justification, acceptation with God; fill the heart with thoughts of the beauty of holiness, as it is designed by Christ for the end, issue and effect of his death; – and thou wilt, in an ordinary course of walking with God, have great peace and security as to the disturbance of temptations.[100]

The relationship between a self-critical mode of thinking and prayer were, for Owen, two sides of the same coin; each informs the other and enables the believer to comprehend both a personal inability to advance in the Christian faith and the overwhelming grace of God that makes it possible.

Finally, and perhaps as an incidental issue, Owen's teaching on the effect of sin in the mind does appear to result in his partial rejection of a quite legitimate arena for spiritual experience, namely the gifts of the Spirit. The rationality of faith that Owen expounded seems to result in his undervaluing, even misunderstanding, the more extraordinary gifts; and, in some cases, a wholesale rejection of their importance for the contemporary church. In keeping with his understanding of faith, Owen stated that

> *spiritual gifts* are placed and seated in the *mind* or understanding only; whether they are ordinary or extraordinary, they have no other hold or residence in the soul. And they are in the mind as it is *notional* and theoretical, rather than as it is *practical*. They are intellectual abilities, and no more.... The will, and the affections, and the conscience are unconcerned in them.[101]

In so describing the gifts of the Spirit, Owen was attempting to present a position of acceptance without giving ground to those whom he regarded as being deceived by sin in their usage of these gifts, most notably the Quakers. However, in maintaining this view, Owen did not remain faithful to Scripture, as Ferguson rightly claims:

> Owen may appear to be on weak ground when he represents the working of spiritual gifts as rational rather than affectional. Paul speaks of his understanding being unfruitful when he uses the gift of tongues. It is commonly held that this gift, at least, was not regarded as dominantly rational.[102]

Owen's desire to uphold the gifts of the Spirit as operating at the level of cognitive behaviour becomes clearer in his exposition on the various gifts. Those which he deemed to be common to the contemporary church – words of wisdom, words of knowledge and the gift of faith – are to be considered extraordinary in degree rather than type; an improvement by the power of the Holy Spirit upon that which the natural faculties could supply.[103] Owen's understanding of the more extraordinary gifts differed from this view quite considerably, as this example concerning the gift of tongues will reveal:

> Although this gift was excellent in itself...yet in the *assemblies of the church* it was of little or no use, but only with respect unto the things themselves that were uttered; for as to the principal end of it, to be a *sign* unto unbelievers, it was finished and accomplished towards them, so as they had no farther need or use of it.[104]

Whilst Owen did not deny the possibility that God may choose on occasions to work miraculously within the contemporary church, he did deny these gifts a common function within the Christian community. He believed these gifts to have been withdrawn by God as a natural and regular outworking of the Body of Christ at the cessation of the apostolic era. It was in making this assertion that Owen provided the clearest declaration of the relationship between excessive claims on the gifts of the Spirit and the deceiving power of sin in the mind:

It is not unlikely but that God might on some occasions, for a longer season, put forth his power in some miraculous operations; and so he yet may do, and perhaps doth sometimes. But the *superstition* and folly of some ensuing ages, inventing and divulging innumerable miracles false and foolish, proved a most disadvantageous prejudice unto the gospel, and a means to open a way unto Satan to impose endless delusions upon Christians...so the pretence of such [miracles]...is the greatest dishonour unto religion that any one can invent.[105]

Thus Owen declared any claim to excessive use of the extraordinary gifts of the Spirit a sinful deceit of the mind. This implication of his doctrine of sin is clearly polarised to many claims of spiritual experience throughout the Christian era and, indeed, amongst his peers for, as Ferguson concludes, '[the claim to the reception of apostolic gifts] disguised the existence of a deep delusion, as far as Owen was concerned, as his constant attacks on "Inner Light" theology demonstrate.'[106] Thus it may be argued that, in this regard only, the implications of Owen's understanding of the effect of sin on the mind prove to be contrary to historic Christian experience and theology.

Sin in the Affections

The natural consequence of sin in the mind is to disturb and corrupt the affections. The importance of this psychological category cannot be overestimated: 'affections are in the soul, as the helm is in the ship; if it be laid hold on by a skilful hand, it turneth the whole vessel which way he pleaseth.'[107] Again,

Our affections are upon the matter our all. They are all we have to give or bestow; the only power of our souls whereby we may give away ourselves from ourselves and become another's. Other faculties of our souls, even the most noble of them, are suited to receive in unto our own advantage; by our affections we can give away *what we are and have*. Hereby we give our hearts unto God, as he requireth.[108]

Furthermore, it is the redemption of the affections in man which is central to the story of salvation itself and which thereby forms the basis of experiential faith:

> But that the holy God should as it were engage in the contest and strive for the affections of man, is an effect of infinite condescension and grace...It is our affections he asketh for, and comparatively nothing else...All the ways and methods of the dispensation of his will by his word, all the designs of his effectual grace, are suited unto and prepared for this end, – namely to recover the affections of man unto himself.[109]

Given this context for sin, then, the focus of our affections, driven by our voluntary thoughts, is the measure of the standing of the individual before God. If the affections are given towards earthly matters and ungodly desires, then the individual is in a state of sinfulness. If the affections are given up to the contemplation of Christ and matters of a spiritual nature, then the individual is in a state of grace. The experience of grace in the soul will naturally tend towards the outward living of a life of faith. It is from such a supposition that the process of sanctification, through mortification and the benefits of Christ being wrought in the soul by the Holy Spirit, can take root and bear fruit.

The affections were understood by Owen to be that faculty of the inner person that determines responses in the light of rational consideration by the mind. The affections are thus the driving forces behind choices made by the individual. Commenting on the spirituality of John Owen, Packer defines the affections as 'the various dispositional "drives", positive and negative, with their emotional overtones – love, hope, hate, fear and so on – which elicit choices by drawing man to or repelling him from particular objects.'[110]

This concept of the affections was common amongst many of Owen's contemporaries and there was little divergence concerning their function. William Fenner[111] perhaps represented the wider tradition when he wrote that

> The affections are motions. They are the motions of the heart...the feet of the soule: for as the body goes with its feet to that which it

loves, so the soule goes out with its affections to that which it loves.... The affections are the wings of the Soule. If the birds wings be lime-twig'd and glued to the ground, she cannot flye up; now a carnall man his affections are glued and lime-twig'd to the things of the world, or the things of this life; and therefore it is impossible he should flie up unto God.[112]

Others too were keen to understand the affections as a part of the reflected image of God and integrally linked to the mind through the actings upon the affections of reason:

[The affections] contain in them a part of mans holiness and of the Image of God.... In Man they are then holy whenas they are agreeable to the nature of the object; as when a man loveth that onely [sic] which ought to be loved, and hateth that which by the will and word of God ought to be hated.... Thus they being ordered by reason and the word of God are not contrary to holiness, but a part of it.[113]

Owen contended strongly with his theological adversaries concerning the nature of the affections in Adam prior to the Fall:

All the affections [were] subservient to the rule of reason for the performance of all natural actions...whereby he was enabled to yield obedience unto God for the attaining of that supernatural end whereunto he was created.... Our nature was then inclined to good only...there was then no inclination to sin, no concupiscence of that which is evil, no repugnancy to the law of God, in the pure nature of man.[114]

Firmly situated in the Reformed tradition, it is perhaps inevitable that Owen was, in part, reliant upon the Aristotelian tradition for his understanding of the affections. He wrote of 'consequential affections' as those aspects of the individual that sustain communion with Christ: 'Christ having given himself to the soul, loves the soul; and the soul having given itself unto Christ, loveth him also.'[115] Owen referred to four aspects involved in loving Christ, the first of which is *delight*. In expounding this idea, Owen used the words of Aristotle for definition: 'the rest and complacence of the mind in a suitable, desirable good enjoyed.'[116]

Owen stressed the notion that the affections have a dominant function in the ethical behaviour of the individual. Whilst the mind is the primary source of the entry of sin into the life of the individual, it is the affections that ultimately grant sin a home in the life of the believer: 'The *affections*...naturally are the principal servants and instruments of sin.'[117] This is not to say that the affections themselves are anything but neutral. It is only the actings of the mind upon them that produce in them any ethical response. Thomas Pierce[118] spoke for the Reformed understanding of this matter in his treatise, *The Signal Diagnostick*: 'Our affections in themselves are indifferent things; apt to be cleaving to any object, whether evil, or good, as they shall happen to be directed, by carnal Appetite or Reason.'[119] The power of sin in the affections is, quite literally, overwhelming: 'Let grace be enthroned in the mind and judgment, yet if the law of sin lays hold upon and entangles the affections, or any of them, it hath gotten a fort from whence it continually assaults the soul.'[120]

Owen also recognised the manner in which sin is at work in the affections. Although his treatment of this was far more concise than that of sin in the mind, it is still a vital aspect of his writings since he thinks of this type of spiritual malaise to be endemic throughout his society to an alarming degree:

What influence [the affections] have in blinding the mind and darkening the understanding is known. If any know it not, let him but open his eyes in these days, and he will quickly learn it...We may every day see persons of very eminent light, that yet visibly have unmortified hearts and conversations; their affections have not been crucified with Christ.[121]

The activity of sin upon the affections is primarily one of seduction from truth. In this manner, Owen likened the individual to a boat on the sea, driven and tossed about by the winds of temptation that afflict the affections.[122] Other poetical allusions to describe the affections were made by Owen's contemporaries, such as by Thomas Morton[123] in his treatise entitled *On the Three-fold State of Man*: 'in the affections [sin] may well be compared to a mad man set on hors-backe [sic], yea on a wilde horse, which can neither stay himselfe or bee stayed by any other meanes, till he hath runne himselfe out of breath and life in all outrage of sin.'[124]

Perhaps the greatest effect of affections enslaved to sin is that they are

> greatly moved, they cloud and darken the mind, and fill it with strange apprehensions concerning God and themselves. Every thing is presented unto them through a glass composed of fear, dread, terror, sorrow, and all sorts of disconsolations.[125]

Owen makes specific his doctrine by suggesting five examples of corrupt affections, namely: (1) Pride and confidence in one's own wisdom, (2) the love of honour amongst one's contemporaries, (3) an adherence to corrupt religious traditions and spiritual errors, (4) spiritual sloth in personal piety and (5) a love of sin and hatred of the truth.

Sin in the Will

The concept of the will was central to Owen's anthropology. Indeed, the very existence of the will was considered by Owen to be a major aspect of defining personhood: 'This is the most eminently distinguishing character and property of a person. Whatever is endued with an intelligent will is a person.'[126] In defining the will itself, Owen offered up two aspects: 'first, as a rational, vital faculty of our souls; secondly, as a free principle, freedom being of its essence or nature.'[127] These two ideas need to be outlined separately.

First, the will is 'a rational, vital faculty of our souls'. As the function of the affections is to compel or repel the individual towards certain objects, so the function of the will is to act upon what has been learned. Owen described it as '*a rational appetite*, – rational as guided by the mind, and an appetite as excited by the affections...it chooseth nothing but "sub ratione boni", as it hath *an appearance of good.*'[128] Thus the will is guided by both the mind and the affections, responding only to that which it deems to be good: 'Moral actions are unto us or in us so far good or evil as they partake of the consent of the will.'[129]

By so describing the will, Owen was again taking recourse in the teachings of Calvin and Aristotle. For Calvin, the rational guidance of the will by the mind was of utmost importance:

> the power of the free will is not to be considered in any of those desires which proceed more from instinct than mental deliberation. Even the Schoolmen admit (*Thomas*, Part I., *Quaest.* 83, art. 3) that there is no act of free will, unless when reason looks at opposites. By this they mean, that the things desired must be such as may be made the object of choice, and that to pave the way for choice, deliberation must precede.[130]

This understanding of the will being 'rational as guided by the mind, and an appetite as excited by the affections' also mirrors the Aristotelian ideal of that which is good is also desirable and that one's desires are rooted in the virtues attributed to certain objects or individuals. To quote Owen again,

> Good is [the will's] natural and necessary object, and therefore whatever is proposed unto it for its consent must be proposed under an appearance of being either good in itself, or good at present unto the soul, or good so circumstantiate as it is.[131]

Secondly, Owen described the will as 'a free principle, freedom being of its essence or nature'. This idea, founded on Augustine's *Epistle lxxxix*, cannot be understood apart from Owen's highly developed pneumatology. Adhering to his Augustinian roots, Owen suggested that, in its present condition, the will has no innate qualities of itself by which it is able to choose the good, since its very nature has become corrupted: 'It is principally with respect unto the *will* and its *depravation* by nature that we are said to be *dead in sin*.'[132] Rather, its perfection derives from its union with the divine – a union that is achieved through the indwelling of the Holy Spirit. By this, the individual is led into a love for God, which is impossible for the will without the divine prompting: 'This, therefore, in our conversion to God, is renewed by the Holy

Ghost, and that by an effectual implantation in it of a principle of spiritual life and holiness in the room of that original righteousness which is lost by the fall.'[133] Furthermore, the will is inspired by the Holy Spirit in its quest for the common good inasmuch as it recognises the divine goodness in others, which is its motivation. Such love and charity, which is a divine grace within the will, inspires its choices for the good: '[The Holy Spirit] gives us a new heart and puts a new spirit within us, writes his law in our hearts, that we may do the mind of God and walk in his ways.'[134]

It is within that pneumatological context that Owen claimed the will to be, by nature, 'a free principle'. This concept of 'freedom' must be considered in two forms, both of which are Augustinian in origin.[135] First, the will is 'voluntas', a term used to denote Owen's understanding of the will as foundational to personhood. It is that aspect of personality from which all actions proceed. It is not, however, a faculty of 'discovery', since Owen attributed this function to the mind:

> Nothing in the soul, nor the will and affections, can will, desire, or cleave unto any good, but what is presented unto them by the *mind*, and as it is presented. That good, whatever it be, which the mind cannot discover, the will cannot choose.[136]

Second, the will is 'arbitrium'; a term that suggests the ability to choose between alternatives and varying courses of action. According to Owen, the will is 'a free principle' as 'arbitrium', in that it is aware of its choices and its responsibility to choose the good. However, the will is not free on the level of 'voluntas', at least in the fallen state of humanity. Owen did not believe the will to be able, in and of itself, to turn towards God in love. Therefore, the work of the Holy Spirit in this regard is to redeem the will in 'voluntas' such that the 'arbitrium' may function in a godly manner:

> There is, therefore, necessary such a work of the Holy Spirit upon our wills as may cure and take away the depravation of the...freeing us from the state of spiritual death, causing us to live unto God, and determining them in and unto acts of faith and obedience...and that freely and of choice.[137]

Concerning the relationship of the will to sin, Owen wrote thus:

> Now the will is the ruling, governing faculty of the soul, as the mind is the guiding and leading. Whilst this abides unchanged, unrenewed, the power and reign of sin continue in the soul, though not undisturbed yet unruined.[138]

The will, left untamed, is wont to run into sin 'as the horse into battle';[139] 'the bent and inclination of the will itself is to sin and evil always and continually.'[140] This inclination has a negative effect on the functioning of the will:

> The will, in the depraved condition of fallen nature, is not only habitually filled and possessed with an aversion from that which is good spiritually...but also continually acts an opposition unto it, as being under the power of the 'carnal mind', which is 'enmity against God'.[141]

It is prevented in its perversion by the fear of the Lord and the promise and expectation of eternal life. However, whilst the effect of sin on the will may be restrained by godly considerations, it can never be eradicated in its completeness.

The will consents to sin in two particular ways. The first is full consent, since 'the convictions of the mind being conquered and [there is] no principle of grace in the will to weaken it.'[142] The example of Ahab's murder of Naboth is given in this regard as a deliberate act of will with full consent.[143] Secondly, the will consents to sin in attendance 'with a secret renitency and volition of the contrary', such as was the case with Peter's denial of Jesus.[144] Certainly, it was Peter's will to deny his Master but 'yet, at this very time, there was resident in his will a contrary principle of love to Christ, yea, and faith in him, which utterly failed not.... Though [the will] consented, it was not done with self-pleasing.'[145] Yet, paradoxically, the power of the will is its very '*liberty, freedom*, and *ability* to consent unto, choose, and embrace, *spiritual* things'.[146] The believer, who is no longer under the state of nature, is free to choose, by an act of the will, that which is good: 'in those who are renewed by the Holy Ghost and sanctified, it acknowledgeth and teacheth a freedom of will, not in an indifferency and flexibility unto good and evil, but in a power and ability to like, love, choose, and cleave unto God and his will in all things.'[147]

The will operates differently in the life of the believer than it does in that of the unbeliever. For the believer, the will inclines to do good since 'grace hath the sovereignty in their souls'.[148] But the will is able to consent to sin against its better judgment. Conversely, the will in unbelievers is under the power of the law of sin; there is no power in the unbeliever to do anything other than sin:

> Take away all other considerations and hinderances...and they would sin willingly always. Their faint endeavours to answer their convictions are far from a will of doing that which is good.... They do not, they cannot, so choose that which is spiritually good...; only they have some desires to attain that end whereunto that which is good doth lead, and to avoid that evil which the neglect of it tends unto.[149]

The Destruction of the Image

Given all that has been noted above with regard to the effect of sin on the psychological categories, it hardly needs stating that, for Owen, the defacement of the image of God in man was an incontrovertible fact; we are not the same now as when Adam was first created. The interruption of the created order by sin has had a devastating effect:

> And this beauty originally consisted in the image of God in us, which contained the whole order, harmony and symmetry of our natures, in all their faculties and actions, with respect unto God and our utmost end. That, therefore, which is contrary hereunto, as is all and every sin, hath a deformity in it, or brings spots, stains, and wrinkles on the soul. There is in sin all that is contrary to spiritual beauty and comeliness, to inward order and glory; and this is the filth and pollution of it.[150]

However, the issue of whether the image of God in man has been totally lost or is only marred is a more complex one. In approaching this problem, Owen again held these two seemingly polarised ideas in tension, adhering to the classical Reformed understanding in continuity with that of the Reformers of the sixteenth century.

Calvin was clear that fallen man is totally bereft of the image of God and that 'there is nothing but rottenness and infection in us'.[151] His view on this was repeated strongly elsewhere, for example in his *Commentary on Job*: '[Fallen man's] proper nourishment is sin and there is not so much as one drop of goodness to be found in them...[they] have no other substance in them than sin: all is corrupted.'[152] Again in his *Commentary on Deuteronomy*, 'It is true that our Lord created us after His own image and likeness, but that was wholly defaced and wiped out in us by the sin of Adam: we are accursed, we are by nature shut out from all hope of life.'[153]

However, elsewhere Calvin appeared to take a more conciliatory approach in that something of God still remains even in sinful man, even though 'it was, however, so corrupted, [as to become] a fearful deformity'.[154] This idea was elucidated in his *Institutes* when he stated that '[the image is] sullied and all but effaced by the transgression of Adam'.[155]

Calvin, however, was able to hold these two ideas together by differentiating between the spiritual and the natural: at the Fall, man is deprived of spiritual gifts but only corrupted in natural gifts. This was an idea he pursued most especially in his *Institutes*:

Man's natural gifts were corrupted by sin, and his supernatural gifts withdrawn; meaning by supernatural gifts the light of faith and righteousness, which would have been sufficient for the attainment of heavenly life and everlasting felicity.... Hence it follows, that he is now an exile from the kingdom of God, so that all things which pertain to the blessed life of the soul are extinguished.... Among these are faith, love to God, charity towards our nature, the study of righteousness and holiness.... On the other hand, soundness of mind and integrity of heart were, at the same time, withdrawn, and it is this which constitutes the corruption of natural gifts. For although there is still some residue of intelligence and judgment as well as will, we cannot call a

mind sound and entire which is both weak and immersed in
darkness.... Therefore, since reason, by which man discerns
between good and evil, and by which he understands and judges,
is a natural gift, it could not be entirely destroyed; but being partly
weakened and partly corrupted, a shapeless ruin is all that
remains.[156]

Calvin can summarise his position thus: 'True it is when we come
into this world we bring some remnant of God's image wherein
Adam was created: howbeit the same image is as disfigured as we
are full of unrighteousness, and there is nothing but blindness and
ignorance in our minds.'[157]

Furthermore, Calvin suggested that what remains of the image
of God in man is actually used to the dishonour of God; the natural
gifts which are left in man are used against God: 'Wherefore...in
consequence of the corruption of human nature, man is naturally
hateful to God.'[158] The consequence is that 'all this tends to their
destruction, for no part or faculty of the soul is not corrupted and
turned aside from what is right'.[159] To this extent then, the image
of God which remains in man performs a function the very opposite
to that which was intended in its original creation. In accordance
with Calvin's dynamic understanding of the image of God as a
movement towards God in love, it is exactly that which is lost
both in the natural and spiritual aspects of man.

This is an approach that Owen fully endorsed. Like Calvin
before him, Owen categorically stated that

[Men] are not able of themselves, by their own reasons and
understandings, however exercised and improved, to discern,
receive, understand, or believe savingly, spiritual things, or the
mystery of the gospel...they are dead...they have lost that power
of living unto God which they had.[160]

This was an understanding common among Owen's Reformed
contemporaries, for example Samuel Young:

We grant Man is dead in Trespasses and Sins (not Sick only, as
some make him). As no Natural Action can be done without a

Principle of Natural Life, so no Spiritual Action without a Principle of Spiritual Life.[161]

And yet Owen was also able to claim that 'because these [rational] faculties are the principle and subject of all actual obedience, it is granted that there is in man a natural, remote, *passive power* to yield obedience unto God, which yet can never actually put forth itself.'[162] The division between the natural and the spiritual enabled Owen to come to the same conclusion as Calvin on the corruption and loss of the image of God in man:

> In life *spiritual* the soul is unto the principle of it as the body is unto the soul in life *natural*; for in life natural the soul is the quickening principle, and the body is the principle quickened. When the soul departs, it leaves the body with all its own natural properties, but utterly deprived of them which it had by virtue of its union with the soul. So in life spiritual, the soul is not, in and by its essential properties, the quickening principle of it, but it is the principle that is quickened. And when the quickening principle of spiritual life departs, it leaves the soul with all its natural properties entire as to their essence, though morally corrupted; but of all the power and abilities which it had by virtue of its union with a quickening principle of spiritual life, it is deprived.[163]

The Body and the Outworking of Sin

To what extent, and in what manner is sin at work in the body? The Reformed tradition, as exemplified by Calvin,[164] drew a clear link between the soul and the body in that the latter is primarily the instrument for the outworking of the persuasions of the former. Owen stood firmly in this tradition. It must be stressed, however, that Owen did not hold a negative idea about the physical body in the sense that the Platonists did:

> Not that the mass of the body is to us an obscure and dark prison, as the Platonists dream, whence, when we obtain a view of divine things being formerly enveloped by that mass, it is immediately suggested to the mind that the bond of union between mind and body must be instantly dissolved.[165]

Rather, the soul and body are integrally linked in that both are vital constituent elements in the make-up of human beings:

> The soul and body are so united as to constitute *one entire nature*. The soul is not human nature, nor is the body, but it is the consequent of their union. Soul and body are essential parts of human nature; but complete human nature they are not but by virtue of their union.[166]

Since it is the case, however, that the body acts on the persuasions of the soul, the body cannot be held directly responsible for the activity of sin in the individual. Notwithstanding, the link between body and soul does mean that sin has an immense impact on the physical body.

Owen believed that, prior to the Fall, humanity had the possibility of immortality; to be subject to neither death nor decay in accordance with its creation in the image of God and the covenant relationship between man and God.[167] However, the introduction of sin irrevocably altered that state of being inasmuch as death, both physical and spiritual, was the resultant punishment for Adam's disobedience to God. The effect of this disobedience on the physical body was devastating:

> Upon the body, also, it hath such an influence, in disposing it to corruption and mortality, as it is the original of all these infirmities, sicknesses, and diseases, which make us nothing but a shop of such miseries for death itself...so they are the direct, internal, efficient causes...in subordination to the justice of Almighty God, by such means inflicting it as a punishment of our sins in Adam.[168]

Again, 'The Scripture, in the description of the effects of this depravation of our nature, calls in the body and the members of it unto a partnership in all this obliquity and sin: the "members" of the body are "servants unto uncleanness and iniquity," Romans 6:19.'[169] The body then, although not directly responsible for sin, is often the agent of sin. Therefore, the body needs must be a part of the process of sanctification whereby the image of God is restored in the life of the believer.

The Influence of Satan

For Owen, the influence of Satan was a very real problem; one that greatly exacerbates and compounds the inherent weakness of every individual, post-Fall. It is important, however, to put Owen's teaching on Satan into its proper context, noting first his mature and Scripture-based approach to the topic. Owen did not give excuse for anyone to avoid personal responsibility for sin. Neither did he understate the influence of Satan and thereby lead his readers into a false sense of security concerning this spiritual enemy. His was a thoroughly balanced and considered approach, which did not ignore a very complex theological issue and yet managed always to retain its pastoral insight.

Without doubt, Owen maintained seventeenth-century orthodoxy by believing in the literal existence of Satan. Nothing in his writings suggests that the name is used merely in reference to the problem of evil in general: '[Satan] is the grand seducer, the deluder of the souls of men, the first author of lying, whose principal design it is to win over the faith and assent of men thereunto.'[170] This personification of Satan accords with much of the preaching and writings of his contemporaries. One such example from Faithful Teate will suffice: 'The Devil counts it not lost labour to play with your children in the streets, to teach them sinful words, apish gestures, and to tread out such pathes [sic] in the wilderness for them, as their little feet may take pleasure to trample in.'[171]

As to the origin of Satan, Owen appeared to accept the understanding of him as being an angel who fell from grace. Forthwith, his nature became corrupted and his desire was then to bring about the same corruption to the rest of God's creation in general and humanity in particular:

> He was the head of the first apostasy from God. Having himself fallen away from that place and obediential part of the creation wherein he was made, the first work he engaged in...was, to draw mankind into the guilt of the same crime and rebellion; and ever since the revelation of the means of recovery for man..., he hath pursued the same design towards all unto whom that way of recovery is proposed.[172]

Again,

> Nothing could ever give satisfaction unto the malicious murderer, as the breach he had occasioned between God and man, with his hopes and apprehensions that it would be eternal. He had no other thoughts but that the whole race of mankind, which God had designed unto the enjoyment of himself, should be everlastingly ruined. So he had satisfied his envy against man in his eternal destruction with himself, and his malice against God in depriving him of his glory.[173]

Concerning the biblical record, Owen believed Satan to be the serpent in Genesis 3. It is Satan who firsts tempts Adam and Eve and it is he who is responsible for the entry of sin into their lives and, subsequently, creation as a whole. He acknowledged that Satan's activity in this event was one of great cunning: 'Satan designed his attempt, and from whence he hoped for his success. It was not an act of *power* or rage; but of *craft*, counsel, subtlety, and deceit.'[174]

Despite this, however, it is not possible to interpret Owen as suggesting that Satan alone is responsible for sin, either in the event of the Fall or in the subsequent behaviour of Adam's descendants. There is no chronological priority outlined by Owen with regard to Satanic activity or human culpability with regard to the operation of sin. The work of Satan and the weaknesses inherent in the mind, will and affections go hand in hand in opposing the will of God in the life of the individual: 'He blinds their minds...he inflames their lusts...he presents occasions...he suggests temptations, with false and corrupt reasonings.'[175]

Satan does not use only one method to persuade individuals into sin. Owen suggested that Satan would use any means at his disposal; there is in satanic activity an element of surprise that would be lost if his methods were predictable in any way. Thus Owen was able to state that 'Satan tempts sometimes *singly* by himself, without taking advantage from the world, the things or people of it, or ourselves',[176] but in the same way, 'Sometimes he makes *use of the world*, and joins forces against us, without any helps from within. So he tempted our Saviour...'[177] and likewise,

'Sometimes he takes *assistance from ourselves also*...he hath, for the compassing of most of his ends, a sure party within our own breasts.'[178]

Owen did not underestimate the influence of Satan on the individual. It must also be said, however, that he did not overestimate this influence either. Certainly Owen believed Satan to be a powerful force and a true enemy of God and man. However, nowhere did he insinuate that it is possible to lay the blame for individual sin at the door of this spiritual being. Mankind is culpable for sin and must face up to that fact before the judgement throne of God despite any influence which Satan has in exacerbating the problem.

Conclusion

Owen understood the outworking of sin to be prevalent in every part of the individual; most especially in the psychological categories of mind, will and affections, but in the body also. Since the Fall, this outworking has utterly defaced the image of God in the individual and destroyed the covenant relationship which existed between Adam – our federal head – and God. The influence of Satan cannot be underestimated in this regard and he serves to exacerbate and exploit the weaknesses inherent in fallen humanity in an attempt to thwart the purposes of God and diminish his glory. Humanity is utterly helpless in the face of sin, unable of itself to do anything about this calamitous situation that is entirely of its own making.

Such then is Owen's general understanding of sin; a constant theological framework by which he was able to interpret the spiritual well-being of the society in which he lived. And it is to that which we now turn to trace the development of Owen's thoughts on sin in response to the political, social and ecclesiological turmoil that so strongly hallmarks the history of seventeenth-century England.

3

SIN AND SOCIETY

Thus far, we have considered Owen's writings on sin within the individual. However, Owen also placed a great emphasis on the corruption of sin that is active in institutions and society in general, or what might be termed corporate and national sin. Owen believed that the nation of England itself was accountable before God for sinful actions and attitudes, as was the institution of the national church. This is, of course, a far more abstract notion but one that is predominant in many of Owen's treatises and, most especially, in his sermons for Parliament. This is not to say that Owen had any developed notion of corporate sin in the sense taught by some evangelical and charismatic writers today.[1] Rather, Owen's understanding was that, when sinful individuals meet and work together, their activities and decisions are bound to reflect the sinful nature inherent in those individuals. Sin in society and the church is an inevitable result of sinful people living and working together. The purpose of this chapter, then, is to come to a clearer understanding of exactly how Owen perceived spiritual dislocation and fragmentation through sin to be rife in society. His teachings are complex and wide-ranging but, as is characteristic of the man, they are imbued with a depth and profundity that go to the very heart of the issue.

Throughout his ministerial career, Owen was very much a political animal. He could hardly have been otherwise, most especially during his early years. Confrontation with the politics of the day was unavoidable, given the civil turmoil of the period. However, more than that, Owen was responsible for shaping events too. Along with Hugh Peter,[2] Philip Nye[3] and Thomas Goodwin,[4] Owen was primarily responsible for defining the theological basis upon which Cromwell and the Parliaments of this era governed. Owen's role as one of Cromwell's chaplains, an appointment which took him both to Ireland and Scotland with the Parliamentarian armies, resulted in his being thrust into the very heart of the political and military machinations of his day.[5] Owen was understandably hesitant to undertake this role; his primary calling was that of a pastor and he had no desire to leave his congregation at Coggeshall. It was the persuasive efforts of his brother, Philemon, one of Cromwell's standard-bearers, which led to his acceptance of this position.[6] If the congregation at Coggeshall were unhappy at losing Owen, they were surely silenced by a letter sent to them by Cromwell himself.[7] Happily for Owen, he was able to spend his time preaching in Dublin for believers hungering after the gospel.[8] The evidence is incontrovertible that Owen was not present at the siege and massacre at Drogheda.[9] In Scotland though, Owen was more intimately involved with the Cromwellian army, preaching to the troops at Berwick on Isaiah 56:7.[10] Owen believed that Cromwell's army was doing the work of God and he exhorted the troops thus:

> It is glorious in respect of the exaltation it hath above and the triumph over all its opposers. To see a house, a palace, hung round about it with ensigns, spoils and banners taken from the enemies that have come against it, is a glorious thing: – thus is this house of God decked.... The Lord hath affirmed, that not only every one that opposeth, but all that do not serve this house, shall be utterly destroyed.[11]

With such a clear understanding in his own mind of the cause of righteousness for which the Cromwellian armies fought, it is inevitable that Owen's understanding of sin should be shaped by what he saw and experienced at this time.

It was during the 1650s that Owen was most influential in matters pertaining to politics and society. However, that is not to imply in any way that his teaching on sin in society is limited to that decade. This was a matter of concern for Owen throughout his life and he has much to offer across the forty-year span of his literary career. In order to assess his thoughts in this regard, it is necessary to contextualise Owen in the wider sphere of the society into which he was directing his writings. In doing this, we shall be examining related topics to this theme of sin in society. Central to this are the defining principles of 'nationhood' during the seventeenth century and, crucially, the millennial expectations that were so important during that era.

What becomes clear from any historical analysis of this period is the immense tumult that England underwent in almost every aspect of its existence. Civil, ecclesiastical and theological upheavals hallmark this era and it is therefore in this context that we must consider Owen's writings on sin and society. It is not our present purpose to reproduce the wealth of detailed historical research already published on this period of English history.[12] However, we must consider certain aspects of the social and religious setting of the period.

The experience of the 1640s was not just of civil war but also unprecedented economic hardship. Poor harvests were the norm with those of 1646 through to 1650 registered as deficient or worse. Compounding the problems, the rate of inflation was running far higher during this decade than in either the preceding or the following ones and textile exports were at a lower level than in the first three decades of the seventeenth century. The inevitable effect of these problems was a famine that had a widespread and devastating effect on the disadvantaged majority.[13]

Undisciplined behaviour and social insubordination was the inevitable result as the poorer sections of society struggled for survival under heavy taxation coupled with low wages. The views and aspirations of these people were to some extent expressed through the convictions and activities of the Diggers and, most especially, the Levellers in both the religious and political realms.[14] It was these groups who represented the desire held by many for household suffrage in the face of an advancing parliamentary system which was as totalitarian in its own way as any monarchy had ever been. There was some clamour for the sovereignty of the people, enshrined in a republican constitution alongside a single-chambered Parliament, the election of magistrates and the redistribution of seats. However, this was more radical than that desired by the majority of Englishmen. Nevertheless, it was true that these principles were foundational to the Leveller cause. Ideas of individuality, the right of association and equality before the law accorded well with the aspirations of the under-classes. Hill gives numerous examples of the practical outworking of this and the manner in which the common people began to exert their influence on the political process through both elections and demonstrations.[15]

Fierce resentment focused on the ruling classes – both aristocracy and monarchy – for the economic problems and the masses were ready to rise in opposition against the perceived tyranny of their masters. Again, the Levellers paved the way for this. John Lilburne had published a pamphlet in January 1647 entitled *Regal Tyranny Discovered*, which called for the trial and execution of the king. Leveller influence within the army resulted in petitions sent to Cromwell from most of the regiments demanding the same end.[16] Ultimately, the Levellers would be the prime movers in bringing Charles to justice, before the face of a reluctant Cromwell. As Brailsford has commented, 'It is the Levellers... who must bear before history the responsibility for this act of retributive justice – or shall we call it in plain words revenge?'[17] However, even they, and Lilburne in particular, held grave reservations as to the legitimacy of the final process of law undertaken to secure his execution. Not that they doubted the principle of execution but only that a non-representative House of Commons was not fit for such an awesome undertaking.[18]

Coupled with this social upheaval and ferment of ideas was relative liberty of the press, albeit short-lived. The reintroduction after 1660 of heavy restrictions, which had been in place before 1641, dealt this a serious blow. Nevertheless, the favourable circumstances of these two intervening decades did provide an enticing opportunity for many dissenting factions within society to contribute ideas and propaganda to an expectant and receptive audience. The impact of that was widespread. However, for our purposes, it is enough to note the increasing anti-clericalism and irreligious attitudes of that period, to the extent that John Webster could declare all clergy 'magicians, sorcerers, enchanters, soothsayers, necromancers, and consulters with familiar spirits'.[19]

This was not a new phenomenon, dating back as it did at least to the *Twelve Conclusions* of the Lollard partisans in 1395. These had condemned the subordination of the English Church to Rome along with what they perceived to be dubious Romish practices. Particular criticism focused upon transubstantiation, clerical celibacy, the consecration of physical objects, prayers for the dead, pilgrimages, images and the exalted position of the priesthood in temporal and spiritual matters. Iconoclastic attitudes may not have been new in the 1640s but rarely had they held such sway over the general population.

What is clear in every generation, but never more so than in the mid-seventeenth century, is the link between political and social stability and the nature and impact of ecclesiastical authority. It was, then, perhaps inevitable that the result of this religious and social upheaval would threaten the established Church, most especially in the intellectual sphere. Increasing philosophical scepticism making its way into English minds from the Continent, not least through the influence of Hobbes[20] and Spinoza, compounded the effects of internal religious dissent.[21] Although he writes of the tensions within Europe generally, Cragg sums up the mood of this period in England well when he states that 'The role of reason was magnified, that of revelation was depressed. The scriptures were subjected to intensive and often to unsympathetic scrutiny. Miracles were challenged. Prophecy was reassessed. Christian thought faced a threat which might have stripped it of all its uniqueness and its authority.'[22]

Conversely, the increasingly widespread influence of astrology threatened ecclesiastical authority too. Such eminent men as the Duke of Buckingham, Oliver Cromwell and Richard Overton regularly sought the advice of astrologers.[23] Hill suggests in his book *The World Turned Upside Down* that, in the early 1640s, the sale of almanacs outstripped those of the Bible.[24] There was no longer an unquestioning acceptance of certainties previously preached. Issues of doctrinal importance – predestination, election, assurance of faith, even the very existence of God, sin, heaven and hell – all came into question in an increasingly sceptical society. John Wilmot, the Earl of Rochester, perhaps spoke for this tradition in one of his poems when he rejected hell, the devil and personal immortality as

> senseless stories, idle tales,
> Dreams, whimsies and no more.
> Our sphere of action is life's happiness,
> And he who thinks beyond thinks like an ass.[25]

England was clearly facing difficult times. In many ways, it seemed that the nation was at a crossroads. As everyone looked to the future, those in authority were anxious to maintain their power and privileges whilst the underclasses were keen to make their lot a better one. The very identity of the nation was seen by many to be in need of redefinition and Owen's understanding of corporate sin would have a significant role to play in that process.

The Idea of 'Nation' and Nationalism

To assess Owen's impact more fully in this regard, we need first to examine the contemporary understanding of 'nation' and the relationship of citizens to the system of rule. We will be able to gain thereby an understanding of how Owen perceived England, practically, to have fallen short of God's standards. As we work through this idea, we shall discover that concepts of 'nation' and 'nationalism' in seventeenth-century England comprised a complex network of thought: economic, social, ethical and spiritual.

The seventeenth century saw the beginnings, or at least the initial evolutionary stages, of a revolution in concepts of society, not least regarding economic factors. That which MacPherson describes as 'possessive individualism' was becoming a foundational concept of political and economic theory during this period. He describes the underpinning idea of this concept as being 'that man is free and human by virtue of his sole proprietorship of his own person, and that human society is essentially a series of market relations'.[26]

This development is attributable mainly to the varying influences of Hobbes, Harrington[27] and later, Locke.[28] The writings of Hobbes and Harrington began to have influence in the 1650s. Locke's influence came a decade later with the 1666 publication of his first treatise, *Essay concerning Toleration.* Interestingly though, Locke had already enjoyed an acquaintance with Owen during the 1650s, he being a student at Christ Church during Owen's period as Vice-Chancellor.[29]

The implications of their economic theories had variable impact on contemporary theological thought. Both Hobbes and Locke interpreted their ideas ostensibly in terms of moral rights and obligations firmly based on their understanding of the nature of humanity. In his *magnum opus Leviathan*, Hobbes stressed that the foundation of true humanity is freedom from the oppressive will of others. Locke, meanwhile, developed the notion that all men are equally free by their very nature and that individual freedom is only limited by the freedom of others. As he wrote in his journal for 1678,

> A civil law is nothing but the agreement of a society of men either by themselves or one or more authorised by them, determining the rights and applying rewards and punishments to certain actions of all within that society.[30]

Harrington expressed his ideas in his work *Oceana* with less overtly ethical overtones. He was concerned more with change and stability in the political realm than he was with individual moral obligation. Nevertheless, we must not underestimate his impact in the realm of theology, particularly, as we shall see below, through his impact on the emerging Republican movement. Predating all these ideas by a decade or so, as we have already noted, were the writings of the Levellers. They took a broadly similar approach to the relationship between the individual and society and they most certainly had influence on theological development.[31]

Paradoxically, whilst concepts of possessive individualism on the grounds of economic viability were developing within the English social structures, so was the concept of mercantilism which, to some extent, ran contrary to this. Mercantilism, whilst not a new idea for England in the seventeenth century,[32] was most certainly a predominant aspect of national identity during this era. The fundamental basis of mercantilism was the development of

trade, not for the good of the individual merchants, but as a means
of increasing the power and influence of the State. Thus legislation
in trading matters, most especially regarding overseas powers,
was ultimately to defend State independence and the security of
the nation. The success of this policy in the seventeenth century is
questionable. In his work *Nationality in History and Politics*, Hertz
suggests that some aspects of trade benefited from this policy.
However, the overall effect was detrimental. He cites the woollen
trade as a particular example of this, a casualty of the wars with
Spain under both Elizabeth and Cromwell. Indeed, Hertz attributes
the causes of the wars of this period, in part at least, to the policy
of mercantilism, a claim most certainly evidenced in the case of
the Protector.[33] The relative merits of mercantilism, however, are
not our chief concern. It is enough for us to note the importance
of this concept in defining the idea of 'nationhood' in seventeenth-
century England.

Such economic developments, both possessive individualism
and mercantilism, suggest a prevailing thought about national
identity in the seventeenth century which leads us to the very crux
of Owen's approach to corporate responsibility before God. At its
simplest, ideas of national identity during this period were very
different from our present understanding. Certainly there was a
consciousness of 'the nation' based on nationality – cultural and
linguistic formulas providing the definition of this – but, as Hayes
comments, 'only exceptionally, after the waning of tribalism and
before the eighteenth century A.D., had patriotism been fused with
the consciousness of nationality to produce genuine nationalism'.[34]
England's relationship with other nations was not a fundamental
aspect of national identity. Rather, it found its basis in how the
citizens related to their rulers and the system of rule. To quote
Hayes again,

> The inter-state...relations of [this period] had to do less with
> attempts to build up homogeneous nationalities and to serve
> nationalist ends than to increase the wealth and prestige of reigning
> families or favoured classes within a community.[35]

For England, then, the function and role of the monarchy during Owen's period provided the defining principle for the sense of nation and nationality. The monarch controlled all aspects of the nation's activity: political, economic, social and spiritual. The monarch defined national traditions and cultural norms. The monarch acted, in a symbolic sense, as the focus for national unity and independence. The attitudes, behaviour and actions of the monarch dictated the spiritual health, or otherwise, of the nation. The relationship of the masses to the ruling monarch became a yardstick by which to measure the spirituality of the nation. Furthermore, the monarch was the foremost representative of the nation before God. Consequently, the nation could be intrinsically guilty of sin through its relationship with its system of rule; if the system of rule was corrupt in God's eyes, then the people themselves were culpable for tolerating irreligious rule. The godliness or otherwise of the monarch was therefore a foundational concept for Owen's understanding of corporate sin in society.

Sin and the Monarchy
Given his upbringing within a Puritan family with Welsh roots,[36] it is perhaps not surprising that, during the 1640s, Owen's thought was in line with those who were heavily critical of Charles I. The perception was of a monarch overtly sympathetic to Catholicism, denying the true Protestant faith. His marriage to Henrietta Maria, the Roman Catholic sister of Louis XIII, did nothing to assuage these fears. His treacherous treatment of the people culminated in the Civil Wars. Of vital importance here is the acknowledgement that almost all those who longed for change and reform, at this stage including Owen himself, did not oppose monarchy as a concept but only Charles himself. There had been some very strong Republican ideologies expounded during the 1640s, predominantly from the Levellers.[37] However, these were only a minority of anti-Royalists on the fringe of English politics at this time and cannot be recognised as in any way representative of the mainstream political thought of their day. The prevailing view amongst the population of England was that a good Christian king was the most desirable option for rule. Many writers were ready to expose

the problems of other forms of government, as can be seen from this representative example by Dudley Digges[38] in his 1643 work *The Unlawfulnesse of Subjects Taking Up Arms*:

> That we should clearly discerne, we have greater hopes under a vertuous King...and greater feares under a vicious nobility or Senate.... Because his interest is the same with that of the People, which is strong State security.[39]

Furthermore,

> The diffusive body of the people hath not greater, nay, not equall power with the King, because they have not any legall way of expressing themselves.... Secondly, the representative body hath not greater nor equall power with the King...for the people cannot authorize them to doe, beyond what themselves were enabled to, therefore if actions of this nature were unwarrantable in the diffusive body, they are so in the representative.[40]

Digges was certainly no anti-Royalist. Indeed, the very opposite. His fervent Royalist attitudes had been committed to paper in many popular works, not least the one quoted above – a passionate treatise devoted to the doctrine of passive obedience. His work passed through several editions before his death from camp-fever in October 1643. However, his views were not especially polarised in this specific matter from those of a predominantly different political persuasion than his own. This is confirmed by an anonymous anti-Royalist letter sent to James Ussher, Archbishop of Armagh,[41] two years after Digges wrote his work, which states that '[Parliament] desire no other King to Rule and Govern these kingdomes, then [sic] His Majesty, nor no other Lawes, then are, and what he shall confirme'.[42]

Monarchy was not the problem. Charles I clearly was. In a 1645 sermon preached at Uxbridge, Christopher Love[43] summed up the mood of his camp when he said: 'Tis the sword...that must end this controversie, wherefore turne your plowshears into swords, and your pruning hooks into spears, to fight the Lords battels [sic], to avenge the blood of Saints which hath been spilt.'[44]

Love's sermon was controversial for two reasons. First, the circumstances of his preaching were the cause of much malicious gossip and alarm. Love had only gone to the church at Uxbridge in order to hear Master Martiall preach. However, Martiall did not turn up and the congregation called on Love to preach without prior notice. He chose to deliver the sermon he had used the previous evening at Windsor Castle. Love's opponents, however, made mischief in the days following by suggesting that he had actually pushed Master Martiall down the pulpit stairs to prevent him preaching and only after that taken the task upon himself! More seriously, and of wider impact, was the terminology he used in attacking Charles and justifying the Parliamentary cause. The degeneracy of the King in the eyes of those who opposed him meant that the Civil Wars almost took on the status of holy wars; an attitude that would have immense repercussions in January 1649.

Owen's first parliamentary sermon was entitled *A Vision of Unchangeable, Free Mercy*.[45] In this, he revealed himself as standing in the mainstream of the Reformed movement opposed to Charles I by regarding the Parliamentarian cause as synonymous with the will of God. Preached at the close of the first Civil War,[46] Owen spoke of the nation unshaken by the course of events and recognised that Charles' defeat was the work of divine providence:

> Unto this day, there is the like conformity to be found to the pattern of God's eternal decrees; though to the messengers not made known aforehand by *revelation*, but discovered in the *effects*, by the mighty working of Providence. Amongst other nations, this is the day of England's visitation, "the Day-spring from on high" having visited this people, and "the Sun of righteousness" arising upon us "with healing in his wings;" – a man of England hath prevailed for assistance, and the free grace of God hath wrought us help by the gospel.[47]

In typical fashion, Owen did not hark back to the rights and wrongs of what had gone before. Rather, he urged the Parliamentarians to look ahead and play their part in restoring the godliness of the nation from its state of corruption. In doing this, Owen focused on three issues in particular; pride, corruption and the need to promote the gospel among atheists.[48]

However, Owen was adamant in his reasoning for the corruption of the godliness of the nation; it was none other than the antichristian spiritual practices that had so ensnared the nation:

> How comes it that this island glories in a reformation, and Spain still sits in darkness? Is it because we were better than they, or less engaged in antichristian delusions? Doubtless no. No nation in the world drank deeper of that cup of abomination. It was a proverbial speech amongst all, 'England was our good ass' (a beast of burden) for (Antichrist whom they called) the Pope.... O Lord, how was England of late, by thy mercy, delivered from this snare![49]

As for where the blame for the corruption lay, Owen placed it firmly at the feet of ungodly authorities, only stopping short of mentioning Charles I and Archbishop Laud by name:

> Which was worst of all, they had centred in their bosoms an unfathomable depth of power, civil and ecclesiastical, to stamp their apostatical errors with authority, – giving them not only the countenance of greatness, but the strength of power, violently urging obedience; and to me the sword of error never cuts dangerously but when it is managed with such a hand.[50]

Owen's desire to link the sins of the nation with those in civil and ecclesiastical authority is further evidenced by his 1649 sermon, *Righteous Zeal Encouraged by Divine Protection*.[51] Preached to Parliament the day after Charles's execution, this has proven to be one of the most controversial acts of Owen's public career. His sympathisers have since defended this sermon by stating that it is well balanced and non-controversial in character; that Owen desired neither to offend, nor to interfere, politically. It has been commented, even by Goold in his 'Life of Dr. Owen', that this sermon makes no real mention of the regicide, far less does it comment on the rights and wrongs of that act. Goold is prepared to accept the possibility that Owen may have approved of the regicide but no more than that. Regarding the text, Goold comments that 'It is remarkable however, that there is throughout a systematic and careful confining of himself to general statements, the most explicit allusion to the event of which, doubtless every mind at the moment was full, being in [one solitary] two-edged sentence'.[52] This view is untenable and seems to be an attempt to defend Owen from an unsavoury aspect of his life. Rather, as we shall see, what we find in this sermon is Owen fully condoning the actions of the previous day. To be sure, he did not mention Charles by name but he did use terminology that we might expect from a theologian and not a politician.

In *Righteous Zeal Encouraged*, Owen forged a link between the ungodliness of Charles and the sins of the nation. The idea he drew upon was a parallel of that between King Manasseh and Judah: that because of the sins of the king, the nation suffered punishment from God.[53] To quote Owen on this vital point:

> The second thing here expressed is, the procuring cause of these various judgments, set down, in verse 4, "Because of Manasseh ...for that which he did in Jerusalem." The sins of Manasseh filled the ephah of Judah's wickedness.... Oftentimes in the relation of his story doth the Holy Ghost emphatically express this, that for his sin Judah should be destroyed.... In the civil politic body the head offends, and the members rue it: Manasseh sins, and Judah must go captive.[54]

The king sins and the people, alongside the monarch, are culpable. God punishes the people for three reasons. First, the influence of the masses on the king tempts him into sin. Secondly, through their fear of the king, the people willingly deny the true faith and indulge in ungodly ways and worship. Thirdly, the people did not restrain their king from his life of sin. As Owen commented, 'if the blind lead the blind, both will, and both justly may, fall into the ditch.'[55]

Given the context, the intentional parallel with contemporary events is clear. Owen believed the sentence passed on Charles to be just in the eyes of God. Furthermore, he recognised that the current paucity of true spirituality in the country was inevitable

given the culpability of the corporate body before God. Contrary
to the claims of Goold, Owen was aware that his sermon was
controversial, acknowledging that '[God's] builders must hold
swords and spears, as well as instruments of labour'.[56] Nevertheless, he is unrepentant. A thinly veiled reference to recent events
in his introduction to the printed version of the sermon makes this
abundantly clear: 'Yea, while sin continueth in its course here...,
great works for God will cause great troubles amongst men. The
holy, harmless Reconciler of heaven and earth bids us expect the
sword to attend his undertakings for and way of making peace.'[57]

The Millennial Hope

In recognising the need to use the sword to make way for peace,
Owen must have adhered to a system of political rule other than
the monarchical system as exemplified by Charles I. That may be
a renewed monarchy or it may be another system altogether. We
will consider Owen's growing republican tendencies below.
However, to understand the shift in his opinion in this regard, we
need to set his beliefs in the context of the millennial expectations
that were so manifest during Owen's lifetime and to which he
himself aspired. It is not our purpose to reproduce the works of
Ball, Toon and Hill, on the millennial expectations of this era.[58]
However, it is important to stress the fact that hopes for the
imminent return of Christ were a driving force for Puritan theology
during the seventeenth century. Indeed, the eschatological
emphasis of Puritan works from this era may well be regarded as
one of the greatest legacies left by these writers to future
generations of believers.

The accepted wisdom of this period was a belief in the literal
and physical return of Christ. The importance of the event itself
cannot be isolated. It is a continuation and completion of the work
undertaken by Christ in his first advent, the salvation of the
individual and the consummation of the Church as the Bride of
Christ. Certainly, there were differences in emphasis and degree
as to the nature and extent of this work. Nevertheless, for all those
who wrote on this topic during this period there was agreement
on the fact that the event of the Parousia has implications not only

for soteriology but also for christology and ecclesiology too. There was most certainly a belief in the divine necessity for the Parousia; that God could not be true to his own nature if he were to leave the work of salvation partially completed. That which had begun in the incarnation and atonement of Christ had necessarily to find completion in the final act of judgement and glorification through the Second Coming of Christ.

There was also during this period what Haller describes as 'among the English generally, apocalyptic urgings...[that] led not to a pursuit of a millennium but to the aspiration after nationality'.[59] This describes a nationalistic tendency within parts of the Puritan movement that equated the nation of England with the kingdom of Christ: the idea that the English were the chosen people of God at that time. There is no evidence to suggest that Owen succumbed to such a nationalistic view but he did recognise the special place of his country in salvation history. This idea he expressed in emotive, almost triumphant language: 'What is England, that it should be amongst the choice branches of the vineyard, the top-boughs of the cedars of God?... For the present, the vineyard of the Lord of hosts is the house of England.'[60] Again, 'To some people, to some nations, the gospel is sent. God calls them to repentance and acknowledgement of the truth...[to] England, the day wherein we breathe.'[61]

If a label is required, then we may describe Owen's teaching on this topic as post-millennialist.[62] Owen's views in this regard were most explicitly outlined in his parliamentary sermons, delivered in 1646 and the seven years following. It is certainly the case that he wrote less fervently on the topic after 1652 but his ministry continued to exhibit an innate sense of urgency that can be understood only in the light of his eschatology.

Sensing the need for ambiguity concerning this issue, Owen was critical of those among his contemporaries who somewhat superstitiously 'observe days and times' in an attempt to forecast the date of the Lord's return.[63] There were many people anxious to perform this ministry with various dates suggested. Johannes Alsted[64] of Herborn suggested 1657. Peter Sterry, in a sermon given to Parliament in November 1651, warned that as the Flood could be dated to 1656 years after the creation of the world, so the return of Christ could be expected in 1656 AD.[65] John Napier[66] from Scotland drew on his mathematical abilities and, after analysing the statistics, proclaimed 1688 as the crucial year. It would be tedious to examine too many other examples. However, we gain a flavour of the style and content of these predictions from just two specific treatises. The first is that of Samuel Hartlib[67] entitled *Clavis Apocaliptica*, published in 1651. In this work, the author analysed the books of Daniel and Revelation in order to determine the date of the Lord's return, which he claimed for 1655:

> The Saints shall be given into the hands of the fourth beast...and when three and a half times, Anno 1655 shall come to an end, the judgment of the Ancient shall sit, and then his power is taken away, so that it wholly is abolished, and comes to an end.... But the world therewith is not destroied [sic], but the Kingdom and dominion, and the greatness under the whole Heaven shall be given to the people of the Saints of the Most High, whose Kingdom is an everlasting Kingdom, and all dominions shall serve and obeie [sic] him.[68]

The second example is that of an astrologer called William Lilly,[69] who published his treatise *The Starry Messenger* in 1645. This dealt with the significance of an unusual sighting in London on 19 November 1644 at 9.45 a.m. – the birthday of Charles I – where three suns appeared in the sky. Lilly outlined twenty-nine such occurrences throughout history from AD 51 (which he claimed for the year of Paul's conversion) through to a similar event in 1639 over Oxford. Lilly claimed that the 1645 sighting '[was] caused by those tutelary Angels, who, by God's permission, and under him, have the Government of the English Commonwealth'.[70] From this event, he warned England of famine, infectious disease, persecution of nobility and gentry and a Great Plague that will sweep through England.[71] He warned King Charles that 'it premonisheth you, above all other People, to make your peace with God in time',[72] and he concluded thus:

> Surely the world is not yet at an end: But whosoever shall see, or
> have the unhappinesse to survive the two or three years next
> succeeding, will wonder at the strange Metamorphosis and
> Catastrophe of Humane Chances in Christian Common-wealths,
> where Jesus Christ is professed with so much pretended Zeal, but
> his Doctrine practised with so slender Devotion.[73]

That Owen was more conservative than some of his peers in his
attitude towards analysing the importance of events that seemed
to mark the last days is evidenced in his late treatise *Seasonable
Words for English Protestants*. Whilst some of his contemporaries
treated the plague and the great fire of London as signs of an
imminent end to the created order, Owen regarded them only as
warnings from God against national sin:

> God hath not left this land without warnings in heaven above, and
> in the earth beneath. Was there no warning given us in the wasting,
> *desolating plague?* no warning in the consuming, *raging fire?* no
> warning in the *bloody* [Dutch] *war* that ensued thereon? no warning
> in all the *prodigious appearances* in heaven above that we have
> had?[74]

Notwithstanding his moderate approach to the issue, Owen was
keenly aware that his generation was in the last days. Even as
early as 1643, Owen wrote thus:

> The glass of our lives seems to run and keep pace with the
> extremity of time. The end of those 'ends of the worlds' which
> began with the gospel is doubtless coming upon us. He that was
> instructed what should be till time should be no more, said it
> was...the last hour, in his time. Much sand cannot be behind, and
> Christ shakes the glass; many minutes of that hour cannot remain;
> the next measure we are to expect is but 'a moment, the twinkling
> of an eye, wherein we shall all be changed'.[75]

Owen believed that a period of righteousness and peace would
precede the coming of Christ in judgement. It would be a time of
great prosperity for the people of God. It would also mark the

annihilation of the power of the Roman Catholic Church, which Owen identified with the Antichrist. This identification of the Papacy with the Antichrist was not new. It had been common at least since the marginal notes in the Geneva Bible on 2 Thessalonians 2:3-9.[76] The idea of an individual Pope being identified with this biblical figure preceded this[77] but it was the printing press that paved the way for the escalation in ideas and formularies concerning the notion. Christopher Hill suggests that Thomas Brightman[78] influenced Owen to the extent that he believed Rome would fall in 1650 and the Antichrist would meet its demise in 1686.[79] Whilst Owen did indeed expect the fall of Antichrist, we must disagree with the analysis of Hill since Owen was very careful never to suggest dates and even warns thus: 'Take heed of *computations*. How woefully and wretchedly have we been mistaken by this!'[80]

Further to the destruction of Rome, this final period of history would also see many Jews coming to faith and there would be purity in doctrine and worship. His view is most fully expressed in Chapter Twenty-six of the *Savoy Declaration of Faith and Order* in a paragraph that is generally ascribed explicitly to the pen of Owen:

> As the Lord in his care and love towards his church hath in his infinite wise providence exercised it with great variety in all ages for the good of them that love him and his own glory; so according to his promise we expect that in the latter days Antichrist being destroyed, the Jews called, and the adversaries of his dear Son broken, the churches of Christ being enlarged and edified through a free and plentiful communication of light and grace, shall enjoy in this world a more quiet, peaceable and glorious condition than they have enjoyed.[81]

In the light of Owen's beliefs about the corporate responsibility of England before God, his sermons reveal the man taking an almost prophetical stance before the political leaders of his day. In a sermon which he preached before Parliament in 1649 entitled *The Shaking and Translating of Heaven and Earth* Owen used Hebrews 12:27[82] to analyse the significance of the civil turmoil of late. In this sermon, he argued that the things to be shaken are no less than the political and ecclesiastical regimes that stand in opposition to God's truth.[83] This shaking of the political and ecclesiastical realm was a pre-requisite to the coming of the Kingdom of God:

> There will, on this ground, be no bringing in of the kingdom of the Lord Jesus until indeed that kingdom in the sense here insisted on is to cease... that shaking and commutation must be for the bringing in of the kingdom of the Lord Jesus.[84]

Owen translated the word μεταθεσις not as a removal but as a 'changing'. He did not believe in the destruction of these oppressive regimes but in the irrevocable alteration of their content in line with the will of God. What this suggests is that, at this stage in 1649, Owen did not advocate a full move towards Republicanism but recognised the need for a renewed monarchy:

> Removal is of the matter, translation of the form only. It is not, then, a destruction and total amotion of the great things of the nations; but a change, translation, and a new-moulding of them, that is here intimated.[85]

Although the foundational text for this sermon is from Hebrews, Owen also considered in some depth various passages in Daniel and the Book of Revelation to determine their prophetic fulfilment.[86] He concluded from this the alignment of some of the references in these portions of Scripture with contemporary Europe and that the establishment of Christ's Kingdom was imminent. By analysing the prophetic writings of both Daniel and John in this manner, Owen was part of a much wider and long-established interpretative tradition. The prime movers in this regard were: John Napier (*A Plaine Discouery of the whole Reulation of Saint Iohn*, 1593); Arthur Dent (*The Ruine of Rome*, 1603); Thomas Brightman (*Revelation of the Revelation*, 1609 and *Exposition...of the Prophecie of Daniel*, 1614) and Joseph Mede, whose works in this regard were prefaced by William Twisse (*Clavis Apocalyptica*, 1627 and *Daniel's Weeks*, 1643). These four men represented the mainstream regarding the interpretation of Daniel and the Book of Revelation. Although hundreds of other treatises on these topics were published alongside their works, few of the other authors were able to match their creativity and maturity of thought.[87]

Owen did not depart in general from the teachings of these writers. His purpose in *The Shaking and Translating* was not to provide a commentary to these controversial biblical writings. Nevertheless, he did feel it necessary to analyse some of the most perplexing aspects of their texts. In doing so, he rejected the preterist and futurist models, which suggested that the events in these books had either already happened or would occur in the future. Rather, Owen endorsed the approach taken by Napier, which is the historicist view. Many of the events written about by Daniel and John had already happened, some were in the process of being accomplished and some are still to be fulfilled.[88] God had been, and clearly still was, working his purposes out through human history and those in authority were therefore obliged to acknowledge their responsibilities within the divine plan.[89]

Given this approach, Owen's purpose was to make his hearers aware of the great spiritual battle in which they were engaged and to convince them of taking the Lord's side to taste victory. Again, Owen suggested that not only does England have a special place in God's plans and that He shall prevail, but that the glory of victory shall be for no other purpose than to glorify God:

> Consider, then, I pray, what you have in hand. Wait upon your King, the Lord Christ, to know his mind.... The time is come, yea, the full time is come, that it should be so; and he expects it from you. Say not, in the first place, this or that suits the interest of England; but look what suits the interest of Christ, and assure yourselves that the true interest of any nation is wrapped up therein...the truth is...Babylon shall fall, and all the glory of the earth be stained, and the kingdoms become the kingdoms of our Lord Jesus Christ.[90]

Owen was aware of the importance of contemporary events, acknowledging especially the pain of the Civil War. However, he claimed that, in the light of the electing purposes of God, out of the ashes 'a beautiful fabric is seen to arise'.[91] There was no hindering the purposes of God. These were evident through the current strife and England had grown through it: 'Some say, this war hath made a discovery of England's strength, what it is able to do. I think so also.'[92] Through the bitter struggle there had been a stripping of pride from the nation, a rooting out of atheistical corruption alongside a growing awareness of how much spiritual work remained undone. Time was short but Owen believed that with the gracious help of God the work required was possible to achieve and, indeed, necessary to prepare the way for the return of Christ.

Owen was acutely aware of the biblical motif that to whomsoever much is given, of them much is required. Thus, his constant plea to Parliament was for their support for the work of the gospel throughout England, and Wales in particular,[93] and a recalling of the nation to a state of national and corporate righteousness. In the light of these, Owen was aware of the power and prevalence of sin and he spoke often of it; the sins of the nation lay before God and England would not escape judgement. Using Augustinian terminology, Owen spoke of sin 'blocking the passage' to God's grace.[94] God distinguishes no nation or individual in this regard – all sin and fall short of God: 'God hath always something against a people, to make the continuing of his grace to be of grace, the not removing of his love to be merely of love, and the preaching of the gospel to be a mercy of the gospel, free and undeserved.'[95]

For Owen, there was no distinction between the sacred and the secular; each is a vital part of God's created order and each has a part to play in God's redemptive purposes. Nowhere is this more clearly revealed than in Owen's famous pronouncement, 'Up and be doing, you that are about the work of the Lord.'[96] Whilst not a remarkable statement in itself, Owen's words take on a different hue when it is realised that they were spoken not to clergymen but to Parliamentarians and soldiers after their part in the siege of Colchester in 1643. Clearly, Owen perceived the work that they were doing to be under the same hand of God as the work of any Christian minister.[97] In *Righteous Zeal Encouraged*,[98] preached the day after the execution of Charles I, he did not shy away from warning those in authority of the awesome nature of the future that confronted them, nor of their responsibilities in the same. His prophetic words about the judgment of God upon England were powerful indeed. He spoke of this in the context of a God for whom the honour of his name is at stake; a God who will not fail the nation lest the derision fall on him:

> He is engaged in point of honour. If they miscarry in his way, what will he do for his great name? Yea, so tender is the Lord herein of his glory, that when he hath been exceedingly provoked to remove men out of his presence, yet because they have been called by his name, and have visibly held forth a following after him, he would not suffer them to be trodden down, lest the enemy should exalt themselves and say, Where is now their God? They shall not take from him the honour of former deliverances and protections. In such a nation as this, if the Lord now, upon manifold provocations, should give up parliament, people, army, to calamity and ruin, would not the glory of former counsels, successes, deliverances, be utterly lost? would not men say it was not the Lord, but chance that happened to them?[99]

Despite the essential role that England was playing in God's elective purposes, Owen believed the nation to be under the judgment of God because of its sins.[100] Inherent in the national sin were two related issues; superstitious false worship and cruelty. For Owen, these were inextricably linked and deserving of God's wrath.[101] The onus was therefore on England to turn from its sin, its oppression, its persecution, its intolerance, its self-seeking and its false worship, and return to the Lord in repentance. Only then would the nation receive the reflected glory and honour due to it as a people elected and set apart by God.

The Re-admittance of the Jews to England
Central to Owen's belief that the millennium was fast approaching, was the need to see the conversion of the Jewish people. His reading and understanding of Scripture made this a prerequisite to the Parousia. It is therefore appropriate at this point to give some consideration to what has become known as the Jewish

Question and Owen's role in that debate.

The Jewish Question was a major political and theological debate of the 1640s and 1650s. Since the act passed by the Council of Edward I on 18 July 1290, the Jewish people had been officially banished from the Realm of England. To claim, however, that there were no Jewish people in England during this period would be plainly inaccurate. There is plentiful evidence of Jewish settlers in England at this time, although most often they publicly declared an allegiance to Roman Catholicism whilst practising their own religion in private.[102] However, in the 1640s there began a considerable movement to re-establish their presence and give them limited but official status. This desire came about, in part, through hopes for their conversion to the Christian faith. This desire was obviously not new in England and can be dated back at least to the fifteenth-century influence of the Bohemian Hussites and perhaps even Wycliff and Hus themselves. However, these contemporary hopes were primarily founded upon the expectation of Christ's imminent return and the need for the conversion of the Jews to facilitate that. The issue became a pressing one for Cromwell through the actions of a Jew called Menasseh ben Israel, who resided in Holland. He petitioned Cromwell to address the issue and this became the focal point of the debate. This provided the foundation for the Puritan divines to consider the English response to the Jewish people and the nation's ensuing sinfulness in refusing to act in a positive manner.

The first petition to reach Cromwell came from Menasseh ben Israel's son, Dormido, in November 1654. The petition requested

> that true & vnfalliable states Pollicie bee admitted opening the gates to my nation to the ende they may (vnder the Diuine protection & that of yr. highnese) freely vse theire excersise in the obseruance of ye most holly lawes giuen by god on mounte Sinay, graunting them libertie to come with theire famillies and estates to bee dwellers heere with the same eaquallnese and conuieneces, wich ye inland borne subjects doe injoy.[103]

This request met with the approval of Cromwell,[104] not least because of his millenarian expectations. Unfortunately, his advisers

were less well disposed and the slow course of events following
the initial contact meant that Menasseh himself was not able to
meet with Cromwell before September of the following year. His
petitions finally went before the Council of State on 13 November
1655. He asked for the following issues to be taken into account:
that the Jews should be readmitted as ordinary citizens; that there
should be religious toleration, a public synagogue and a Jewish
cemetery; that there should be freedom of trade for Jews; that the
Jewish people should be permitted to try their own cases according
to Mosaic law with recourse to English civil law; that the
programme of readmission should be adequately supervised; and
that all anti-Semitic legislation in England should be annulled.[105]

The examining sub-committee of the Council of State issued a
number of objections to Menasseh's petition. There were concerns
about the scandalous nature of Jewish worship and the fact that
Jewish marriage and divorce customs were contrary to English
law. On another level, the Council of State was apprehensive about
the impact of Jewish resettlement on trade, social stability and the
ability of Jewish people to remain true to their swearing of oaths.[106]
Crucially, however, they did not rule out the possibility of
readmission in principle. To that end, twenty-eight delegates for
the Whitehall Conference were appointed, primarily clergymen
but also representative lawyers and merchants, to meet with the
Committee in December 1655 and discuss the issues. The
Conference itself was unable to come to a consensus and therefore
had to reconvene on a further four occasions throughout
December.[107] Despite Cromwell's efforts to gain a positive
outcome by appointing philo-Semitic Hugh Peter, Peter Sterry
and John Boncle to the Conference after it had opened,[108] there
was a reluctance to agree to Menasseh's requests. The merchants
were primarily concerned that England would suffer economically
if the Jews were readmitted whilst the majority of delegates were
happy to consider re-admittance under certain safeguards relating
mainly to the practice of their religion.

There is no record of Owen's stance on this issue. What is
clear, however, is that an invitation was sent to him as a delegate
to the Whitehall Conference on 16 November. He is listed as one

of the twenty-eight who received a summons by the President of the Council of State, Henry Lawrence, in the Council of State Order Book entry for 15 November 1655.[109] Certainly Owen was, that very week, dealing with a dispute concerning Dr. Michael Roberts, the Principal of Jesus College in Oxford and his schedule would have been very full.[110] Whether or not he attended, some of his closest colleagues, most notably Nye, Goodwin and Joseph Caryl, did actively participate in the proceedings and it would be safe to assume that Owen's opinions were similar to theirs. Owen's colleagues joined a powerful third faction at the conference, consisting primarily of clergymen, who were anxious for the readmittance of the Jews without precondition. In the light of the tragic historical relations between England and the Jewish people alongside the dangerous and threatening treatment of Jews on the Continent that needed alleviating, this was seen not only as desirable but as a Christian duty. The millenarian hope was quite naturally at the forefront of their minds in this regard. Joseph Caryl stated that

> In our Nation the good people generally have more beleeved the promises touching the calling of the Jews, and the great riches and glory that shall follow to Jews, and us Gentiles...[the faithful] have (and do stil) [sic] more often, and earnestly pray for it, than any other Nation that we have heard of.[111]

Despite an impassioned plea from Cromwell in the closing session of the Whitehall Conference, the delegates left in perhaps more confusion than that in which they had arrived. Nothing concrete came out of the proceedings. By the middle of January 1656, Jewish readmission was no longer a live issue for the Parliament of the day; the matter disappeared into obscurity without there even being a report published by the Council of State on their findings.

What part does such a debate play in our consideration of Owen's doctrine of sin during this period? The answer lies in the perceived failure of the political authorities, and therefore the nation at large, to prepare the way for the return of Christ. Whilst Owen's specific stance concerning the Whitehall Conference

cannot be firmly ascertained, he clearly stood in the mainstream
of his peers in linking the conversion of the Jews to the return of
Christ. Evidence of this is found primarily in his parliamentary
sermon of 13 October 1652, entitled *Christ's Kingdom and the
Magistrate's Power*. Owen was categorical in his belief, stating
that 'what *kingdom* soever the Lord Christ will advance in the
world, and exercise amongst his holy ones, the beginning of it
must be with the Jews'.[112] He was, however, less sure of the process
than many of his contemporaries and was determined to commit
himself to neither process nor date:

> Nothing is more clear to any, who, being not carried away with
> weak, carnal apprehensions of things present, have once seriously
> weighed the promises of God to this purpose. What the Lord Christ
> will do with them, and by them, is not so clear; this is certain, that
> their return shall be marvellous, glorious, – as life from the
> dead...these things are, or may be, for any thing we know, afar
> off.[113]

Nevertheless, the importance of the conversion of the Jews was
not lost on Owen. A sense of the culpability of the English people
rested heavy upon him in this, as in other regards: 'The Jews not
called, Antichrist not destroyed, the nations of the world generally
wrapped up in idolatry and false worship, little dreaming of their
deliverance, – will the Lord Christ leave the world in this state,
and set up his kingdom here on a molehill?'[114]

For Owen, the re-admittance of the Jews to England and their
subsequent conversion was no mere academic issue. His
millenarian ideals forced on him the adoption of this position even
if he were less willing to make rash pronouncements on the issue
than some of his more radical colleagues.[115] Owen would no doubt
have viewed the reluctance of the Whitehall Conference and
Council of State to take on such a programme as one further
example of the grave standing of the nation before God. England's
hope depended entirely on an act of repentance on a grand scale
alongside a reordering and restructuring of the institutions of power
that could facilitate the return of Christ and the inauguration of
his kingdom on earth. Whilst the intensity of Owen's

millenarianism declined over the next few decades, he never lost the fundamental hope that his beloved nation would not be found wanting on the last day.

Owen and Republicanism

We have seen that a vital aspect of the standing of the nation before God was the political system that governed the nation. Owen was strongly opposed to the style of monarchy which Charles I embodied and the decisions he took during his reign. However, we have also noted that, at the time of the king's execution, Owen was not opposed to the principle of monarchy as such. His hope was for a renewed Protestant monarchy that would bring glory to the nation and thereby glorify God. However, the contention of this writer is that Owen's political views underwent a dramatic change in the decade that followed the regicide. This change of opinion, which marked Owen's movement towards Republicanism, is especially pertinent to the theme of our study. This is perhaps one of the most difficult areas of his thought to unravel since he never dedicated himself to writing a treatise overtly expressing his political ideas. However, it is possible to follow the strands of his thoughts on this issue through his varied writings, most especially from the parliamentary sermons he preached during this time.

Such a thesis runs counter to the general tradition of opinion on Owen's political views. Ever since Asty's memoirs on Owen, there has been a clear attempt to divorce him from Republican tendencies. This has been an effort to absolve him from responsibility over the issue of Oliver Cromwell's fated move towards becoming king and the subsequent rejection of Richard Cromwell. Toon, in his biography of Owen, is especially keen to play down Owen's Republicanism. He does so against the claims of Matthews concerning Owen's Preface to the *Declaration of the Faith and Order Owned and Practised in the Congregational Churches in England*.[116] Matthews suggests that '[Owen is] repeating a fiction from the doctrinaire stock-in-trade of his [Republican] party, which he had swallowed with the credulity of a recent convert'.[117] Toon summarily dismisses Matthews' idea by calling it 'an extraordinary statement'.[118] This I believe to be an erroneous reading of history. Not only is Toon's opinion incorrect, it is asserted through scurrilous and mischievous methodology unbecoming of a man interested in historical accuracy. Toon defends his position thus: 'Against Matthews it must be emphasised that no evidence *(if the Preface is not taken into account)* exists to prove that at this time Owen was a doctrinaire republican who wanted to overthrow the Protectorate.'[119] It is Toon's defence that is extraordinary. He may equally well have said, 'If we get rid of the evidence, we have no evidence to prove that Owen was a republican'! The truth is that the evidence is there for all to see – and not just in Owen's Preface, either. An examination of Owen's writings and sermons from the late 1650s will produce a wealth of evidence to reveal his republican tendencies. Furthermore, we cannot underestimate the importance of Owen's belief about a godly and appropriate form of government since it is a crucial factor in understanding his writings and actions after the Restoration.

Thus far we have noted Owen's understanding that the system of government and the standing of the governing authority before God is, to no small degree, a determining factor concerning the corporate standing of the nation before God. There is a sense in which the nation stands or falls by its chosen form of government. What becomes clear is that after the death of the king and with the beginning of the Protectorate, Owen thought afresh about the form of government that he deemed to be most pleasing to God. It was the conclusions he reached that determined his high standing and political influence over the coming decade.

Owen perceived that by the unmerited grace of God, England at the beginning of the 1650s was at the beginning of a new phase in its history; the brink of a new era, a time 'to mend or end'.[120] Most especially in his parliamentary sermons, Owen was keen to clarify the link between the prevailing sin of the nation and his understanding of England's elect purpose in God's salvation history. Whether the nation continues in sin or repents before God is of the utmost importance if the light of God is to continue to shine on the people:

> Let England consider with fear and trembling *the dispensation
> that it is now under*; – I say, with fear and trembling, for this day
> is the Lord's day, wherein he will purge us or burn us, according
> as we shall be found silver or dross: – it is our day, wherein we
> must mend or end.[121]

Again, 'And if the people love darkness more than light, the
candlestick will be removed. Let England beware!'[122]

Integral to Owen's teachings and political activity during this
period was the belief that Oliver Cromwell was the man who could
bring righteousness and godliness back into the political realm.
Cromwell, as well as being a man of vision, was also a man of
faith. He aligned himself with the Independent tradition although
it is difficult to pin down his denominational allegiances any more
than that.[123] Owen came to Cromwell's attention after preaching
his parliamentary sermon *On the Shaking of Heaven and Earth*.
The following day, they met at General Fairfax's[124] house.[125]
During that afternoon, Cromwell invited Owen to accompany him
to Ireland as his chaplain and thus began a long friendship and
working relationship that would bear much fruit for both parties.
It was with high hopes that Owen served as Cromwell's chaplain.
Before 1656, Owen's allegiance to Cromwell was unwavering
and he truly believed that the Protectorate would act as a precursor
to the imminent restoration of the Kingdom of Christ. This view
is evident in a sermon Owen preached to Parliament in the
aftermath of Cromwell's success in Ireland:

> Be faithful in doing all the work of God whereunto you are
> engaged, as he is faithful in working all your works whereunto he
> is engaged.... God's work, whereunto you are engaged, is the
> propagating of the kingdom of Christ, and the setting up of the
> standard of the gospel.... For my part, I see no farther into the
> MYSTERY of these things but that I should heartily rejoice, that,
> innocent blood being expiated, the Irish might enjoy Ireland so
> long as the moon endureth, so that Jesus Christ might possess the
> Irish.... God hath been faithful in doing great things for you; be
> faithful in this one – do your utmost for the preaching of the gospel
> in Ireland.[126]

However, after 1656, matters began to unravel and over the next two years Owen's allegiance to the Cromwellian ideal irrevocably diminished. This was the result of political activity alongside a related development in Owen's own thought. Perhaps the major political event that was to determine Owen's future relationship with Cromwell centred on the latter being offered the position of king. This was not a new initiative in 1657; the idea had been suggested on numerous occasions, dating back at least to 1649 and most seriously in 1653/4.[127] There had been, especially in 1653, some considerable debate as to whether Cromwell should be crowned king or emperor, the latter title understood as being less offensive to Republicans.[128] However, the *Humble Petition and Advice*, offered to Cromwell on 23 February, which called for the return of the monarchy and the House of Lords, was the most far-reaching attempt to exalt Cromwell's position. Lord Broghill,[129] alongside Cromwell's son-in-law Claypole, put forward persuasive arguments encouraging him towards acceptance of the Crown.[130] These arguments held particular sway for Cromwell given the difficulties he was facing at the time with his Parliaments, army and Major-Generals and he most certainly gave the idea strong consideration. Furthermore, he had become increasingly convinced that only by accepting the Crown could he sustain peace in the three nations and fulfil his vocation in working for Christ's kingdom. The Speaker of the House of Commons formally offered monarchical office to Cromwell on 31 March.

Opposition to the move towards Cromwellian monarchy was strong. From the army Fleetwood,[131] Lambert[132] and Desborough[133] showed open antagonism and Captain Bradford – an old friend of Cromwell – warned him: 'those that are for a crown...have attended your greatest hazards'.[134] Some of his closest friends and advisers counselled against it and the parliamentary process for deliberating the matter with the Lord Protector proceeded for quite some weeks. Thus whilst Cromwell indicated his readiness to accept the crown on 6 May, the final insistences and threats of resignations from Lambert, Fleetwood and Desborough that evening changed his mind irrevocably. On 8 May,

Cromwell finally and formally turned down the offer from Parliament.[135]

However, it was not just the threats from his colleagues on that day which changed Cromwell's mind. We cannot underestimate the influence of Owen on the Lord Protector. After Desborough had met with Cromwell in St. James' Park,[136] he spoke to Colonel Pride[137] about Cromwell's intentions to accept the Crown. Such was Pride's indignation that both he and Desborough sought the help of Owen in preventing Cromwell's intended course of action. Thus it fell to Owen to draw up a petition opposing Cromwell and that carried enormous weight in the subsequent changing of Cromwell's decision.[138] It signalled, too, the demise of the relationship enjoyed between the Lord Protector and his favoured Chaplain. As Cromwell's funeral cortège moved solemnly through the streets of London on 23 November 1658,[139] Owen did have a part to play in that magnificent state occasion.[140] However, the truth is that their relationship had become irreparably damaged. They were no longer close, as he stressed in the course of a defence against a slanderous attack on him in 1670: 'One of the first charges that I meet withal, upon the first head, is...that I "was one of them who promised Cromwell his life upon his last sickness, and assured him that his days should be prolonged".... I saw him not in his sickness, nor in some long time before.'[141]

So what was it that compelled Owen to oppose his friend in such a public and decisive manner? The answer is both political and ecclesiological.

First, Owen was concerned that any restoration of monarchy would be a negative development for the nation. What is clear is that, during this period, Republican writers and ideas had an increasing influence on Owen. He was certainly aware of the ideas of Harrington since a copy of *Oceana* was in his private book collection auctioned after his death. In addition, Owen was personally acquainted with leading republican thinkers,[142] notably Ludlow[143] and Vane,[144] through his involvement with the army officers who met for prayer and worship at Wallingford House.[145] Furthermore, Owen's Preface to the *Declaration of the Institution of Churches* in 1658 shows decidedly republican tendencies.

Owen's move towards republicanism was a major shift in his thinking. Whereas previously it was Charles and not the concept of monarchy that was problematical, now it was the very concept of monarchy itself that was sinful. The old order had gone to make way for the new. This was not to be in the sense of μεταθεσις as outlined in his 1649 sermon, *A Shaking and Translating of Heaven and Earth*, but a spiritual creation *ex nihilo* operating in the temporal realm. Preaching to Parliament after Cromwell's death, Owen encouraged the Parliamentarians in the task that lay ahead for them when he stated that

> It is, as I have said, safety and preservation, both spiritual and temporal, that is here engaged for.... There is a creating power needful to be exerted for the preservation of Zion's remnant. Their preservation must be of God's creation. It is not only, not to be educed out of any other principle, or to be wrought by any other means; but it must, as it were, by the almighty power of God, be brought out of nothing; – God must create it. [146]

Indeed it is in this sermon preached in February 1659 entitled *The Glory and Interest of Nations Professing the Gospel* [147] that we receive perhaps the greatest indication of Owen's development as a republican. In this sermon to Parliament, Owen began by addressing the gathered honourable members in glowing terms with theological overtones:

> Are you not the remnant – the escaping of England? Is not [Parliament] a brand plucked out of the fire? Are you not they that are left, – they that remain from great trials and tribulations? The Lord grant that the application may hold out, and abide to the end of the prophecy! [148]

Owen consolidated his opinion further by stating that the preservation of Parliament as the remnant 'must be of God's creation'.[149] Owen then moved on to encourage Parliament in their task of restoring godliness to the nation. In so doing, he spoke with incredible candour and with great political conviction. In one passage, he seemed to refer to Cromwell and his desire for monarchy with an alarming degree of judgment:

After some years' contending, when the Lord had begun to give us deliverance...the backsliding of some to the cause and principles they had opposed, this evil was also found rising again amongst us; – slighting, blaspheming, contemning [sic], under several pretences, of the Spirit and presence of Christ in and with his saints.[150]

Owen then makes a more specific charge to the assembled Parliamentarians concerning the nature of their responsibilities:

Set yourselves to oppose that *overflowing flood of profaneness*, and opposition to the power of godliness, that is spreading itself over this nation. Know you not that the nation begins to be overwhelmed by the pourings out of a profane, wicked, carnal spirit, full of rage, and contempt for all the work of reformation that has been attempted among us? Do you not know that if the former profane principle should prove predominant in this nation, that it will quickly return to its former station and condition, and that with the price of your dearest blood?[151]

In Owen's address, there is a clear linking of the two primary themes under discussion here. The opposition of monarchy and the move towards a new system of government was clearly, for Owen, an ordinance of God. Opposition to that political change is nothing less than opposition to God and therefore grossly sinful. It lay in the hands of the Parliament of the day to salvage the situation both by asserting its own power – and using that for the good of the nation – and by opposing too any move back to constitutional monarchy. No doubt mindful of the contemporary moves already afoot to restore Charles II, Owen concluded his argument thus:

I pray God we lose not our ground faster than we won it. Were our hearts kept up to our good old principles on which we first engaged, it would not be so with us; but innumerable evils have laid hold upon us; and the temptations of these days have made us a woeful pray.[152]

However, it was not just monarchy in isolation to which Owen was opposed in his criticism of Cromwell over this matter. Owen was acutely aware that, with the re-establishment of the monarchy, there would be an inevitable return to a prelatical form of church government. That was something that was abhorrent to Owen, not least given the current satirical joke of the day, relayed to Cromwell by the journalist Marchamont Needham.[153] In this, Philip Nye was named as Archbishop of Canterbury and John Owen as Archbishop of York![154] Owen's concern for the purity of religion and suitable church structures and forms of government will be examined in more detail in the next chapter. However, it is enough to suggest the link here between monarchy and ecclesiology in Owen's mind. The restoration of the monarchy would indeed lead the nation to be culpable before God if for no other reason than that the church as an institution would be irreparably damaged by that one act.

That being the case, it was natural therefore that the Parliamentarians were seen as God's people for that time. The words expressed about Parliament during this period were overflowing with praise and flattery:

> God hath sent us Physitians.... These Physitians are our Worthies of Parliament, the healers of our breaches, who put oyle into our wounds, and were it not for them (the Lord knows) we should have bled to death and perished in our wounds before this day.[155]

Again, this time in a sermon to Parliament preached after Fairfax's victory at Naseby on 14 June 1645,

> God hath put into your hands the greatest opportunity, and means of providing for all the glory that he expects from England while the world stands, that he did ever put into the hands of any. The measuring line, and plummet of his house is put into your hands as once it was in the hands of Zerubbabel.[156]

Aligned with this, and most pertinent for our present purposes, was a very real sense of the guilt of sin that lay before the nation. These sins were one side of a double-headed coin that spun irrevocably before God; the sins of the nation spurred the king into greater depths of depravity and the king's depravity wrought havoc on the godliness of the nation. It is worth quoting Love at some length to comprehend this point:

> My soul is troubled to consider what an inundation of hurtfull doctrines and poysonfull errours have been preacht and spread up and down throughout our Land...affirming that Kings might do what they list, that the lives, wives, liberties and estates of their subjects are to be disposed by the King according to his owne will.... Oh! the abominable errors which have been nourisht in the bowels of this Nation, touching Free-will, falling from grace, universall Redemption, the abolishing of the Morall Law, denying sorrow for sinne, or seeking pardon for it, with many more; oh this hath layen our Land under sad distempers at this day![157]

In the light of this dilemma, Parliament was perceived as the sole body able to lift the national guilt and to avert the judgment of God, as Tuckney[158] suggested in his sermon to Parliament in 1643:

> (as you are our State-Physicians) you may keep the disease from proving Epidemicall: for as for the general body of this people, it hath wellnigh overspread all; and therefore the representative bodies integrity (if any thing do) must stand for all, one body for another; you representing us all, as well to God as to man, and so being for the present the only meanes that is left of keeping off a nationall guilt, and so the wrath of God from this whole nation.[159]

By 1659 then, all the evidence would suggest that Owen had become a Republican. His desire, as Matthews rightly states, was 'for the restoration of the remnant of the Long Parliament, the Rump, expelled by Cromwell in 1653'.[160] Not only was this a political matter for him, but theological too. Charles I had revealed the worst excesses of monarchical power. Millennial hopes had led Owen and his contemporaries to put their trust in Cromwell but he too had been tempted with the Crown. The power of sin's temptations, it would seem, was no respecter of persons. Owen's thoughts had therefore changed quite radically. It was no longer monarchy that could safeguard the godliness of the nation. That responsibility lay with a parliamentary system based on Republican ideology. If Owen needed further convincing of the truth of this, the political impact of the Restoration on the church would provide just that.

Owen After the Restoration

Many churchmen welcomed and celebrated the restoration of Charles II. None more so perhaps, than Thomas Reeve,[161] Rector of Waltham Abbey, and Joseph Glanvill,[162] whose writings on this topic reach almost to the point of sycophancy. Upon the Restoration, Reeve was moved to comment that

> So far as I can perceive, your Majesty doth but seek your Native Right, the Established Religion, the fundamental Lawes, the Honour of the Highest, the freedome of the meanest, the welfare of the Nation, the Peace of the Kingdome, and [anti-Royalists] may see as well as I that your graces are conspicuous, your qualifications eminent, your carriage affable, your Government mild, your counsailes prudent, your actions heroical, your life spotless, and your conscience sincere, except therefore they would have an Angel to reign over them, where can they have in flesh and blood a more desired man?[163]

It is interesting to note that Owen was well aware of Thomas Reeve and was clearly no admirer of the man. In a letter sent to his friend John Thornton soon after the Restoration, Owen sarcastically exhibited surprise that recently 'Our learned Dr. Reeve preached one sermon without railing'.[164] As for Glanvill's comments on the Restoration, he, like Reeve, was overcome with deep emotion. After copious references to the Old Testament and Greek philosophy, Glanvill states that 'These, I think, are testimonies enough to prove that Kings wear Gods Image and Authority. And therefore Menander calls the King...God's living Image.... The King is the figure of God among Men.'[165]

Owen could not find it in his heart to concur with these views. Given the development of his thoughts outlined above, the Restoration must have been a bitter blow to Owen. Toon suggests that Owen would have viewed this political development as 'from the hand of the Lord',[166] an inscrutable act of providence. This is true, but nevertheless it would have been with a very heavy heart and Owen, if the style and content of his future writings are anything to go by, was never fully to recover from this shocking event.

For Owen, the fact that a monarchy is almost by definition sinful and likely to lead the nation into culpability before God became clearer to him in the years immediately following the Restoration. The treatment that many Independent churchmen suffered in the 1660s was to consume Owen's thoughts, activities and writings during this period. Much of what he wrote concerning religious toleration at this time was borne out of an innate sense of the sinfulness of a political system persecuting the godly. Again, the nation stood guilty before God for allowing the monarch to pursue such wicked ends through government legislation.

In the light of the *Declaration of Breda*,[167] there had been enormous hopes for a just and fair religious settlement when Charles II came to the throne. Concessions were widely anticipated with a generous spirit being shown to almost all religious groupings in society, Muggletonians, Fifth Monarchists and Quakers excepted.[168] Certainly, these hopes looked like being realised in the initial months of Charles' reign. However, they were soon dashed with the imposition of the 1662 Act of Uniformity, which demanded episcopal ordination for all ministers, a strict adherence to the Prayer Book and a renunciation of previous political and religious affiliations.[169] The strict boundaries of this Act prohibited many conscientious clergymen from continuing in their posts and those who refused to accept the terms of the Act were ejected from their livings on 24 August 1662, St. Bartholomew's Day. The irony of the timing of this was not lost on those ejected. St. Bartholomew's Day was the anniversary of the French massacre of the Huguenots in 1572. The loss to the church was incalculable, the statistics only showing part of the story: 1,760 English clergy were ejected, although some 10% later conformed and were re-instated.[170] In addition, 120 Welsh clergymen were forced to leave, alongside 200 lecturers and teachers of theology in the Universities.

Other legislation also created problems for dissenting clergy. The Corporation Act 1661, by which Aldermen and Town Councillors had to take the Oath of Supremacy and denounce the Solemn League and Covenant, restricted participation in local government solely to practising Anglicans.[171] The Quaker Act of the same year suppressed the meetings of dissidents.[172] The 1664 'Conventicle Act',[173] which expired in 1668 but was renewed again in 1670, outlawed meetings of five or more people for religious purposes. The 1665 'Five Mile Act' prevented Nonconformist ministers from living within that distance of areas where they had previously pastored congregations.[174] The ensuing result of these pieces of legislation (collectively known as *The Clarendon Code*), quite predictably was the imprisonment of many men of God. For those who did not suffer this fate, there was much inconvenience caused in other aspects of their lives; payment of fines, physical threats and officially sanctioned vandalism called for great resolve and patience in this difficult period.[175]

Owen, perhaps due to the many influential contacts he had made in the previous decade, was able to avoid imprisonment. Asty, Owen's early biographer, provides the names of those who respected him and may have provided help at this stage in his life:

> his reputation shone out with such lustre as drew the admiration and respects of several persons of honour and quality upon him, who very much delighted in his conversation; particularly the Earl of Orrey, the Earl of Anglesea, the Lord Willoughby of Parham, the Lord Wharton, the Lord Berkley, [and] Sir John Trevor.[176]

Indeed, it is true that his sufferings were small in comparison with many of his contemporaries. His considerable wealth[177] ensured that he was able to make the best of a bad situation and we may legitimately state that he endured not so much suffering as inconvenience. Certainly for the last twenty years of his life, Owen was to lead a nomadic existence. During that period, he resided variously in London, Stadham, Stoke Newington and Ealing. For much of this time, circumstances meant that he was apart from his family.[178] However, he was able to pursue a literary and preaching ministry that was no doubt the envy of many of his less fortunate brethren. Many of his greatest works come from this period, not least his magnificent commentary on Hebrews and his penetrating analysis *On the Holy Spirit.*

However, Owen had a tender conscience towards those who were suffering more than he was. Furthermore, he understood that these pieces of legislation were grossly unjust and affronts to God, in whose name the persecuted clergy were ministering. There was a deep sense for Owen of the corporate and national guilt laid upon the nation through the actions of the monarch in this regard. This guilt manifested itself, as we shall see, in a number of particulars: the injustice of the situation, the destruction of godly consciences and the linking of the good of the nation with the good of the Established Church.

Throughout the 1660s, Owen pleaded for justice for Independent churchmen. That he should have to devote himself to this issue seemed utterly incongruous to Owen in the first place. In an anonymous letter printed in 1667, Owen recognised that

> It seems, therefore, that we are some of the first who ever anywhere in the world, from the foundation of it, thought of ruining and destroying persons of THE SAME RELIGION with ourselves, merely upon the choice of some peculiar ways of worship in that religion.[179]

Owen argued that it was essentially only in matters or rituals and liturgies that they differed from the established church and that these differences, in and of themselves, should be no barrier to reconciliation or indulgence. Indeed in all other matters, Owen was eager to stress their sense of common purpose:

> We are...fully satisfied that our interest and duty, in self-preservation, consist in a firm adherence unto the protestant religion as established in this nation.... We own and acknowledge the power of the king or supreme magistrate in this nation, as it is declared in the thirty-seventh article of religion; and we are ready to defend and assist in the administration of the government in all causes, unto the law of the land, with all other good protestant subjects of this kingdom.[180]

This was not an understanding with which Owen's opponents agreed. In the Appendix to his 1668 treatise, *A Serious Examination of the Independent's Catechism*, Benjamin Camfield was to write,

> Among all the Brethren of the Separation, whom I have either known or heard of, there hath not one been found of that Loyal Disposition, as to call the War against the last King a rebellion, or his Death a Murther, or the Government of O.C. an unjust Usurpation.[181]

Indeed, rather than expressing their loyalty, the Independents were viewed as conniving traitors who were willing to exploit the moment of national weakness – given England's confrontational stance against the Dutch – in order to gain their desired ends:

> Was this a Time to ripp up and aggravate Discontents at Home, when we were set upon with a Powerful Enemy from abroad?...the Puritan Spirit hath not at all altered his old way of Acting; For so did their Forefathers in 88 try how far they could terrifie the State at that time, because it was a Time of great Danger.[182]

The authoritarian treatment of dissenting churchmen, by which – under the 'Conventicle Act' – they were imprisoned or had their goods confiscated without any recourse to law, was clearly, for Owen, sinful. He understood the injustices they suffered to be sinful in three ways.

First, they contravened the law of God's government. Even when Adam sinned God 'gave him the liberty of his own defence, as that which was his right, before he denounced any sentence against him'.[183] If that was God's model of governmental law then Owen implored the magistrates to take heed before setting up an alternative scheme. Furthermore, Owen suggested that the law and light of nature demands the principle of self-defence, since

> it is a contradiction unto common sense in morality or polity, for a man to be convicted of a crime exposing him to penalty, and not be allowed to make his own defence before conviction.... The general ends of penal laws, which alone make them warrantable

in government, are inconsistent with such clancular [sic] convictions as are in this case pretended.[184]

Second, Owen believed the lack of tolerance towards Independent churchmen to be sinful in its affront to godly consciences. The inability of Dissenters to agree to the Act of Uniformity was a matter of conscience: they honestly believed that God did not approve the manner of worship so prescribed in the Act. It was vital that the churchmen follow their consciences because something much greater than a temporal agreement was at stake here. The judgment of God on the last day will be made on one's actions according to conscience and if the latter has been barbarised there will be no hope for the offender. Put into that eternal context, Owen was able to state that

> To impose penalties, then, enforcing men to a compliance and acting in the worship of God contrary unto what they are convinced in their consciences to be his mind and will, is to endeavour the enforcing of them to reject all respect unto the future judgment of God; which, as it is the highest wickedness in them to do, so hath not God authorized any of the sons of men, by any means, to endeavour their compulsion unto it.... Atheism will be the end of such endeavour.[185]

Third, Owen believed that such attempts to bring uniformity of worship were based on the assumption that 'the church and commonwealth may stand upon the same bottom and foundation, that their interest may be every way the same, of the same breadth and length, and to be mutually narrowed or widened by each other'.[186] Owen contested such an understanding, believing that a heretical and inherently sinful institution – the Church of England – was being upheld at the expense of evangelical and godly ministry. This ecclesiological understanding forms a wide-ranging aspect of Owen's treatment of corporate guilt before God and we will examine it separately to comprehend the depth of his teaching in this regard. That will be the focus of the next chapter.

One can conclude that the restored monarchy justified all Owen's fears about the inherent sinfulness of that institution.

Regardless of personality, it seemed that monarchy in the seventeenth-century English context was bound to oppress godly people and stand contrary to the will of God. Owen could find in his heart no way of supporting such a system of rule.

God's Providence
Given all that has been said above about a nation that stands guilty before God but never without the hope of final redemption, how is it that Owen was able to make sense of political events? What justification did Owen have for remaining optimistic about the nation in which he lived? The answer, quite simply, is to do with his understanding of the providence of God.

Since the nation and the church as a national institution were guilty before God of corporate sin, it is inevitable that they should both come under the judgment of God. That judgment however, cannot be stored up until the final day when all humanity will be called to account since that act of God is reserved for individuals only. There must be a sense in which God's judgment in the face of such sin is enacted more immediately and in the temporal realm.

In the light of that, it is pertinent at this point to touch upon Owen's understanding of how God's providence operates in the course of events that make up human history. The concept of providence was an important one in his thinking, especially as the notions of election and predestination formed such an integral part of his Christian worldview. Thus, Owen believed God's judgment and warnings on and towards the corporate bodies to be enacted out through the events of history:

> The anger of God...is by these judgements openly declared against all unrighteousness and ungodliness of men whatever, whether they fail in the worship and duty which they owe to God, or in the duties which it is incumbent on them to perform to one another; moreover, that the solemn revelation of this divine justice consists, not only in those judgements which, sooner or later, he hath exercised upon particular persons, but also in the whole series of his divine dispensations towards men.[187]

The providential acts of God are especially pertinent in this regard since Owen believed that it is providence 'whereby he obstructs the power of sinning.... When sin is conceived, the Lord obstructs its production by his providence, in taking away or cutting short that *power* which is absolutely necessary for its bringing forth or accomplishment.'[188] If the propensity is towards sin, then God will cut short the power of that individual or body. This was true for Owen whether the perpetrator of sin is an individual monarch such as Charles I, or a corporate body such as the national church.

However Owen was very much a realist and he recognised that some events, notably the restoration of Charles II, did not seem to fit into his perceived understanding of God's providence. There remained for Owen a sense of the inscrutable nature, or mystery, inherent in this aspect of God's actions. God's judgment on ungodliness will come in his own time, not that necessarily expected by man:

> In every distress learn to wait for this appointed time.... He that is infinitely good hath appointed the time; and therefore it is best. He that is infinitely wise hath appointed the season; and therefore it is most suitable. He who is infinitely powerful hath set it down; and therefore it shall be accomplished.... Wait, contending also in all ways, wherein you shall be called out; and be not discouraged that you know not the direct season of deliverance.[189]

In the light of world events taking an unexpected turn in which the evils of men seem for a time to triumph, all one can do is to lean in faith on the providential power of God. One has to believe that judgment will come in his own good time. Owen admitted that this is far from an easy task, but requires of us that

> we are to humble ourselves unto in our walking with God.... Let us lay our mouths in the dust, and ourselves on the ground, and say, 'It is the Lord; I will be silent, because he has done it. He is of one mind, and who can turn him?... Oh, let my heart and thoughts be full of deep subjection to his supreme dominion and uncontrollable sovereignty over me!'[190]

What is most clear is that the very concept of providence was essential for Owen if he was to make sense of contemporary events. It was for Owen a driving principle in understanding the successes of the Parliamentarian forces during the Civil Wars and the advances made during the Protectorate of Oliver Cromwell. Owen believed with some passion that he and his comrades were fighting for the cause of the Lord in all their efforts. It is therefore inevitable that he should cast their triumphs over the enemy in the theological framework of God's providential dealings, the destruction of sin and the triumph of godliness. Conversely, when Owen's cause seemed to be all but lost following the restoration of Charles II, it was in no small part his belief in God's providence that offered a continued validation for his theological system. Sin cannot ultimately triumph over good and therefore it must be within the inscrutable mystery of God's providence that the timing for judgment would come.

The judgment of God on the nation was most evident to Owen during the 1660s following the restoration of Charles II. Pertinent confirmation of this fact came through the Great Plague, the fire of London and the Dutch War.[191] This understanding of the Great Fire was of course a very common point of view amongst many of Owen's contemporaries, as two such examples show. The first is from Thomas Brooks'[192] *London's Lamentation on the Late Fiery Dispensation*, published in 1670:

> Consider that the burning of London is a national judgement. God, in smiting of London, has smitten England round: the stroke of God upon London was a universal stroke.... The burning of London is the herald of God to the whole nation, calling it to repentance and reformation; for the very same sins are rampant in all parts of the nation.[193]

The second such example is from Edward Chamberlayne[194] in his 1674 edition of *Angliæ Novitiæ*:

> Gods just indignation, for the notorious impenitency of the Citizens, for their great abominations in abetting and instigating the shedding of the precious innocent Blood, both of Gods

Anointed, and of their other Chief Governors, both in Church and State, for their still going on in their old hainous sins of despising Dominions, and speaking evil of Dignities, till there be no remedy.[195]

Uncharacteristically perhaps, Owen went farther than these two examples, farther even than most of his contemporaries, in apportioning blame for the Great Fire of London. Whilst he did indeed perceive it to be God's judgment on the nation, he also discovered another hand at work as he outlined in his short treatise *A Word of Advice to the Citizens of London*:

Whilst things are in this state and condition among you, it is sufficiently known that the avowed, implacable enemies of your city (I mean the Papists) are intent on all advantages, improving them unto their own ends, their present design being so open and naked as that it is the common discourse of all sorts of persons.... Unto their conduct of affairs you owe the flames of '66; nor will they rest but in your utter ruin, or, which is worse, the establishment of their religion amongst you.[196]

Whatever the temporal circumstances, it was clear to Owen that these national crises were judgments from the hand of God. It was only by a sovereign act of God's grace that the nation could find salvation: 'But the truth is, the land abounds in sin, – God is angry, and risen out of his holy place, – judgement lies at the door...I know *no provoking sin*, condemned as such in the book of God, whereof instances may not be found in this nation.'[197]

However, Owen was far from pessimistic. He did honestly believe that there were encouraging signs for the future and that with the showing forth of repentance and fresh zeal for holiness, God would respond to the pleas of his people. Nevertheless, this optimism was set in the context of realism about the present situation:

Oh, poor England! among all thy lovers thou hast no one to plead for thee this day! From the height of profaneness and atheism, through the filthiness of sensuality and uncleanness, down to the lowest form of oppression and cheating, the land is filled with all sorts of sin. If there be any that can put in an exception as to any provoking sin that is not among us, let them stand forth and plead the cause of this nation. I profess my mouth is stopped.[198]

As we have noted previously, God's providence was central to his understanding of the nation before God. The duty of all believers, therefore, in rooting out corporate sin in their midst, must begin with an appreciation of God's providential activities. If the nation does not recognise and heed the warnings, then there is no way for it to respond to the grace of God in an act of repentance:

> It is a part and duty of spiritual wisdom, as also a due reverence of God, to take notice of *extraordinary occurrences* in the dispensations of his providence; for they are instructive warnings, and of great importance in his government of the world. In them the 'voice of the Lord crieth unto the city, and the man of wisdom shall see his name'.[199]

The situation was very clear for Owen. Even at this late stage when the nation had so abundantly rejected the gracious prompting of God in the recent past, England was not past redemption. The choice for Owen was simple: repent and flourish or reject God and perish:

> When a land, a nation, a city, a church, is filled with sin, so as that God gives them warnings or indications of his displeasure by previous judgements, or other extraordinary signs, if they are not as warnings complied withal by repentance and reformation, they are tokens of approaching judgements, that shall not be avoided.... The state is so with us, that, unless we repent, we shall perish.[200]

However, this understanding of England being at a spiritual crossroads was tempered with Owen's fundamental optimism about the future:

> God may have, for our sins, determined a desolating calamity on this nation; yet if there be not a judiciary hardness upon us, it may

only be partial, and recoverable.... It will be but *partial*; it will be but *for a time;* it will be *sanctified;* – it will *purify* the church, and restore it unto a more glorious state than ever before.[201]

Again,

Here lies the trial of this poor land and nation at this day; judgement is deserved, judgement is threatened, judgement is approaching – the clouds are the dust of his feet. If all sorts of men turn not to God by repentance, – if we are not humbled for our contempt of the gospel and outrage against it, – if we leave not our provoking sins, – evil will overtake us, and we shall not escape. And yet, on the other hand, by a due application unto him who holds the balance in his hand, mercy may glory against justice, and we may have deliverance.[202]

Whether the nation would come under God's judgment or mercy was beyond knowing for Owen. What he did fully grasp however, was the corporate nature of the shared guilt. All may not have indulged in the prevailing sins of blasphemy, iniquity and immorality. Nevertheless, there was a sense in which all were culpable by the lack of mourning and sensibility to the problem amongst Christians. Owen was prepared to accept his own guilt in this manner too:

I do acknowledge here before you, and to my own shame, I have great guilt upon me in this matter, that I have not been sensible of the abominations of this nation, so as to mourn for them and be humbled for them, as I ought to have been. And you will do well to search your hearts, and consider how it is with you.[203]

For Owen, all were culpable and each member of society stood guilty of tolerating sin in society. It was for each individual to take seriously their own responsibility in this regard and throw themselves upon the mercy of God and his providential actions.

Conclusion

Given Owen's consistent involvement in the world of politics before 1660 and his championing of ecclesiological causes after that date, it is inevitable that much of his understanding of sin should focus on corporate and national perspectives. His concern as a pastor and teacher was very much for the state of the individual before God. However, he held that emphasis in tension with his concern for how wider issues ultimately affected the eternal destiny of the individual.

Owen's pastoral heart gave him a concern for corporate issues. He was not an abstract political or social philosopher intent on showing the evils of society merely for the sake of some academic interest. Owen was acutely aware that no man exists in isolation and that the political realm has an immense impact on the well-being of the individual. Therefore, it is not enough for the individual to combat sin in his life if the wider context of society inhibits, or even prohibits, the success of such efforts. Clearly, the two aspects of combating sin need to work in tandem. Personal sin must be the constant object of private mortification whilst sin in society must be the focus for those who are able to offer their influence towards the increasing of godliness in the wider sense.

The impact of Owen's teachings in this regard is difficult to quantify. Clearly through the sermon he preached in January 1649, he gave Parliament a sense of self-justification after the execution of Charles I and gave the embryonic Republican movement a theological basis on which to build in the light of that. It would be wrong, of course, to attribute this solely to Owen. There were many other theologians very influential in this regard; Philip Nye, Joseph Caryl and Thomas Goodwin are good examples of this. However, none had the lasting impact of Owen. As Cromwell's chaplain and regular preacher to Parliament, Owen provided much of the theological impetus in the era of the Protectorate. As such, he was able to inform those in power of concepts of national guilt and sin.

However, there was undoubtedly a sense of failure in Owen's mission to uncover and eradicate the corporate responsibility of the nation before God. After all, by the time of his death in August

1683, how much had really changed? The monarchy was intact and as powerful as it had been at the time of his birth in 1616. Lack of commitment to the Christian cause was still rife within many sections of society and Reformed theology was less popular than at any time for a century. Sin in society was still a very real problem. It would be easy to come to the conclusion that this aspect of Owen's ministry had been but a tiny ripple attempting to withstand the force of a massive tide; ineffective and soon dissipated without trace.

So it might be viewed had Owen not set his own life's work in the wider context of the gracious providence of God. In our efforts to be faithful to Owen, we too are duty bound to locate this aspect of his ministry in the same context. Viewed in that manner, we are able to understand the deep success Owen enjoyed. His ministry in this regard was to convict others of the reality of sin in society. Owen helped to liberate the minds and consciences of godly men and women to make a difference in whatever way they could. He encouraged others to build alternative systems of government, the legacy of which would have a long-lasting impact that transcended his own lifetime. He challenged those in power to take seriously the godliness of the nation and the spiritual needs of the poor and disadvantaged. Owen was convinced of the sin in society that needed addressing. In the short term, he may well have failed to make any immediate impact. However, his legacy in the long-term was immense and cannot be underestimated. Without doubt, Owen would attribute that timing to the providence of God, whose inscrutable mysteries cannot be comprehended, let alone challenged.

4

SIN AND THE CHURCH

The power of sin is prevalent in the individual. Sin is deep rooted in society too. Seeking sanctuary within the established church provides no escape route from sin, for, according to Owen, sin was rife within the church as well. One hallmark of the seventeenth century was the great number of ecclesiological debates that demanded the energies of so many eminent theologians. It comes as no surprise to us, then, that a great proportion of Owen's literary output was devoted to matters of an ecclesiological nature. Indeed, for many, this area of his literary output is the greatest legacy that he has left to the church, for it is as the Father of Congregationalism that he is best remembered and respected. Given his devotion to this area of doctrinal thought, it should not be surprising that his understanding of sin relates to his ecclesiology. What follows, then, is an analysis of the interdependence of these two issues.

Our concern is not to provide a detailed consideration of Owen's ecclesiological thought, but only his understanding of sin within the general arena of ecclesiology. As we examine this aspect of his thought, we recognise a number of differing, though inter-related, issues. First, Owen had a well-developed understanding of the nature of the church founded, as we might expect, on the Reformed teachings of election and federal theology. Second, Owen was consistent in applying his ecclesiology in a practical manner concerning sin. The result of this was that he believed there to be some occasions when it is right to separate as Christians from those institutions and forms of church which are deemed to exist and operate contrary to God's will. Third, Owen was unstinting in attacking those forms of contemporary faith which called themselves 'Christian' and yet, from his own perspective, fell far short of Christian orthodoxy; namely, Arminianism, Socinianism, Quakerism and Roman Catholicism. These themes provide the content of the ensuing chapter.

Election and Covenant

Central to Owen's argument was the concept of election; the biblical doctrine that teaches that God predestines some to salvation, which Owen succinctly described in *A Display of Arminianism*:

> This election the word of God proposeth unto us as the gracious, immutable decree of Almighty God, whereby, *before the foundation of the world, out of his own good pleasure, he chose certain men, determining to free them from sin and misery, to bestow upon them grace and faith, to give them unto Christ, to bring them to everlasting blessedness, for the praise of his glorious grace.*[1]

The practicalities and detail of the relationship of election to saving faith formed the background of the greatest theological battle of the early to mid-seventeenth century, namely, the Reformed Orthodox tradition versus the Arminian school of thought. It was thus inevitable that Owen's writings on sin in an ecclesiological setting should take seriously this doctrine.

For Owen, what he termed 'effectual calling' is primary in the *ordo salutis*, although not chronologically since it is inseparable from regeneration, faith, repentance, justification, adoption and sanctification.[2] Writing extensively on the subject towards the end of his life, Owen stated that the elective purposes of God are primarily for salvation, that God's name may be glorified.[3] Inextricably linked with this idea is holiness in the life of the elect; for Owen, there could be no sign of election without holiness and vice versa:

> Chosen we are unto salvation by the free, sovereign grace of God. But how may this salvation be actually obtained? how may we be brought into the actual possession of it? Through the sanctification of the Spirit, and no otherwise. Whom God doth not sanctify and make holy by his Spirit, he never chose unto salvation from the beginning. The counsels of God, therefore, concerning us do not depend on our holiness; but upon our holiness our future happiness depends in the counsel of God.[4]

Herein lies the importance of Owen's concept of election in relation to his doctrine of sin. Of course, Owen engaged, in detail, in the debate concerning the precise nature of predestination; how, when, by whom and for whom it has been wrought.[5] His most detailed analysis of these concepts is in his early treatise, *A Display of Arminianism*. But, in relation to sin, it is not the practicalities of election which are important so much as the freedom and responsibilities that election brings; freedom to participate in the purposes of God and a responsibility to holy living. Indeed, Owen summarily dismissed the idea that election renders holiness unnecessary since the purposes of God cannot be frustrated, as a 'cavil against the truth'. He stressed the idea that election can only be known by its fruits and not in any way as a part of the revealed will of God. His argument was summarised in concise form when he stated that 'faith, obedience, holiness, are the inseparable fruits, effects and consequents of election'.[6]

Owen understood election to be a work of God in the individual. However, it also has implications for the Christian community. It brings with it responsibilities that can only be worked out through fellowship with others in a church context. When Owen attempted to define specifically the nature of the church, he often wrote in terms of election. The church was to Owen, 'the whole company of God's elect, called of God';[7] 'the whole multitude of them who antecedently are chosen of his Father...to be gathered to [Jesus Christ] out of all nations.'[8] Furthermore, it is 'a society of persons called out of the world...unto the obedience of faith'.[9] This notion of election by God to a life of obedience was fundamental for Owen's understanding of the ability of the church to be corporately guilty of sin. Ferguson summarises Owen's teachings by suggesting four characteristics of the church, namely, 'the ministry of the word, the celebration of the sacraments, the exercise of discipline and the work of evangelism.'[10] That being the case, the church is guilty of betraying its responsibilities by falling short in these areas.

Owen was in no doubt about the reason for the foundation of the church: it is for the sole purpose of leading humanity to its ultimate τελος; the worship of God and life in fellowship with others:

God created our nature, or made man, for his *own worship* and service, and fitted the powers and faculties of his soul thereunto...this nature is so fitted for society, so framed for it as its next end...by the light of nature this acting in society is principally designed unto the worship of God...without *the worship of God in societies* there would be an absolute failure of one principal end of the creation of man.... Hence have we the original of churches in the light of nature. Men associating themselves together, or uniting in such societies for the worship of God, which he requires of them, as may enable them unto an orderly performance of it, are a church.[11]

For Owen, it is the duty of all humanity to meet in church-society, in church-fellowship together, to worship God. Furthermore, Owen believed that there is a sense in which we are not able to become wholly human until we participate in that act.[12] It is through the church (as the gathered people of God, not necessarily as institution) that God interacts with humanity and is thus the arena for the actualisation of the covenant relationship between creature and the Creator.[13]

Central then to Owen's understanding of how the church is capable of corporate sin, was this notion of covenant. In Owen's mind, this had two applications; primarily the covenant between the church and God and, secondarily, the covenant made or informally understood between fellow Christians within a given congregation, which Owen called a mutual (or virtual) confederation.[14]

The covenant between God and His people – the church – was from antiquity. Owen suggested that God initiated this covenant with Moses. Exodus 24 is the record of that instance, 'whereby they were raised and erected into a church-state, wherein they were intrusted with all the privileges and enjoined all the duties which God had annexed thereunto.'[15] In outlining his thought, Owen was not suggesting that this covenant is identical to any one of those already considered in the first chapter of this book:

The covenant which God made there with the people, and they with him, was not the covenant of grace under a legal dispensation, for that was established unto the seed of Abraham four hundred years before, in the promise with the seal of circumcision; nor was it the covenant of works under a gospel dispensation, for God never renewed that covenant under any consideration whatever; but it was a peculiar covenant with God then made with them...whereby they were raised and erected into a church-state.... This covenant was the sole formal cause of their church-state, which they are charged so often to have broken, and which they so often solemnly renewed unto God.[16]

Whilst Owen clearly stressed the peculiar nature of this covenant, he was nevertheless careful not to suggest that the church-covenant made here should be thought of as entirely separate from other forms of covenant relationship with God. Rather, he was anxious to hold these ideas in tension by speaking of the temporary nature of the *form* of the covenant that embraced eternal *principles* that carry on with the people of God in every age.[17] The principles of the covenant of grace were inherent in this church-covenant. Faith and repentance and so forth 'are presupposed unto it' as a natural response to the calling of holy and elect people into all the duties of evangelical worship:

This resignation of ourselves unto the will, power, and authority of Christ, with an express engagement made unto him of doing and observing all his commands, hath *the nature of a covenant on our part*; and it hath so on his, by virtue of the promise of his especial presence annexed unto this engagement on our part, Matthew 28: 18-20.[18]

However, Owen was adamant that, due to their sin and rejection of Christ, the form of this church-covenant made with the Jews 'was utterly taken away; for hereon the Hebrews ceased to be the peculiar church of God'.[19] What remains for the true seed of Abraham – the elect of Christ – are the principles of that covenant which continue as the promise of God to every generation.

The second covenant relationship which binds the church is that made between believers to one another. Owen did not consider this relationship to hold equivalent status as that between man and God.[20] Nevertheless it was an essential aspect of Owen's ecclesiology and important in our analysis of how he believed that the church could fall into sin. Owen, of course, was not alone in this understanding of the church-state in terms of covenant; indeed, it was a prevalent theme within the Congregational movement at this time. Many, if not most, of the Congregational churches in England had a written covenant, at the bottom of which each church member signed his or her name. In each case, there was a twofold emphasis within the text: obedience to the holy ordinances of God and a determination to be stewards of each other's faith in fellowship.

In his book, *Visible Saints 1640-60*, Nuttall gives an excellent treatment of these church member covenants.[21] For our purposes, we shall consider just three of his examples in order to get a flavour of these covenants. The first is that of an Independent church in Bristol, the covenant of 1645:

> That [the congregation] would, in the strength of Christ, keep close to the holy scriptures, the word of God; and the plain truths and ordinances of the gospel, of church fellowship, breaking bread, and prayers; and to be subject to one another, according to the discipline and admonition by the rules of Christ, in the New Testament, or the scriptures.

The Bury St. Edmunds congregation replaced their 1646 covenant two years later with one that accommodated Congregational rather than Separatist principles.[22] The second covenant began thus:

> We whose names are here subscribed do resolve and engage by the help of the Spirit of God to walk in all the ways of God so far forth as he hath revealed or shall reveal them unto us by his word, and in all duties of love and watchfulness each to other as becomes a church of Christ.

Likewise, in Market Weston in 1654, it was agreed that

> Wee doe Covenant or Agree in the Presence of God, through the Assistance of his Holy Spirit, to walke together in all the

Ordinances of our Lord Jesus, so far as the same are made clear unto us; indeavouring [sic] the Advancement of ye Glory of our Father, The Subjection of our Wills to the Will of our Redeemer, and the mutual Edification Each of other in his most holy Faith and Fear.

As for Owen, his views on the subject stood within the mainstream of the Congregational movement in that his own writings on this topic suggested identical ideas and beliefs. In *The True Nature of a Gospel Church*, for example, he stated that this 'mutual confederation', 'this *joining of themselves*, whereon depend all their interest in church powers and privileges, all their obligation unto church duties, is a *voluntary act* of the obedience of faith unto the authority of Christ; nor can it be anything else.'[23] Owen stressed the voluntary nature of this confederation, in common with many of his Congregational peers. In his 1647 treatise, *A Model of the Primitive Congregational Way*, William Bartlet[24] described the true church as 'a free society or communion of visible Saints, embodyed and knit together by a voluntary consent'. Likewise, six years later, John Rogers defined the true Church of Christ in his *An Idea of Church Discipline* in part as 'all her Members freely, and voluntarily, embodying without the least compulsion (having communion with the Father and the Son) [and] all seeking the same End, viz. the Honor and Glory of God in his worship'.[25] Owen understood the nature of the church so described to be the foundation for all decency and order in church life and the means of preventing schism. Thus the aim or end of the church is obedience to the Lord but the means or cause of that is 'a mutual agreement amongst themselves jointly to perform all the duties required of them in that state'.[26] This, of course, was not merely academic teaching on Owen's part. Rather, it was borne out in his own experience as a pastor; the rules in his section on 'Mutual Duties in Church-Fellowship' in *Eshcol*, published in 1647 through his experiences at Fordham and Coggeshall, reveal this most clearly.[27]

Thus far, we have examined Owen's understanding of the make-up of the church; an elect people called by God into a covenant relationship both with the Creator and with each other. However,

if we are to consider Owen's teachings about how the church itself
can fall into sin, one more question needs to be addressed, namely:
what actually constitutes the nature of a true gospel church? In
defining this, Owen drew on an idea that was commonplace
amongst his contemporaries: that of the 'visible saints'. Nuttall
has explored the social consequences of such an idea with the
provision of some delightful anecdotes and stories,[28] so no further
treatment is required here. Owen's understanding of the concept
itself, however, does demand further comment.

The determining measure of qualification for Christ's church,
according to Owen, was the measure of holiness in an individual's
life.[29] Lest such an idea lead to over-judgmental and censorious
behaviour on the part of church leaders, Owen stressed, in a passage
to which some of his over-zealous colleagues would have done
well to pay heed, that

> the judgement which is passed on the confession and profession
> of them that are to be admitted into churches is charitative,
> proceeding on evidence of moral probability, not determining the
> reality of the things themselves; that there are sundry measures of
> light, knowledge, experience, and abilities and readiness of mind,
> in those that are to be admitted, all whose circumstances are duly
> to be considered, with indulgence unto their weakness: and if the
> Scripture will allow us any further latitude, we are ready to
> embrace it. [30]

Owen acknowledged that God alone is able to judge each
individual but that the church is able to judge the external evidences
of a regenerated spiritual life: the fruit of the Spirit of righteousness.
In the light of that, Owen suggested six attributes that must be
visible in the lives of the saints:

> (1.) There is required unto [them] *a competent knowledge* of the
> doctrines and mystery of the gospel, especially concerning *the
> person and offices of Christ....* (2.)...*a professed subjection of soul
> and conscience unto the authority of Christ in the church....* (3.)
> An instruction in and consent unto *the doctrine of self-denial and
> bearing of the cross...* (4.) *Conviction and confession of sin, with*

the way of deliverance by Jesus Christ...(5.)...the constant performance of all known duties of religion...(6.) A careful abstinence from all known sins.[31]

Owen concluded thus:

> [There is not] one word in the whole Scripture intimating any concession or permission of Christ to receive into his church those who are not so qualified.... No man, as I suppose, is come unto that profligate sense of spiritual things as to deny that the members of the church ought to be *visibly holy:* for if so, they may affirm that all the promises and privileges made and granted to the church do belong unto them who visibly live and die in their sins; which is to overthrow the gospel.[32]

The Justification for Separation

Given the above, there could be occasional necessity for separation from individuals and institutions that are deemed to fall short of the mark in some way. Indeed, this topic engaged Owen's pen to no small degree and, as we shall see, many of his writings were for justifying not only himself but also his fellow Congregationalists against the charge of needless schism. However, we need to emphasise that this was a difficult area for Owen as an individual. He was no schismatic. Indeed, Owen put much effort in his later years into trying to create an accommodation between the Presbyterian party and Independents. The stance that Baxter took ensured that these efforts were doomed to failure. The depth of Owen's desire to facilitate such unity amongst Protestants becomes clear in a letter he wrote to Richard Baxter in January 1669 in which he stated

> I [was] in earnest in what I proposed, in reference to the Concord you design. For the desire of it is continually upon my heart, and to express that desire on all occasion, I esteem one part of that Profession of the Gospel which I am called unto. Could I contribute any thing towards the Accomplishment of so holy, so necessary a Work, I should willingly spend my self, and be spent in it.[33]

Owen's fervent desire, throughout his ministry, was to see unity among Christian brethren. Division amongst Christians was abhorrent to him: 'He who doth not pray always, who is not ready with his utmost endeavour to remedy this evil, to remove this great obstruction of the benefit of the gospel, is scarce worthy the name of a Christian.'[34] He believed that a unity of love would mirror the spiritual unity that already exists between them because of the union with Christ that is the inheritance of every believer. There was, for Owen, a clear difference between schism, which was unwarranted by Scripture, and separation, which had become a necessity for many believers.

Owen's appreciation of the need for separation was not born out of mere academic reflection. This issue had taxed him from the beginning of his ministerial career. Certainly Owen had not always been a Congregationalist; the publication in May 1644 of *The Duty of Pastors and People Distinguished* affirmed his broad commitment to the Presbyterian ecclesiastical model of ministry. However, his commitment to that model soon waned, and his congregational ideas rapidly advanced, not least due to his understanding of the centrality of election. The correlation between the two ideas was a natural one for Owen since election by God is primarily an election to salvation and, crucially, holiness. An integral aspect of growing in holiness is to divorce oneself from an apostate church. For what reasons, specifically, did Owen regard separation from the Church of England as a necessity? Two reasons: the first, to do with perceived idolatrous practices; the second, because the very notion of a 'national church' seemed to Owen to be anathema to Scripture and thus an untenable position to hold.

Some of Owen's most controversial and influential writings were on the subject of schism in the church.[35] It is not the intention of this writer to attempt a review of his extensive and detailed teaching on this vital topic, but only in so far as separation relates to his doctrine of sin. In a passage from his posthumous publication *The True Nature of a Gospel Church*, which dealt specifically with the reasons for separation, Owen stated quite categorically that '*Communion with particular churches is to be regulated absolutely by edification.* No man is or can be obliged to abide in or confine himself unto the communion of any particular church any longer than it is for his edification.'[36] In the light of that, Owen then listed four reasons why an individual may leave a church due to its lack of provision for edification. First, if it is inconsistent in practice with that which communion ought to be amongst its members. Second, if it is so lost in scandal and bad practice as to make edification impossible. Third, if the behaviour and lifestyle of most of its members runs contrary to the demands of the gospel for Christian holiness. Fourth, if that particular church is incapable of self-reformation.[37] Quite simply, the Church of England, in Owen's estimation, had failed on each of these four counts (and more), thus making separation from that body into Congregationalism inevitable.

In *Eshcol*, Owen had outlined fifteen rules for the saints, one of which stressed the need for 'Separation and Sequestration from the world and men of the world, with all ways of false worship'.[38] Owen was unequivocal in his approach to this, stating that 'He that will not separate from the world and false worship is *a separate* from Christ'.[39] Owen claimed biblical warrant for his views from the following texts: Numbers 23:9; Proverbs 14:7; Hosea 4:15; John 15:19; 2 Corinthians 6:14-18; Ephesians 5:8,11; 2 Timothy 3:5 and Revelation 18:4. Baxter, however, contended against Owen in this regard and accused those who use these texts in this way of abuse and misunderstanding of Scripture.[40] Despite these attacks from Baxter, Owen continued to intertwine his understanding of sin with election to holiness and salvation. The manner in which he did this rendered null and void any commitment to Presbyterianism in the context of a national church that endorsed Romish practices.

Owen's primary concern in this regard was for orthodox Christianity as the sole basis for the Church's creed, doctrine and worship. Initially, we must consider this in the light of Owen's belief that the Church of Rome was the Antichrist. The separation of the true church of God from the idolatrous practices and superstitions of Rome was essential for the promotion of true gospel holiness for Owen, an idea we will further examine. His millennialism compounded his sense of urgency. If the age in which he lived were to witness the return of Christ then the integrity of the Protestant church was of paramount importance. Lest anyone charge Owen with schism from the Church of Rome, he had this to say:

> But what need I insist upon this supposition, when I am not more certain that there is any instituted church in the world, owned by Christ as such, than I am that the church of Rome is none, properly so called?...The foundation of it lies in this clear truth, that no church whatever, universal or particular, can possibly err in fundamentals; for by so doing it would cease to be a church. My denying, then, the synagogue of Rome to be a church, according to their principles, amounts to no more than this, - the Papists maintain, in their public confessions, fundamental errors; in which assertion it is known I am not alone.[41]

Owen and many of his contemporaries developed the Reformers' idea of the Antichrist by extending it to include not only Rome but also the established Church of England. Nuttall is quite right to point out, however, that this was not an entirely new concept. In 1572, the Presbyterians expressed the same sentiment in their *Admonition to the Parliament*: 'All the bad language used in Reform apologetics to describe the "corruptions" of Rome, is now turned against the Elizabethan settlement...the church is "governed by such canons and customes as by which Antichrist did rule his synagogue".'[42] Some understood the close proximity between the English Church and idolatrous Romish practices and doctrine to be a sign of the times. In an undated and unsigned tract based upon an exposition of Revelation 17:14, probably written in 1642, the writer stated that

> The time is [coming] when...we shall be about to finish our testimonie, and then riseth the last warre to lay us as lowe as the graves mouth, but not to be able to bury us, and the reason is the fame that we have, 2 Kings 13.21...That the horns of Antichrist are in it is more than manifest, and our Bishops so blinded that they see it not, and if his Majestie cannot through the thick mist see it, God of his goodness expell the cloud that hinder it.[43]

The political implications for such a view were immense. Charles I was heavily criticised by William Prynne[44] for dispatching letters of protection and warrants of discharge to hundreds of favoured Catholic recusants, priests and Jesuits.[45] Archbishop Laud felt compelled in his own funeral sermon to clear the monarch of Catholic sympathies:

> [Charles I] hath been much traduced by some for labouring to bring in Popery, but upon my Conscience...I know him to be as free from this as any man living, and I hold him to be as sound a Protestant, according to the Religion by Law established, as any man in this Kingdom.[46]

Ecclesiologically for Owen, the impact of such a view was just as immense, resulting in the increasing and eventual overwhelming congregational ideas within him. Owen was not the first to express such a sentiment; in 1636, William Prynne had written that

> I hope these arrogant lofty prelates will not be offended with me, if I make it apparent to them (and others) by their fruits and works, that they are so far from being the sons or successors of Christ and his apostles, or of divine institution, that they are of their father the devil (for his works and lusts they do). The successors from the Jewish high priests who crucified our Saviour, persecuted, silenced, imprisoned, excommunicated his apostles, and so, of diabolical ordination, not divine.[47]

Given this understanding amongst his contemporaries and himself, separation was, for Owen, a necessary act to avoid the charge of culpability by inference with the sins of the Church of England. In *Eshcol*, Owen commented that

> Causeless separation from established churches, walking according to the order of the gospel (though perhaps failing in the practice of some things of small concernment), is no small sin; but separation from the sinful practices, and disorderly walkings, and false unwarranted ways of worship in any, is to fulfil the precept of not partaking in other men's sins.[48]

This work by Owen was published in the same year as William Bartlet's *A Model of the Primitive Congregational Way*, the second chapter of which expressed a similar sentiment. There was, Bartlet suggested, a difference between

> good separation, a separation from evill, from evill and sinfull wayes, and things, and persons, a separation from false worship, from Babels confusion, a separation of the precious from the vile, of the cleane from the uncleane [and the] bad separation from good to evil, from Christ to Belial; from God to the Devill.[49]

Whether there was any link between Bartlet and Owen, and whether they may have influenced one another in this regard, is impossible to state with certainty. However, it is very likely that that was the case, given the close-knit fraternity of Congregational ministers throughout England at that time. In addition, Bartlet was aware of other writings by Owen since in his 1647 treatise he quoted from Owen's 'Country Essay', attached to *A Vision of Unchangeable, Free Mercy*.[50] Regardless of his influences, it is clear that a primary motivation for Owen's move towards Congregationalism was 'our own preservation from sin and protection from punishment, that with others we be not infected and plagued'.[51]

It was because of the strength of his feelings in this regard that the movement towards unity attempted by Baxter and Owen eventually proved fruitless. The two church leaders had been in negotiations for some time at the end of the 1650s, engaged in an honest attempt to find an accommodation between Presbyterians and Congregationalists. Contrary to the suggestion of Wood, that Owen 'had little interest in the effort',[52] these discussions were close to his heart. It is possible that Wood's misunderstanding arises out of the fact that Owen had delayed meeting with Baxter to talk through the proposals. Owen was not dragging his feet, as a letter to Baxter makes clear: 'Sir, The continuance of my Cold, which yet holds me, with the severity of the Weather, have hitherto hindered me from answering my purpose of coming unto you at Acton but yet I hope ere long to obtain the advantage of enjoying your Company there for a Season.'[53] Indeed, Owen was most optimistic that some measure of unity and co-operation could be achieved: 'Upon the whole Matter, I judge your Proposals worthy of great Consideration, and the most probable medium for the attaining of the End aimed at, that yet I have perused.'[54]

The sad truth is that it was Baxter, not Owen, who proved unwilling to compromise. His reply to Owen's optimistic letter was far from helpful. Baxter chose to criticise the very heart of the Congregationalist position and it is worth considering his response at some length:

> The great things which hinder the Presbyterians and Moderate Episcopal Men from closing with you are principally these.
> 1. Because they think that your way tends to destroy the Kingdom of Christ, by dividing it...
> 2. They think, while you seem to be for a stricter Discipline than others, that your way (or usual Practice) tendeth to extirpate Godliness out of the Land; by taking a very few that can talk more than the rest, and making them the Church...neglecting the Souls of all the Parish...They think that Parish-Reformation tendeth to the making Godliness universal, and that your Separation tendeth to dwindle it to nothing. I know that some of you have spoken for endeavouring the good of all; but (pardon my plainness) I knew scarce any of you that did not by an unjust espousing of your few, do the People a double Injury, one by denying them their Church-Rights, without any regular Church-Justice, and the other by lazily omitting most that should have been done for their Salvation.[55]

Baxter's response left Owen with no room for compromise. Unity could never be achieved whilst Baxter remained so intransigent.

The death-knell for these discussions was sounded when Baxter was won over to the Royalist cause in 1659. The publication of his treatise *The Holy Commonwealth* marked a turning point in his views. His Royalist enthusiasm was further evidenced by his preaching for Parliament the day before the vote was taken to recall King Charles II from exile and his ensuing activity within the Royal Court.[56] Baxter's subsequent involvement in discussions to create a just settlement for nonconformists foundered on the rocks of the Book of Common Prayer, despite his best efforts at the Savoy Conference the preceding year.[57] The Bishop of Worcester rejected his personal appeal to receive a Preacher's licence,[58] although Beddard suggests that this was an act of collusion on the part of three local Cavaliers, Sir Ralph Clare, Sir John Pakington and the Bishop himself, rather than an act that had the backing of the Royal Court.[59] Baxter remained a nonconformist but any principles that had united him with Owen were lost in his courting of the institutional church during this dark period of his life and ministry. The desire which Owen had for his flock not to be 'infected and plagued' by the Church of England stood in marked contrast to Baxter's attempts to work within and reform the national church along Presbyterian lines.

The second motivation for Owen's advocating a separation from the established church was the perceived standing of that institution in the nation. Put at its simplest, the very idea of commitment to a 'national church' was anathema to Owen. To be a member of the Church of England bears no relation to the institution of that name[60]; only that the individual is an elect of God and thereby a member of the true church of God. The church, for Owen, was no mere institution. It is the elect of God, his body here on earth, that exists only by the grace of God and for the glory of God. The Presbyterian system that acknowledged the claim of all within the parish to be members of the Church cannot fulfil the biblical ideal of an elect and regenerate people called out of the world into a life of holiness. The notion of a national church, common to the people of the land, is an abrogation of scriptural principles and therefore contrary to any biblical idea of election:

> I would loath to exclude every man from being a member of the church in England, – that is, from a share in the profession of the faith which is owned and professed by the people of God in England, – who is not a member of a particular congregation. [But] subjection to one civil government, and agreement in the same doctrine and worship specifically, either jointly or severally, [does not] constitute one church.[61]

In voicing his opinions thus, Owen was but one voice in a well-founded tradition. Indeed, Jeremiah Burroughs[62] had been expressing the same sentiment over a decade previously:

> That wee may call the Church in England a Nationall Church because of the many Saints in it, who are the body of Christ, I deny not, nor ever did...but that it is by the institution of Christ formed into one politicall Church, as the Nation of the Jewes was, this is no Independency to deny.... What Nationall Worship hath Christ instituted? Doth our birth in the Nation make us members of the Church? These things are so palpably plaine to any that will understand, that tis tedious to spend time about them.[63]

Others, however, were anxious to oppose such a view and took issue with Owen about it. One such minister was Daniel Cawdrey,[64] a Presbyterian minister in Great Billing, Northamptonshire. He had been heavily critical of Owen in his 1657 pamphlet, *Independencie A Great Schism*, to which Owen replied the same year with *A Review of the True Nature of Schism*. The popularity of the movement for church reform according to the Congregationalist principle was considered to be as threatening as the principles themselves which, as Daniel Cawdrey noted, threatened the very fabric of society itself: 'Does this not open a door to all confusion, in Church and State? and give every man (all as well as any) liberty, if they judge anything amiss in Church and State, to turn Reformers, if Superiours cannot or will not Reform it.'[65] Nevertheless, Owen was completely unrepentant. For him, soteriology and ecclesiology could not be divorced since salvation is only a possibility within the true church. This was a view that remained central to Owen's ecclesiology throughout his ministry as he confirmed in one of his last works:

> It is generally said that '*out of the church there is no salvation*;' and the truth hereof is testified unto in the Scriptures...This is true both positively and negatively of the *catholic church* invisible, of the elect; all that are of it shall be saved, and none shall be saved but those that belong unto it, Ephesians 5:25-27.[66]

As Owen's ministry moved towards its final days, the sense of urgency concerning the need for separation in the light of the sins of the church increased. Infused throughout all his writings on this topic is a real sense in which he believed time to be running out. Certainly time was running out for Owen personally and this no doubt increased his sense of zeal. In a sermon preached in November 1676 entitled *Perilous Times*,[67] Owen outlined the imminent danger in which the church – the people of God – found itself. In this sermon, he focused on the corporate guilt of the church before God, and stressed the immediate need for repentance and renewed zeal if the church is to continue to bring glory to God in the nation. In this work, he outlined two predominant themes that indicated the perilous state in which the church found itself.

First, Owen recognised sin abounding in the church through its lack of holiness. Specifically, it did not live up to its calling by God to be separate from the world: 'If any thing under heaven will make a season perilous, this will do it, – when we mingle ourselves with the world, and learn their manners.'[68] Owen suggested some specific examples in this regard; habits of behaviour, manner and topics of conversation, luxurious living and style of dress and attire.[69] There was a certain irony in Owen attacking what he referred to as 'gaiety of attire' amongst professors. Not ten years previously, those at Oxford had been highly critical of Owen for the clothes and the powdered wig with which he chose to adorn himself. Indeed, Owen was considered to be something of a 'dandy', being seen in clothing quite unbecoming to a man of his standing and church tradition. Anthony Wood commented that he

> scorned all formality and undervalued his office by going in quirpo like a young scholar, with powdered hair, snakebone bandstrings (or bandstrings with very large tassels) lawn band, a large set of ribbons pointed, at his knees, and Spanish leather boots, with large lawn tops, and his hat mostly cock'd.[70]

However, the truth is that Owen chose to wear such outrageous clothes to make himself distinct from the various professors and theologians with whom he differed so much in theological and doctrinal outlook. For Owen, his sense of dress was a theological statement of sorts. Those whom he was criticising here were believers who did not want to appear separate from the world. Such an attitude was a travesty of godliness in that it ran contrary to the very nature of the calling of God's people to be 'a royal nation, a peculiar people'.[71] Furthermore, it was a direct denial and forcible denigration of all that Christ achieved on the cross:

> Christ hath brought the hatred of the devil and all the world upon him and against him, for taking a people out of the world, and making them a peculiar people to himself; and their throwing themselves upon the world again is the greatest contempt that can be put upon Jesus Christ. He gave his life and shed his blood to recover us from the world, and we throw ourselves in again.[72]

Owen issued the solemn warning that, for those who conformed to the world, they must also embrace its final judgment: 'If, therefore, you will be like the world, you must have the world's lot; God will not separate.'[73]

Second, Owen warned that the church has abandoned, or was in perilous danger of abandoning, sound doctrinal teaching. Professors of religion had forsaken the truth and Satan had been able to seduce many believers through this temptation into doctrinal error. Owen found a scriptural warning against such practice in 2 Timothy 4:3:

> 'The time will come when they will not endure sound doctrine; but after their own lusts shall they heap to themselves teachers, having itching ears.' When men grow weary of sound doctrine, – when it is too plain, too heavy, too dull, too common, too high, too mysterious, one thing or another that displeases them, and they would hear something new, something that may please, – it is a sign that there are in such an age many who are prone to forsake sound doctrine: and many such we know.[74]

The temptation to seek novelties in faith was perilous in that it leads to the loss of many souls. Indeed, Owen drew a parallel between the spiritual effects of such behaviour and the external effects of the Plague and the Fire of London some ten years earlier.[75]

It is concerning the abandonment of sound doctrine that we perceive the slight bitterness of spirit that came with Owen's old age. Looking back over the years, and comparing days past with the present circumstances, Owen betrayed his ageing attitude when he wrote

> Little did I think I should ever have lived in this world to find the minds of professors grown altogether indifferent as to the doctrine of God's eternal election, the sovereign efficacy of grace in the conversion of sinners, justification by the imputation of the righteousness of Christ; but many are, as to all these things, grown to an indifferency: they know not whether they are so or not. I bless God I know something of the former generation, when professors would not hear of these things without the highest detestation; and now high professors begin to be leaders in it: and it is too much among the best of us. We are not so much concerned for the truth as our forefathers; I wish I could say we were as holy.[76]

Whilst Owen was making a valid point here about the abounding sin within the contemporary structures of the church, it is more than evident that his understanding of the theological setting of years past was viewed through rose-tinted spectacles! What teachings, specifically, was the church in danger of accepting throughout Owen's lifetime? What were the enemies of truth which Owen focused on and did his utmost to oppress? It is to these perceived heresies that we must now turn.

Arminianism
Owen dedicated much of his writing during the 1640s and early 1650s to a powerful and polemical attack on the contemporary heresy of Arminianism. This doctrine was based on the ideas and teachings of Jakob Hermandszoon, better known today as Jacobus Arminius. Arminius was born in South Holland in 1560. He was educated in Utrecht and went to the Lutheran University in

Marburg before finishing his theological education in Geneva. Acclaimed by none other than Beza himself, he travelled through Europe developing a university career. He was ordained in Amsterdam in 1588. By 1592, Arminius had moved away from an accepted orthodox position and he faced charges the following year of having sympathy with the Church of Rome. Amid much controversy, Arminius took up an appointment as professor of theology at Leyden in 1603 and two years later took the position of Rector of the University. Suspicion of Arminius had grown considerably by the end of 1607 and, the following year, he successfully refuted charges of Socinianism. He accepted a platform at Dort in 1609 to vindicate himself despite his failing health. This conference was abandoned when Arminius had to return home – ultimately to die on October 19th at the age of forty-nine. His death, however, only fanned the flames of Arminianism and its influence was considerable by the beginning of Owen's ministry.[77]

Owen regarded Arminianism as a very real threat to perceived Christian orthodoxy and thus needful of complete and utter denunciation. Without doubt, this theological scheme, which denounced the rigid Calvinist understanding of predestination and reprobation, had become acceptable to many prominent English theologians and its influence was widespread.[78] However, we note that English Arminianism was not simply one body of teaching after the writings of Arminius; the situation was far more complex than that. As was the fashion in the seventeenth century, theologians used terms such as 'Arminian' as much to vilify and mock an opposing point of view as in its purest sense. To the Reformed mind, Arminianism taught justification by works. This reflected Catholic teaching and was thus linked to pro-French, Roman sympathies.

Many who were called 'Arminians' were not really followers of Arminius at all but were guilty only of holding anti-Calvinist ideologies. That said, the threat of Arminianism, whether in its pure form or not, was very real to the traditional Reformed position and writers such as Owen were absolutely right to recognise that fact. The Arminian assault opposed Reformed orthodoxy in

England on two fronts and Owen's writings were in response to both.

First, Arminianism was especially popular amongst the ecclesiastical authorities. Since the end of the Elizabethan period, there had been a growing dissatisfaction with Calvinist theology among the hierarchy of the Church of England. To that extent, the groundwork for the acceptance of the controversial Dutch doctrine was laid before 1613 when Arminianism entered England through the visit and influential teachings of Hugo Grotius.[79] Grotius, who died in 1645, was a theologian who knew both the pleasures of high office and the indignity of prison. He wrote a treatise, *De Satisfactione Christi*, that refuted Socinianism but, towards the end of his life, his theology became less and less orthodox from a Reformed stance. Socinians, Arminians and Roman Catholics accepted his theological ideas and it has been jocularly said of him that more religious groups have claimed his theology than towns have claimed the honour of being Homer's birthplace![80] Regardless of Owen's considerable attacks on Grotius' ideas, his influence was immense on seventeenth-century theological development, both in England and on the Continent. In his biography of Grotius, Jean L'Evesque de Burigny quoted Gerard Vossius[81] as stating, 'He is one of the greatest ornaments of our times, or rather the miracle, the eternal honour, of Holland, and of his age.... If we would do him justice, there is none we can place above him, nor even any we can compare with him.'[82]

The strong foothold that Arminianism gained in England at the end of the sixteenth century was especially true of Cambridge. The anti-Calvinist revolt had begun under William Barrett,[83] a fellow of Caius College. In 1595, he preached a sermon attacking the Calvinist interpretation of the doctrine of assurance. Lancelot Andrewes,[84] who went on to become Bishop of Ely in 1605, continued in a similar vein. Likewise at Oxford, Laud was responsible for undermining traditional Calvinism and the future Archbishop soon faced accusations of Arminianism. This culminated in his execution in 1644 for heresy. It is important to note, however that Laud always protested his innocence, right up to his death. In his funeral sermon, which he preached himself from the scaffold, he said, 'I die in the presence of Almighty God and all his holy and blessed Angels, and I take it now on my death, That I never endeavoured the subversion of the Laws of the Realme, nor never any change of the Protestant Religion into Popish superstition.'[85] Those responsible for his execution, however, held a more denigrating opinion, as William Prynne expressed:

> He [appears] as Criminall, as Treasonable, as Arch a Malefactor ...wherein he most protested, most laboured to assert his Innocency against so many pregnant Evidences and cleer [sic] Demonstrations of his guiltinesses, as will render him execrable to all true Protestants for eternity[86]

Regardless of whether Laud's claims for himself were accurate, it is certainly the case that, with the accession of Charles I to the throne, Arminianism received official sanction. It would be impossible to claim that the result of this was the wholesale denunciation of Puritanism since John Goodwin[87] is an example of a form of Puritanism that remained broadly acceptable to the ecclesiastical authorities. However, it is certainly true that Puritans from the moderate and high Calvinist traditions found themselves placed increasingly on the margins of ecclesiastical power and influence. Continuing in the recent Jacobean tradition, despite James' fluctuating antipathy towards Arminianism, Charles ensured the increase in an Arminian episcopate that would eventually transform the prevailing culture of the Anglican administration. For example, Neale went to Winchester, Montaigne[88] to York, Howson[89] to Durham, Buckeridge[90] to Ely and Montague[91] to Chichester. As Tyacke suggests, 'King Charles became the architect of an Arminian revolution which had at most been dimly foreshadowed in the last year of his father's reign.'[92] That revolution was primarily one of osmosis. At no point did Archbishop Laud openly accept Arminianism; rather, he sanctioned such episcopal installations over a period that those who surrounded him were amenable to Arminian doctrines. With some justification, Wallace has suggested in his book *Puritans and Predestination*, that, most notably, Montague and Cosin[93] in

England and Chappell[94] and Bramhall[95] in Ireland were appointments of this nature.[96]

The Episcopal antipathy towards Calvinism in favour of Arminianism entered the public domain in England with the controversy concerning Richard Montague. Although his first published work in sympathy with Arminianism was printed in 1624 whilst he was still a Rector in Essex, he was granted preferment soon afterwards as Bishop of Chichester in 1628. His undisguised attacks, not only on Catholicism but also on the Calvinist doctrines of the grace of God, unconditional election and the perseverance of the saints resulted in much criticism from Calvinist quarters.[97] Despite this, he soon enjoyed the benefits of preferment and subsequently became a chaplain to Charles I. Alongside this provocative move came injunctions from the king in 1622 to silence Puritan teaching on Sunday afternoons in favour of children's catechism. These were followed by orders for preachers to refrain from speaking on matters of predestination and election but to leave such weighty theological matters to the Bishops and deans.[98] In addition to this, the liberty of the press was severely reduced as books criticising Montague were forbidden whilst writings in support of Arminianism were 'tolerated'; a charge laid against Laud at his subsequent trial.[99]

It would be wrong, however, to suggest that the style of Arminianism endorsed by the Episcopal sympathisers of the Church of England was a direct imitation of the Dutch model; they differed considerably in practice if not always in theology. The English-Episcopal Arminian model tended towards the Anglo-Catholic, with great emphasis laid on sacramental worship, ceremonials and ornaments such as candles, crosses and 'east-end' altars in the place of communion tables. A 'high' view of the priesthood was encouraged which related closely to recognition and support of the divine right of the monarchy.

It would be true to say that the General Baptist Arminian assault of the 1640s adhered more closely to the Dutch model. This sectarian group opposed the Laudian abuses and the perceived idolatrous ways of the national Church in the same manner as the orthodox Calvinists. However, they maintained a similar Arminian outlook whilst not endorsing the practices of the Church of England. Their Arminian sympathies were strongest in London, made public with the 1645 publication of their treatise entitled *The Fountain of Free Grace Opened.* However, their exceptionally aggressive and creative use of the press enabled their ideas to spread further afield than London throughout the decade. Their chief and most able protagonist was John Goodwin, whose most notorious work in this field was entitled *Redemption Redeemed.* This work was originally started by Goodwin in reply to Samuel Lane's *A Vindication of free-grace.*[100] However, his intentions changed after a few years and Goodwin's thesis became much wider, most notably in response to the writings of William Twisse.[101] Goodwin's teachings came under much sustained criticism from the Reformed wing of the church but in his Epistle Dedicatory for *Redemption Redeemed,* he made light of the criticisms with which he had to contend:

> My long deprivation and want of respects from men, is now turned to an athletique habit, somewhat after the manner of those, who by long fasting, lose their appetites, and withall either contract, or finde an ability, or contentedness of Nature, to live with little or no meat afterwards. I can from the dunghill whereon I sit, with much contentment and sufficient enjoyment of my self, behold my Brethren on Thrones round about me.[102]

The hatred of Arminian theology, whether held by episcopacy or sectarian groupings, which Owen and his Calvinist contemporaries felt, was intense. Francis Rous[103] voiced the fears of all in that tradition when he wrote,

> I desire we may consider the increase of Arminianism, an error that makes the grace of God lackey after the will of man. I desire we may look into the belly and bowels of this Trojan horse, to see if there be not men in it ready to open the gates to Romish tyranny, for an Arminian is the spawn of a Papist, and if the warmth of favour come upon him, you shall see him turn into one of these frogs that rise out of the bottomless pit.[104]

Likewise, Thomas Edwards,[105] in 1646, complained: 'O how is
the scene changed within these few years! Those Doctrines of
Arminianism and Popery which in Episcopall men we cryed out
so of...are delivered and received with great applause.'[106]

Owen's first published work, *A Display of Arminianism*, was
an attack on the controversial doctrine. Owen's treatise did not
offer a complete critique of Arminianism but only on two major
points of dispute, namely that concerning predestination and the
limits of human free will. His vital work on the atonement, *The
Death of Death in the Death of Christ* (1647), written to confound
the teachings of the sectarian Thomas Moore of Lincolnshire,
continued his assault on this perceived heresy. He clarified his
views in his Preface to William Twisse's *The Riches of God's
Love* in 1653 when he wrote that

> Of all the weighty parcells of Gospell truth, which the Arminians
> have chosen to oppose, there is not any about which they so much
> delight to try and exercise the strength of fleshly reasonings, as
> that of God's eternall decree of Reprobation.[107]

However, Owen was not alone in combating Arminianism in print.
Amongst a multitude of other tracts and treatises, he was joined
most notably in print in 1647 by John Stalham's[108] *Vindiciæ
Redemptionis* and Samuel Rutherford's[109] *Christ Dying and
Drawing Sinners to Himselfe*. All these works focused on the
atonement as an effectual act of grace for the elect, not something
that merely made salvation a possibility. This approach, however,
led to a strengthening of the understanding of a limited atonement
which, in part, resulted in a divergence between high and moderate
Calvinists.

In his anti-Arminian works from this period, Owen was acutely
aware that the true importance of the debate was not so much to
do with anthropology as with a right doctrine of God. In the light
of this, Owen attacked Arminianism by firmly establishing his
arguments in the framework of classical Calvinist orthodoxy.
Discussion ensued on such points as the efficacy of the atonement,
the nature of predestination and the irresistibility of God's grace.

Central to Owen's argument was the correlation between election
and sin. If Owen were to allow that Adam had a propensity to evil
before the Fall, he would attribute to the nature of God the same
potential weakness reflected in Adam as his image:

> But what! did God create in Adam a proneness to evil? was
> that a part of his glorious image in whose likeness he was
> framed? Yea, saith Corvinus, 'By reason of his creation, man
> had an affection to what was forbidden by the law.'[110]

Furthermore, such an idea would be to attribute a grave injustice
to God. That God should create man with an affection for evil and
then judge him for his weakness in submitting to that affection,
was an unthinkable concept for Owen:

> But yet this seems injustice, that 'God should give a man a law to
> keep, and put upon his nature a repugnancy to that law;' as one of
> them affirmed at the synod of Dort.... Let them only who will be
> wise beyond the word of God affix such injustice on the righteous
> Judge of all the earth...we [must] overthrow the...odious heresy.[111]

In *A Display of Arminianism*, Owen went to the very heart of his
differences with the Arminians, namely the doctrine of original
sin. Owen no doubt agreed with Burgesse's[112] comment that a
thoroughly biblical approach to the issue was of paramount
importance:

> As for the Doctrine of it, its easie and difficult; easie, because we
> palpably and evidently find the effects thereof; Difficult, because
> the exact knowledge of its being chiefly by divine Revelation; No
> wonder if those, who attend to Aristotle more than Paul, and desire
> to be rationales rather than fideles, have grossely [sic] stumbled
> in the dark they walk in.[113]

Owen contended strongly with the Arminian position concerning
the status of Adam before the Fall:

All [his] affections [were] subservient to the rule of reason for the performance of all natural actions...whereby he was enabled to yield obedience unto God for the attaining of that supernatural end whereunto he was created.... Our nature was then inclined to good only...there was then no inclination to sin, no concupiscence of that which is evil, no repugnancy to the law of God, in the pure nature of man...[114]

Owen believed that, prior to the Fall, humanity was immortal; subject to neither death nor decay in accordance with its creation in the image of God and the covenant relationship between man and God. However, the introduction of sin irrevocably altered that state of being inasmuch as death, both physical and spiritual, was the resultant punishment for Adam's disobedience to God. The effect of this disobedience on the physical body was devastating:

Upon the body, also, it hath such an influence, in disposing it to corruption and mortality, as it is the original of all these infirmities, sicknesses, and diseases, which make us nothing but a shop of such miseries for death itself... so they are the direct...causes...in subordination to the justice of Almighty God, by such means inflicting it as a punishment of our sins in Adam.[115]

Owen attributed the entry of sin into the created order to the fall of Adam and Eve, described in Genesis 3. For Owen, that historical act had massive repercussions for the rest of humanity inasmuch as Adam represented them in a covenant relationship with God. This covenant was broken and thereafter Adam and his descendants came under the dominion of sin: 'He was not only a natural head, but also a federal head unto us...and his transgression of that covenant is reckoned to us.'[116] Owen's key text in regard to the implications of the Fall was Romans 5:12-14[117] which he called 'the proper seat of this doctrine'.[118] Certainly he was aware of the various syntactical and grammatical difficulties arising from this passage but this did not complicate the issue for him and he was confident that the theological implications remained the same regardless of the translation problems:

We all sinned in him. Εφ ω παντες ημαρτον Rom. v. 12, whether
we render it relatively 'in whom,' or illatively 'being all have
sinned,' all is one: that one sin is the sin of us all, – 'omnes eramus
unus ille homo.' We were all in covenant with him; he was not
only a natural head, but also a federal head unto us.[119]

Owen rightly observed that the clarifying issue was not so much
the grammatical construction but the context in which Paul wrote
these words. Owen refuted the Pelagian understanding, believing
that this passage refers to the actual sins of men; that Adam is a
prototype for sin and that the rest of humanity relates to him only
in that sin is common to all. For him, there was an integral link
forged between the sin of the first man and that of his descendants;
the sinfulness of humanity is *directly related to*, and not merely
imitative of, the sinfulness of Adam:

> There is the *derivation* of a polluted, corrupted nature from him:
> 'Who can bring a clean thing out of an unclean?' 'That which is
> born of flesh is flesh,' and nothing else; whose wisdom and mind
> is corrupted also: a polluted fountain will have polluted streams.
> The *first person* corrupted *nature*, and that *nature* corrupted *all
> persons* following.[120]

Elsewhere, he clarified this theological position by stating that
'The disability and corruption of nature, by reason of original sin,
[has been] propagated unto us all by our first parents.'[121]

The Arminian position undermined Owen's understanding of
election in that it questioned the eternal nature of God's decree,
the constancy of the same and the particularity of it. Owen traced
their error back to an acceptance of Platonic ideology whereby
the notion of election can be upheld distinct from particular
application.[122] Owen focused upon the Dutch Remonstrant error
in this regard: 'Nos negamus Dei electionem ad salutem extendere
sese ad singulares personas, qua singulares personas.'[123] Owen
was incredulous of this philosophical idea, stating that it 'is such
a riddle as no Œdipus can unfold'.[124]

With specific regard to sin, the denial by the Arminian party of
a Reformed doctrine of election results in a logically altered

sequence concerning effect and cause of God's predestination. For Owen, the activated truth of election, by the gracious activity of God, is the cause of salvation of which holiness and spiritual rectitude is a fruit. The Arminian position, however, reverses the order; that moral obedience is the cause and pre-requisite of God's election in the life of the individual. The Arminian order proved unacceptable to Owen since it stood in complete opposition to his doctrine of God, most especially his understanding of the work of the Holy Spirit in sanctification. For Owen, no one is able of himself or herself to be holy and obedient since the effects of the Fall have destroyed man's spiritual capabilities. To claim otherwise is to nullify the need for sanctification, even the need for atonement. Arminianism was, therefore, a strike at the very root of Owen's understanding of sin and all its related doctrines.

Socinianism
The theological movement known as Socinianism was that stemming from the teachings of Fausto Sozzini, known as Socinus. This theologian was born in Tuscany in 1539 into an affluent family. He enjoyed the life of a ducal courtier devoting his time to poetry but he left Italy in 1574 in order to devote himself to academic pursuits. In Basel, he partook of the religious discussions and began his literary career with the publication of *De Jesu Christo Servatore*, seeking to incorporate all the fundamentals of his beliefs. In 1578, after the publication of three more tracts, he moved to Poland and remained there for the last twenty-four years of his life. Socinus attached himself to an Antitrinitarian church in Cracow but, due to his refusal to undergo a second baptism, he was never officially recognised as a member. The turn of political events after 1586 resulted in the confiscation of his property in Italy and his flow of income from that country ceased. His following in Poland, however, increased and his influence resulted in the publication of *Prælectiones theologiæ* in 1592, a work based upon the lectures he had given over the previous few years. Socinus' popularity was challenged in 1598 when he was physically set upon and his books and papers burnt. Fearing for his life, he left Cracow and settled in Luslawice. He presided over

synods and theological conferences for the Polish Brethren before his death there in 1604 at the age of sixty-five.[125]

A humanistic optimism hallmarks Socinus' teachings that supposed the ability of man to follow Christ and thereby achieve salvation. He believed that natural reason alone is adequate to understand and interpret the Scriptures and was thus mistrustful of any mystic tendencies.[126] It was, however, his antitrinitarianism and christology that set him apart from orthodox faith and provided the fundamental beliefs amongst his followers to which Owen was so opposed.

Re-interpreting the opening chapter of John's Gospel, Socinus taught that the Logos was indeed Jesus, but not the eternal Logos. The use of such language stressed only the dignity of Christ, not any claim to divinity. The important implication of this for our purposes is that concerning the atonement of Christ. The function of the atonement, according to Socinus, was not to satisfy the justice of God but rather to demonstrate how individuals may be saved. The resurrection is of more importance, since it verifies the truth of Jesus' teachings and death. Such an understanding is intertwined with the notion that original sin is a fallacy; free will continued after the fall and one man's sin could not have confounded the ability of others to respond to God. Thus the very concept of predestination is absurd since a divine injunction of that nature is contrary to the very principle of free will. Rather, the process of faith in the individual is a result of natural tendencies, reliant primarily upon reason, which has no need of supernatural intervention. The imitation of Christ through self-denial is the path of Christian discipleship and it is that which is met by God's gift of assurance by the power of his Spirit in the heart of the believer.

Socinianism grew in England primarily through the influence of John Bidle.[127] His various tracts published in the 1640s had challenged Christian orthodoxy, most notably with regard to the doctrine of the nature of the Godhead in general and the Person of the Holy Spirit in particular. Most notable among his publications in this period are the *Twelve Arguments*, September 1647, and his *Confession of Faith touching the Holy Trinity*, published in

November 1648. Periods of imprisonment had neither silenced
him nor prevented the widespread publication and acceptance of
his teachings. In his tract *A Confession of Faith*, Bidle denied the
divinity of Christ. He stated that it was not possible for God to
satisfy himself in any act of atonement. Throughout the 1650s, he
and his contemporaries went on systematically to oppose the
Reformed interpretation of every main tenet of faith;
predestination, original sin, the Trinity, free-will, the priesthood
of Christ, baptism and the Lord's Supper amongst others.

During and beyond the 1650s Owen, alongside many of his
contemporaries, clearly believed Socinianism to be the major threat
to religious orthodoxy in England. McLachlan identifies the
following people, in his book *Socinianism in Seventeenth-Century
England*,[128] alongside Owen as the chief anti-Socinian writers in
England: Nicholas Estwick, Francis Cheynell,[129] Nicholas
Chewney, Matthew Poole, Edmund Porter and Matthew Wren.[130]
But even in the 1640s the threat was becoming clear to Reformed
pastors. Witness this quotation from Francis Cheynell in 1643:

> The Socinians have raked many sinkes, and dunghils for those
> ragges and that filth, wherewith they have patched up and defiled
> that leprous body which they account a compleat body of pure
> Religion...the Devill hath done more mischiefe in the Church by
> counterfeit Protestants, false brethren, then [sic] by professed
> Papists, open enemies.[131]

Again,

> The Socinian Errour is Fundamentall, they deny Christs
> Satisfaction, and so overthrow the foundation of our faith, the
> foundation of our Justification; they deny the Holy Trinity, and
> so take away the very Object of our Faith; they deny the
> Resurrection of these Bodies, and so take away the foundation of
> our hope; they deny originall sinne, and so take away the ground
> of our Humiliation, and indeed the necessity of regeneration; they
> advance the power of Nature and destroy the efficacy of Grace.[132]

Owen arrived at his antipathy towards Socinianism as much through a development in his own understanding (that Christ's death was an absolute necessity for God's vindicative justice) as by its ascendancy in English society. His two greatest works of this period were apologetic treatises against Socinianism; *A Dissertation on Divine Justice* (1653) and *Vindiciæ Evangelicæ; or, the Mystery of the Gospel Vindicated and Socinianism Examined* (1655). The latter was a work commissioned for the Council of State.[133]

Owen was not the first English writer to attack Socinianism. A multitude of tracts published at the time criticised Socinianism. Four such works of importance, and all published prior to Owen's writings on the topic, were *God's Glory Vindicated and Blasphemy Confuted, &c.* (1647 anonymously), *The Holy Spirit Vindicated* (1648, William Russell), *A Treatise of the Holy Ghost* [134] (1648, Nicholas Estwick), and *The Blasphemer slaine With the Sword of the Spirit* (1653, Matthew Poole).[135] However, Owen's attack on Socinianism, based upon a firm and intricate understanding of the issues involved, was outstanding in both clarity and detail. He acknowledged the great learning of his adversaries and revealed an intimate familiarity with their works, as his frequent references suggest.[136] Nevertheless, he was unflinching in his assault on this heresy since it attacked the very heart of a true doctrine of God and Christian anthropology.

In contending against Bidle, Owen argued for the historical importance of the Fall of Adam, and the consequent effects of that act on all humanity:

> That which is common to all things in any kind, and is proper to them only of that kind, must needs have some common cause equally respecting the whole kind: but now of the evils that are common to all mankind, and peculiar and proper to them and every one of them, there can be no cause but that which equally concerns them all; which, by the testimony of God himself, was this fall of Adam, Romans 5:12, 15-19.[137]

The tendency towards a philosophical approach here was not contrary to his general approach since, at times, Owen was prepared to develop his theology within a largely philosophical framework. This methodology was required in his writings against Socinianism perhaps more than at any other time, given the learning of his opponents. That was most especially the case with Bidle, whose classical and philosophical training was comprehensive. Indeed, McLachlan quotes an early biographer as stating that 'he did so Philosophize, as it might be observed, he was determined more by reason than authority; however he did not much dissent from the common doctrine'.[138] Owen therefore combined philosophical reason with biblical authority to create a doctrinal *tour de force* in countering the claims of his theological enemies.

In contending against Bidle, Owen stressed the defacing of the image of God in man through sin and the mortality and condemnation that Adam's sin has brought on his descendants. Crucially, Owen also stressed the effect of sin on the mind. He drew on the scriptural analogies of light and darkness, seeing and blindness, to compare the effect of sin and the work of Christ in the mind of the individual. Owen utterly confuted the Socinian idea that the mind is capable of itself to comprehend the truth of God apart from the actings of grace on the soul. In launching a personal attack on Bidle, Owen underlined his thoughts on the Socinian movement in general; that it is this very acting of sin in the mind that has resulted in their erroneous doctrines:

> nor can I say that it is well for Mr. B. that he finds none of those effects of sin in himself, nothing of darkness, bondage, or disability, or if he do, that he knows where to charge it, and not on himself or the depravedness of his own nature; and that because I know none who are more desperately sick than those who, by a fever of pride, have lost the sense of their own miserable condition.[139]

Quakerism

The sect known as the Quakers arose as a formidable social and religious grouping in the 1650s under the guidance of George Fox, who was born in 1624 at Drayton-in-the-Clay, Leicestershire, the son of a weaver. Fox received an orthodox Christian upbringing and counted himself obedient to the doctrines of Christ. In 1643, he left his family and travelled the country. During this period, his religious quest took on new directions and he began to have 'openings', or intuitive perceptions of truth. These 'openings' led to his increasing dissatisfaction with institutionalised religion and he began to speak out against 'the great idol of religion'. His following increased and they began to practise silent worship together, calling themselves The Children of Light, or Friends in Truth. During the worship, some took to shaking and quivering, earning the nickname, The Quakers. Fox suffered much persecution as his ideas gained popularity; he was stoned, put in the stocks, beaten and imprisoned. Missionaries went abroad with the teachings of Quakerism, travelling to Ireland, North and Central America, the West Indies, Holland and Turkey. Despite massive persecution, Quakerism flourished and was an immensely popular style of religious practice by the time of George Fox's death in 1691.[140]

Whilst the beliefs and practices of Quakerism were diverse in the extreme, its central religious tenets were based around a theological system epitomised in these words of Fox:

> [Christ]...hath given us a Light, which is the Life in himself; and saith believe in the Light so we Believe in that which Christ has given us...namely the Light, which is the Life in him, by which we may see him...and this light shining in our hearts, it gives us the knowledge of the glory of God in the face of Christ Jesus...having the witness in ourselves that God is true in all his Promises and Prophets and Types and Shadows in the law, concerning his Son, Christ Jesus.[141]

His intense sense of vocation, that he should lead people away from the trappings of idolatrous religion towards an 'inner light' experience, proved immensely popular and won him a numerically powerful following. Quakerism found its deepest roots in the north of England and the Midlands, initially in Nottinghamshire.[142] His immediate congregation (though nothing so formal as an organised society came into being until 1652) was taken from the separatists and Seekers, who were looking for new insights. The inclusion of

the Westmoreland Seekers in 1652 brought intellectual strength
to the movement and they were responsible for the silent Meeting
innovation for worship.[143]

The primary focus of the Quakers during the Interregnum was
political and social rather than spiritual. A systematic presentation
of their religious doctrines only appeared from the 1670s onwards,
their religious beliefs standing in opposition to orthodox Calvinism.
Of particular importance for our purposes is their wholesale
rejection of the doctrine of predestination and their proclamation
of the possibility of universal salvation. The notion of the 'light
within' resulted in a form of perfectionism, which was an absolute
denial of the power and nature of sin as taught by Owen and his
contemporaries.

Indeed, Owen gave no credence whatsoever to the claims and
practices of the Quakers. Calling them 'poor deluded souls', he
derided them for their vapid practices and theological doctrine,
useless in the combat of sin:

> In the height of their outward appearances, as they came short of
> the sorry weeds, begging habits, macerated countenances, and
> severe looks, of many monks in the Roman church, and dervises
> among the Mohammedans; so they were so far from restraining
> or mortifying their real inclinations, as that they seemed to excite
> and provoke themselves to exceed all others in clamours, railings,
> evil-speakings, reproaches, calumnies, and malicious treating of
> those who dissented from them, without the least discovery of a
> heart unto mankind, or love unto any but themselves; in which
> frame and state of things sin is as secure from mortification as in
> the practice of open lusts and debaucheries.[144]

Earlier he had insisted, 'Convince any of them of the doctrine of
the Trinity, and all the rest of their imaginations vanish into
smoke.'[145]

Owen's primary attack on the theological system of the Quaker
brethren came in his 1658 treatise, *A Defense of Scripture*. In this
work, Owen's contention against the Quakers' theological system
centred on four principles. First, that they claim the inner light to
be not natural but spiritual. Second, that the light itself is salvific.

Third, that the light is equal to the written Word of God in authority and efficacy and fourth, that the light is Christ and residing in all men equally. Each one of these Quaker proposals had an impact on their doctrine of sin and Owen was vehement in his denial of each precept.

First, concerning the nature of the inner light, Owen accepted that there is within every rational creature an inner light. However, far from this being an innately spiritual 'light of Christ', Owen understood it to be the natural force of reason, the faculty of understanding. For Adam, that light enabled him to develop a perception of God that resulted in obedience to the Creator. However, through the Fall humanity has come to a state of blindness and darkness. In terminology that reflected his Calvinistic differentiation between the spiritual gifts that were lost and the natural gifts that were only marred at the Fall, Owen stated that

> The remnant inner light, common to all, with such elements of truth as remain, allied with the natural force of conscience, is natural and may properly be so called. It has been an attribute of human nature from our first creation, and to this day remains as an essential part of our makeup and being. We thus declare that this light is not that light granted by Christ as the Mediator of the New Covenant.[146]

Were Owen to conceive of the light within as the Quakers did, he would have been unable to defend any notion of depravity in a Calvinistic sense. Certainly the Quakers acknowledged the Fall and the reality of sin but their understanding was coupled with a potential for perfectionism unacceptable to Owen.

Second, that the light within is salvific was anathema to Owen. If he were to concede that a natural ability was able to lead to salvation, that would be a denial of God's grace and an acceptance of the semi-Pelagianism of the Arminian party. Owen contended against the Quaker position, and went a stage further, when he stated that 'Not only is this light insufficient for salvation, but it cannot even grant the power to understand what is truly needful for salvation – these are matters which are not naturally, but spiritually discerned'.[147] Owen was willing to accept that the light within acts as a rule of conduct and a guide given by God for holy living; even that it may work as a means towards salvation. However, he was adamant that this is not identical with that salvation itself. Such ideas were, for Owen, a denial of the importance of the atonement and the work of the Holy Spirit in regeneration since they render inessential the need of this gracious activity of God. Crucially for Owen, the spiritual light that is in humanity since the Fall, the 'new, divine, spiritual light by which their eyes are opened and they perceive spiritual matters',[148] is granted only to the elect. It is not an inner light common to all humanity but only one which illuminates the spiritual path of those predestined to salvation:

> Christ does not bestow spiritual light and grace on any man, except through the Word and the Spirit, and no man may be a participant in that light except he be born of the Spirit and be a saved believer in the gospel as revealed in God's Word, the Bible.[149]

Third, Owen denied that the light within is equal to the written Word of God. The effect of sin is so all encompassing as to render the individual unable to gain a true knowledge of God by individual effort and reliance upon natural abilities. It is only by the illuminating power of the Holy Spirit working in the heart of the individual that the reality of a depraved spiritual state is discovered in the pages of Scripture. To deny the importance of the Word of God is a symptom of arrogance and pride and those who hold to the Quaker ideal 'stand self-condemned of most base ingratitude, and so are accursed of God'.[150]

Owen believed the nature of this aspect of the Quaker heresy to be founded in their fundamental lack of contextualisation; any analysis of the 'light within' must by necessity be placed within a strictly trinitarian-christological frame of reference:

> In all discussions of 'inner light,' the aid of the Father of Lights is first to be earnestly entreated and invoked. From Him descends every good gift and all that is wholesome, and it is He who shines in our hearts, displaying the light of the knowledge of His glory

in the face of Jesus Christ. Thus freed from the dominion of darkness we may rightly be directed to the true knowledge, and right worship, of God.[151]

God is the Author and Source of all light. Owen went on to contend in the same passage that light is an essential part of the very essence of God. Conversely, because of sin, humanity sits in darkness. Since 'Jesus Christ is the true light and life of man,'[152] any consideration of 'inner light' must take into account the christological dimension.

Owen rejected the Quaker idea that the light within is Christ himself. Basing his argument on 2 Corinthians 3:17 in comparison with Romans 8:9, Owen suggested that, far from all men enjoying liberty, many are still in bondage to sin. Therefore, the light that is common to all cannot be Christ, by whom comes freedom. Furthermore, Owen stated that 'Christ is called the light *of* men, not the light which is *within* men. He is the cause of all light, but all light is not Him. Christ is not that remnant and corrupted natural light of creation of which we have been speaking.'[153] Again, to suggest that Christ is the light within would be to make a mockery of any coherent understanding of sin. Every person is devoid of spiritual abilities and gifts and lives in darkness until the spiritual light of Christ – through the renewing work of the Holy Spirit – acts upon them. The light within all therefore cannot be Christ but only a corruptible and corrupted natural ability.

During the 1650s and beyond, Quakerism perhaps even more than Socinianism was perceived as the greatest threat to Reformed orthodoxy. This was not so much the case because of any cohesive and developed theology that it taught so much as the immense popularity of the movement itself. This was most especially true of rural communities but its popularity stretched even to the political and military authorities of the day.[154] Owen was therefore justified in producing such an attack on the ideas of the Quakers with such clarity and detail. Owen understood Quakerism, like Socinianism and Arminianism, not only to undermine a true understanding of the nature and effect of sin but also to be a heretical deviation from the orthodox doctrine of God. Such ideas must not gain any ground if the nation as a whole, and individuals in particular, were to grow in godliness and holiness.

Roman Catholicism

Arminianism, Socinianism and Quakerism were undoubtedly important areas of polemical debate for Owen at various stages of his ministry. However, his most sustained attack in the ecclesiological realm, most especially in his latter years, was waged against the Church of Rome and the heresy he perceived therein. Owen was fundamentally clear on one point; that the Church of Rome was an abomination, standing at the very heart of the antichristian element in society that needed challenging. Interpreting Catholicism as the whore of Babylon in the light of Revelation 17,[155] Owen, of course, was not alone in his beliefs but merely reflecting the Puritan anti-Catholic train of thought. In his book *Visible Saints 1640-60*, Nuttall gives a number of historical examples of Protestants aligning the Church of Rome with the Antichrist: Luther, John Whitgift[156] in 1563, William Whitaker[157] in 1582 and James Ussher in the Articles of Religion written for the Church of Ireland.[158] These examples are not comprehensive but only serve to illustrate a common trend within the Protestant tradition. This tradition, although rooted in centuries of mistrust, was highlighted by the perceptible sympathy of the Royal Court to Catholicism since the 1620s.[159] This had been compounded in 1639 by the Catholic contribution to the Scottish war[160] and the increasing presence of Catholic sympathisers in the army. The next few years saw an increasing paranoia about the treachery of Catholicism in England that only abated in strength of action but not in belief by the 1650s.

Owen perceived Rome as the fountainhead of the heresies which had turned the nation from God. The Papacy had acted as 'a Trojan horse'[161] leading the people of England away from God and, through allegiance to Rome, the nation had been seduced and fallen into great sin.[162] It is worth quoting Owen at some length to comprehend the passion of his belief in this regard:

Every age hath its peculiar work, hath its peculiar light. Now what is the light which God manifestly gives in our days?... Plainly, the peculiar light of this generation is that discovery which the Lord hath made to his people of the mystery of civil and ecclesiastical tyranny. The opening, unravelling, and revealing the Antichristian interest, interwoven and coupled together, in civil and spiritual things, into a state opposite to the kingdom of the Lord Jesus, is the great discovery of these days. Who almost is there amongst us now who doth not evidently see, that for many generations the western nations have been juggled into spiritual and civil slavery by the legerdemain of the whore, and the potentates of the earth made drunk with the cup of her abominations? – how the whole earth hath been rolled in confusion, and the saints hurried out of the world, to give way to their combined interest? Hath God not unveiled that harlot, made her naked, and discovered her abominable filthiness? Is it not evident to him that hath but half an eye, that the whole present constitution of the government of the nations is so cemented with antichristian mortar, from the very top to the bottom, that without a thorough shaking they cannot be cleansed?[163]

Owen's writings on Roman Catholicism were detailed and wide-ranging, attacking the denomination on almost every aspect of its teaching and practice.

The experience of faith and, more specifically, the experience of the power of religion was, for Owen, the foundation of all true belief and religious practice. Loss of that experience inevitably leads to heresy of the worst kind: 'The loss of an experience of the power of religion hath been the cause of the loss of the truth of religion; or it hath been the cause of rejecting its substance, and setting up a shadow in the room of it.'[164] For Owen, Catholicism represented the greatest evil of all in this regard. It retained the general notion of true religion but framed in an outward image based on ignorance and superstition:

For the religion of [the Church of Rome], at this day, is nothing but a dead image of the gospel, erected in the loss of an experience of its spiritual power, overthrowing its use, with all its ends, being suited to the taste of men, carnal, ignorant, and superstitious.[165]

Thus, Satan is able to use Catholicism to blind people to the truth of their lost state in following the empty ritualism of that denomination.[166] In the heresy that is the Church of Rome, Owen detected three primary ways in which the experience of faith was denied; christology, worship and discipleship.

First, concerning the person of Christ, Owen credited the Church of Rome of wanting to do what is right in principle but failing to do what is right in practice. Since God is invisible to us, it is only right that the believer should desire – and need – a representation of him to become the focus of faith. It is through this representation of Christ that 'believers have an experience of the power and efficacy of the divine truth contained therein'.[167] By means of that representation, it is possible to 'have experience of its transforming power and efficacy, changing them into the likeness of the image represented unto them'.[168] For Owen, that representation is found quite properly in the Scriptures. It is through the Word of God that Christ is revealed and it is through obedience to that Word that the believer becomes transformed in the power of the Spirit. However, Owen recognised that the officers of the Church of Rome had, historically, kept the reading of the Scriptures from the ordinary people, claiming that it was dangerous for them. Therefore, representation of Christ needed another expression, giving rise to images and idols that have become the focus of faith. This process Owen likened to the experience of the Israelites in the desert in Exodus 32 when they made for themselves a golden calf. In time, these images had replaced the gospel of Christ, attempting to provide the Catholics with all the experiential faith they need, since finding the representation of Christ in the Word of God was anathema to them:

'No,' say these men, 'we cannot understand how it should be so; we do not find that it is so, – that Christ is made nigh unto us, present with us, by this word. Wherefore we will ascend into heaven to bring down Christ from above; for we will make images of him in his glorious state in heaven, and thereby he will be present with us, or nigh unto us. And we will descend into the deep, to bring up Christ again from the dead; and we will do it, by making first crucifixes, and then images of his glorious resurrection, bringing him again unto us from the dead. This shall be in the place and room of that word of the gospel, which you pretend to be alone useful and effectual unto these ends.'[169]

Such apostasy arises out of a right desire – to represent Christ as the focus of faith – but out of wrong practice – the abandonment of the Scriptures in return for worshipping idols.

Owen accused the Church of Rome of refusing to sit under the authority of the Word of God and thereby of elevating itself onto the very throne of God. This happened in three ways. First, by proclaiming Scripture as only a 'partial revelation of the will of God'. Secondly, by claiming that Scripture can only be the Word of God alongside 'an accession of testimony from [those] men that call themselves the Church of Rome'. Thirdly, by stating that the original translations of the Old and New Testaments are so corrupt as to be unreliable as 'a certain standard and measure of all doctrines'.[170] Owen wrote disparagingly of those Catholics who

pretend themselves to be the only keepers and preservers of the Word of God in the world, the only 'pillar and ground of truth'.... [But rather] through the craft of Satan and the prejudice of their own hearts, lying under the power of corrupt and carnal interest, have engaged to decry and disparage that excellency of the Scripture which is proper and peculiar unto it.[171]

For Owen, such attitudes were suggestive of the greatest apostasy in and of themselves. Furthermore, Owen was convinced that the inability of the Catholic Church to accept Scripture as the Word of God rendered it incapable of giving direction to others concerning sin and its combat in the life of the individual:

The consideration of the present state and condition of the generality of professors, the visible evidences of the frame of their hearts and spirits, [manifest] a great disability of dealing with the temptations wherewith...they are encompassed.[172]

This is a belief that remained with Owen throughout his life as a cross-reference to *The Reason of Faith*, published in 1677, will reveal:

On all occasions they insinuate such objections against [scripture], from its obscurity, imperfection, want of order, difficulties, and seeming contradictions in it, as are suited to take off the minds of men from a firm assent unto it or reliance on it... [and] the first tendency of these courses is to make men atheists.[173]

That being the case, the Roman Catholic Church stands condemned before God in its own blasphemy and its inability to lead others away from sin on the true paths of God. As Owen concluded,

This, therefore, is evident, that the introduction of this abomination ...took its rise from the loss of an experience of the representation of Christ in the gospel, and the transforming power in the minds of men which it is accompanied with, in them that believe.[174]

Second, concerning the manner of worship enjoyed by the Church of Rome, again, Owen based his ideas on the foundation of experience. The ideal of worship is beautiful and glorious, something that will reveal something of the wonder of heaven to the human soul. Again, Owen recognised that the Church of Rome wanted to adhere to the principle of this but that the practical application was far from godly:

Having no light to discern [evangelical worship's] glory, they could have no experience of its power or efficacy. What, then, shall they do? The *notion* must be retained, that divine worship is to be beautiful and glorious. But in the spiritual worship of the gospel they could see nothing thereof.... To this end they set their inventions on work to find out *ceremonies, vestments, gestures, ornaments, music, altars, images, paintings, with prescriptions of great bodily veneration:*.... Without it they know not how to pay any reverence unto God himself.[175]

To the end of his days, Owen was convinced that 'Babylon was the original of apostasy from the natural worship of God unto idolatry in the whole world.'[176] That which had begun from spiritual, even evangelical roots had moved into idolatry of the worst kind, namely image-worship and the worship of the saints departed.[177] In *Perilous Times*, Owen drew attention to the sinfulness of the church in its acceptance of empty ritualism; what he termed 'outward duties, but inward, spiritual decays'.[178]

This betrayal of godly worship by the Church of Rome was most clear in the Lord's Supper. Owen, of course, stood in the mainstream of Reformed Orthodoxy in his understanding of this Christian rite, namely that it is a symbolic act of remembrance in which the believer becomes united with Christ through faith.[179] It is a very real experience of union for the believer as the soul is fed with spiritual food that nourishes 'unto eternal life by a spiritual incorporation with him'.[180] An altogether different concept from that which was taught by the Catholics:

> For hereby they provided that all these things which are spiritual in this communion should be turned into and acted in things carnal: bread shall be the body of Christ carnally, the mouth shall be faith, the teeth shall be the exercise, the belly shall be the heart, and the priest shall offer Christ unto God. A *viler image* never was invented; and there is nothing of faith required herein; – it is all but a fortifying of imagination against all sense and reason.[181]

As far as Owen was concerned, not only was this view theologically erroneous, it also misunderstood the very basic concept of Christian worship. The beauty and glory therein is spiritual and for the soul and no outward adornments or rituals can enhance this. Indeed, externalising inward truths can only detract from the true nature of worship and thereby create nothing less than an abomination in the eyes of God. To summarise Catholic worship, then, 'the whole of it is but a deformed image of that glory which they cannot behold.'[182]

Third, concerning the graces and duties of the believer. Owen rooted his argument in the idea of headship of the Church. Christ is the only true head of the body and the Church of Rome had usurped that position by acknowledging the Pope in his stead (or, at the very least, as co-head if such a thing were possible). Therefore, any duties of obedience were inevitably offered to the wrong head and were, by their very nature, idolatrous:

> And hereon they conclude the insufficiency of Christ to be this *sole head* of the church; another they must have...And this was their pope, – such an image as is one of the worst of idols that ever were in the world. Unto him they give all the titles of Christ, which relate unto the church; and ascribe all the powers of Christ in and over it, as unto its rule, to him also.[183]

Again, Owen suggested that such apostasy was linked with experiential faith. The recognition of another authority can only be assumed by the loss of experience of the power of true spiritual authority, the Spirit and the Word, who are able to order the affairs of the church to the glory of God.

Christ, as head of the church, has set up rule and discipline for its ordering and existence. The end of that rule and discipline is to bring glory to God through the peace, purity and holiness of the church set in the context of the reality of future judgement. Clearly, for Owen, this was a rule and discipline exercised purely in the spiritual realm, without the assistance of any secular power, as witnessed to by first century Christians. The Church of Rome had fallen far short of that example by its desire for world domination and secular power throughout the nations. Thus, the Church of Rome exercised its desire for rule and obedience in the temporal realm rather than the spiritual. Whilst grave sinfulness continued among its professors and followers, there was a uniformity demanded in terms of canonical obedience and ecclesiastical jurisdiction. The underlying motivation for adherence to its discipline, rather than being a desire to glorify God, had become something altogether different:

> So was there an image composed and erected of the holy discipline of Christ, and its blessed ends, consisting of these two parts, *outward force* and *feigned subjection*. For hardly can an instance be given in the world of any man who ever bowed down to this image, or submitted unto any ecclesiastical censure, out of a conscientious respect unto it. Force and fear rule all.[184]

Consequently, the history of the growth of influence of the Church of Rome had been written in blood. Inquisitions, the execution of the martyrs, plots and murdering of princes, wars and the destruction of nations and peoples were the methods by which Papal rule has extended throughout the world. In their perverted desire to see Christ glorified, they had abandoned the very principles of peace and love and reconciliation which bring glory to his name:

> It is that wherein 'the god of this world', by the help of their blindness and lusts, hath put a cheat on mankind, and prevailed with them, under a pretence of doing Christ honour, to make the vilest representation of him to the world that can be conceived.[185]

Towards the end of Owen's life, some feared the possibility of the creation of an English Catholic state under James Duke of York upon his succession to the throne after Charles. William Lloyd[186] represented this tradition when he wrote that

> 'Tis obviously known how destructive both to itself and the Community is the Partnership of Regal Power; but this must be infinitely mischievous when shared by a Foreiner [sic], whose interests are necessarily contrary to those of our Prince and Nation, as the Popes certainly are...for the Pope is not content with a bare co-ordination, but demands the Preference for his spiritual Sword, and claims a power to depose Kings and dispose of Kingdoms.[187]

However, despite such writings there was, amongst the majority of the population, a benign acceptance of Catholicism. Practising Catholics remained a small minority in England and the imposition of Popery on the nation at that time may have been very difficult to achieve. Nevertheless, Owen and his Reformed contemporaries were acutely aware that, only a hundred years previously, a reigning monarch had indeed brought Catholicism back to the nation, albeit for a short period. His intense hatred of Catholicism was far from anachronistic and crude. The perceived threat was still very real.

Owen was not alone in putting his hatred of Catholicism into print. An extreme, although not unrepresentative, example, is that of Henry Care[188] who, in 1680, beseeched his readers to think of themselves

forced to fly destitute of bread and harbour, your wives prostituted
to the lust of every savage bog-trotter, your daughters ravished
by goatish monks, your smaller children tossed onto pikes, or
torn limb from limb, whilst you have your own bowels ripped
up...or else murdered with some other exquisite tortures and holy
candles made of your grease (which was done within our memory
in Ireland), your dearest friends flaming in Smithfield, foreigners
rendering your poor babes that can escape everlasting slaves, never
more to see a Bible, nor hear again the joyful sounds of Liberty
and Property. This, this gentlemen is Popery.[189]

A more creative example came from the pen of Robert Wild,[190]
who in 1679, published a poem entitled *Oliver Cromwells Ghost:
or Old Noll Newly Revived.* In this work, he had the spirit of the
Protector offer his opinions on the late Catholic threat to stability
in England:

Ye Powers! I thought my Countries Innocence,
(When in fierce Whirlwinds you had born me hence)
And by the Pow'r of your most just Command,
Restor'd the Scepter to the Owners hand
Would have sufficient bin to Wall you free
From the Assaults of such an Enemie.
I little thought, when last I took my leave,
And sadly entered my unwelcome Grave,
That e're the Porphry Idol could command
So great a friendship in our Native Land;
As by that means to hope to circumvent,
With black Design, both King and Government.[191]

Owen himself had many salient points to teach his readers
concerning the perceived link between Catholicism and his
understanding of sin in the church. The Church of Rome had fallen
short of the standards of God. It was no more than an empty shell;
an idolatrous image designed to lead men away from the true paths
of godliness in the pursuit of political and ecclesiastical power
and domination for its rulers. As a confessing body, it was riddled
with sin and stood in opposition to God and, as such, would be

condemned from the Throne of Judgement. Ultimately, its apostasy was founded upon one fundamental principle, namely, the loss of '*their experience of the power of every gospel truth unto its proper end,* in communicating unto us the grace of God, and transforming our minds unto the image and likeness of Jesus Christ.'[192] Experiential faith is at the heart of true religion. It was the loss of that experiential faith which left the Church of Rome wanting and ultimately condemned that institution in the eyes of God:

> The broad light which ariseth from the evidence [shows that] the Pope and his church for many ages have given themselves so to be [the Antichrist], by their idolatries, persecutions, murders, Luciferian pride, trampling on the power and persons of kings and all sorts of persons, in conjunction with the characteristical notes of times, places, rise, progress, nature, and actings of that church-state in the Scripture.[193]

Conclusion

Owen's primary concern, as we have seen, was for the state of the individual before God. That was always going to be the focus for his teaching on sin. However, given the centrality of his understanding of the primacy of election and federal theology within the context of Christian community, it is hardly surprising that he had much to say regarding sin and the church. Indeed, it is within this sphere that Owen was, arguably, most influential with his teaching. The resurgent Dissenting movement was indebted, to no small degree, to what Owen had to say concerning the need for separation from iniquitous bodies. His writings on the various sectarian movements of his day provided the foundations and framework for Cromwellian legislation and the determination of degrees of toleration. Most importantly perhaps, Owen gave a credible voice to the consciences of many individual believers who were unhappy with the state of religious faith and were looking for a more positive and godly system of church-community.

To what extent his criticisms of the various institutions and sectarian theologies mentioned above were valid is difficult to discern. Certainly, the passage of time has rendered aspects of his argument invalid. However, to judge Owen with hindsight is hardly fair and certainly not a good way of doing historical theology. The man and his ideas need assessing by the criteria of his day and, if we are to be true to that, we are bound to recognise the incisiveness of his thought in this regard. Owen's treatment of Arminianism was profound and without equal among any of his contemporaries. Likewise, his appreciation of the dangers of Socinianism and the emerging Quaker movement reveal a man who had an uncanny ability to grapple with difficult theological issues. Owen was unstinting in his attack on the national church and, again, his arguments were lucid and thoroughly biblical.

Likewise, his objections to Catholic theology and practice were justified from a contemporary Reformed stance. Owen can be forgiven for fearing the possibility of a renewed upsurge in Catholic popularity. The vociferous nature of his opinions may rest uneasily with the ecumenical spirit of the early twenty-first century. However, we must interpret him within the context of his own society. In his defence, then, we must make the simple interjection that he was a man of his time and such assaults on the Church of Rome were very much a part of the society in which he lived.

Thus far, we have noted that Owen had an immense awareness of the danger and threat of sin, within the individual and within society and the church too. The defeat of the power of sin can only be found in the cross of Christ. However, believers have a responsibility in the light of their election and that is to live out a life of holiness. And it is to this final issue which we must now turn.

5

SIN AND THE NEED FOR HOLINESS

At the very heart of Owen's teachings on corporate and individual spirituality, we find an emphasis on the need for holiness. Not only was this central to his understanding of the restoration of the image of God in man, it provided a foundation for his political and ecclesiological hopes and aspirations too. The creation of a just and godly society that would be a precursor to the millennium motivated Owen in the political realm. The creation of a church that honoured God in its structures and doctrine was inevitably a foundation stone upon which he was able to build a coherent ecclesiology.

The purpose of our final chapter, then, is to relate Owen's teaching on holiness to his understanding of sin. In so doing, we shall see how this emphasis in his teachings influenced his involvement both in church and in politics. However, what is central to Owen's teaching on holiness is the standing of the individual before God; how the believer has a responsibility to mortify sin within the context of union with Christ. We must never forget that Owen was primarily a pastor and his concern for the individual believer was always paramount. Certainly, holiness in the church and society is vital. However, that is only achievable if the sum total of those individuals take seriously their responsibility to conform to the image of Christ themselves.

Corporate Holiness
During the 1640s, Owen's concern for increasing the spiritual maturity of believers inevitably demanded parallel growth within the church. The Catechisms that he wrote during this period[1] and his treatises on the nature of the church,[2] among other writings, stand as testimonies to this fact. Owen's pastoral concern was natural given that he was ministering to congregations during this period in two parishes only a few miles apart in Essex: All Saints,

Fordham (1643-46) and thereafter at St. Peter's, Coggeshall.
Indeed, the lot had fallen to Owen to restore the spiritual state of
the congregation in Fordham after the desertion of the previous
Rector, the Laudian John Alsop.[3] Given his role as chaplain to
Archbishop Laud, Alsop was presumably of a 'high church'
persuasion, probably with Arminian sympathies. After
confirmation of his death in France, where he had fled after Laud's
execution, the parish sequestration period was finished and Owen
was asked to move on to another parish in order to make way for
Alsop's successor.

It is undoubtedly the case that Owen spent much of his time
there visiting his congregation in their homes and nurturing them
in the ways of the faith. In his Preface to *Two Short Catechisms*,
Owen reminds his parishioners of his endeavours in this regard:

> You know, brethren, how I have been amongst you, and in what
> manner, for these few years past, and how I have kept back nothing
> (to the utmost of the dispensation to me committed) that was
> profitable unto you; but have showed you, and taught you publicly
> and from house to house, testifying to all repentance towards God,
> and faith towards our Lord Jesus Christ.[4]

Such enterprises would not have been new to the parish of
Fordham. Despite the appointment of Alsop, it had previously
enjoyed a rich tradition as a parish in the Reformed tradition.[5]
The catechetical style and methodology practised by the Puritans
and exemplified in Baxter's treatise *The Reformed Pastor*, which
more often than not was accompanied by detailed expository
preaching, had not always found favour with the Fordham
parishioners. Parish records recount one incident, in March 1628,
when a parishioner by the name of John Potter climbed through
the window of the church in the night and removed the pulpit as a
protest against Rector Robert Cotton's long sermons![6] For all such
earlier protestations, Owen would have employed the same pastoral
style at Fordham and he undoubtedly took that with him to his
work at St. Peter's, Coggeshall. Indeed, so successful was Owen's
ministry in Coggeshall that he soon had a congregation numbering
two thousand.[7]

While his overriding desire was to pastor his flock, Owen's political concerns came to the forefront soon after his move to Coggeshall. It is appropriate at this point to note again his concern for holiness in the actions of political and military leaders. His concern for the world of politics far exceeded that of many of his contemporaries and we are able to trace a number of different influences upon Owen in this regard.

Certainly his personal background as the son of a Puritan minister with Welsh roots meant that he would have been aware of the tensions between church and state since his childhood. Furthermore, he had made many contacts during his time at Oxford with others that would later take on eminent positions in the world of politics. The very nature and disposition of the man was such that he would want to engage and wrestle with contemporary debate in a number of intellectual spheres.

However, if we were to search for one particular incident during this period that was formative of Owen's political outlook, we might find the answer in what occurred on 12 June 1648. On the afternoon of that day, Sir Charles Lucas,[8] a Royalist leader, was riding through the parish of Fordham (which Owen had recently left) with his troops on the way to the siege of Colchester. Sir Charles' brother, Sir John Lucas,[9] was the Church patron. Short of ammunition, they stopped at All Saints' church and proceeded to strip the roof of its lead in order to make bullets. A fierce fracas ensued during which it seems that some of Owen's old parishioners died. Evidence for this comes from a remaining piece of wall from Fordham Hall, the Lucas residence, spattered with blood in such a way that suggests the severing of a main artery. The evidence suggests that this injury, which would undoubtedly have been fatal, corresponds to the date of the roof-stripping incident.[10]

We can only guess the intensity of emotion that this incident stirred up in Owen. There was injustice in the desecration of the house of God for such an ignoble cause. There was injustice in the manner in which the community of Fordham had suffered such cruel fatalities. This event would surely have stirred up in Owen a more fervent belief that the Royalist cause was sinful and that the need for holiness and righteousness in the political realm was of immediate importance. We have scant information about his exact role as chaplain to General Fairfax during the siege of Colchester. Writing to Fairfax some months after the siege, Owen spoke of 'those blessings of Providence wherewith the days of my pilgrimage have been seasoned, that I had the happiness for a short season to attend your excellency, in the service of my master, Jesus Christ'.[11] It is most probable that he approved of Fairfax's orders to execute Sir Charles Lucas on 28 August 1648 and thereafter to imprison Sir John Lucas, both of whom thereafter became known as the Colchester martyrs. After this time, Owen's writings and sermons seem to emphasise the need for holiness in the political realm. This emphasis culminates, during this period, in his parliamentary sermon after the execution of Charles I and his appointment as Oliver Cromwell's chaplain.

It was as Cromwell's chief religious adviser, alongside Hugh Peter, that Owen continued to show concern for holiness in the corporate realm; not just politically but socially too. In May 1651, Owen had taken on the role of Dean of Christ Church, Oxford and in September 1652, he was nominated by Cromwell to the position of Vice-Chancellor. He devoted much of his time at Oxford to the reform of the institution itself. This was primarily as a member of the Board of Visitors.[12]

The spiritual and intellectual welfare and discipline of his students was a primary concern for Owen but he faced an uphill struggle in this regard. The lack of discipline amongst the students, both academically and in their private lives, motivated Owen to work for substantial change. Forthwith, undergraduates had to give an account of the sermons they had heard, preaching duties were made obligatory, and Hall conversation was to be conducted only in Latin. Further to this, each student's expenses were kept to a strict budget and he tried, unsuccessfully, to have repealed the Annual University Act because of its encouragement of frivolous behaviour. As a member of the Board of Visitors, Owen was not afraid to exact the severest of punishments on those whose behaviour and lack of learning brought disrepute on the University:

Upon consideration of a speech lately made by Mr. Busby, Student of Christ Church, at the funerall of Mr. Hoult of Baliol College, at Magdalen Parish in Oxon: contayning matter of profanation and abuse of Scripture, tending much to the palliation and extennuation of grosse miscarriages, to the strengthening of the hands of the wicked and sadning of the hearts of the godly, whereby God hath beene much dishonoured, and the University scandalised and prejudiced...wee the Visitors of the University of Oxon doe hereby order: That the said Mr. Busby be deprived of all the profits and privileges of his Student's place in Christ Church for a full halfe yeare...[13]

Toon also cites a case of his having two Quaker girls whipped after their attempts to preach to the students![14] Clearly, for Owen during this period, the relationship between sin and personal holiness was no mere academic issue; it went to the very heart of his everyday business at Oxford.

This is not to suggest that Owen's efforts did not meet some resistance. In September 1657, he had to write to Henry Cromwell[15] to justify his reforms[16] and this opposition from Convocation may have hastened political events to no small degree. Less than a month later, Richard Cromwell removed Owen from his position as Vice-chancellor in favour of Dr. John Conant,[17] Rector of Exeter College. Cromwell's shortsighted action may have precipitated Owen's alleged participation in his overthrow.

Owen's concern for a right sense of holiness and godliness in academic institutions was not confined to the University at Oxford. In March 1650, Owen had been appointed a trustee for the University of Dublin. Issues of holiness amongst students there were taxing him, at the instigation of the Commissioners in Ireland in a letter sent to him in July 1651:

In order thereunto we desire that you...will seriously consider what laws, rules, orders and constitutions are fit to be established in the said College. Wherein we desire that the educating of youth in the knowledge of God and principles of piety may be in the first place promoted, experience having taught that where learning is attained before the work of grace upon the heart, it serves only to make a sharper opposition against the powers of godliness.[18]

The importance of creating some order in the University of Dublin was paramount for Owen. Thus when Cromwell's ship landed at Ringsend little more than a month later, Owen almost immediately travelled to nearby Dublin to attend to University matters and preach the gospel to the people gathered in that city.

We are bound to note the irony that, whilst Owen was in a position to promote holiness and godly order in Ireland, his political master, at the same time at Drogheda, was presiding over an army indulging itself in acts of cruelty and barbarism in the name of the same God.[19] There is no evidence that Owen was concerned by the paradoxical nature of these events. Indeed, when news of Drogheda reached England, the ministers proclaimed from the pulpits that God's justice had been meted out on the Irish rebels.[20] Consequently, 30 October was set aside as a Day of Thanksgiving. Perhaps one man's sense of holiness is another man's understanding of sin. For Owen, holiness could be enacted as much through the sword as through the daily devotions. We have seen that to be the case concerning the execution of Charles I and Drogheda is but another example of Owen's ethical understanding of the relationship between sin and holiness.

On the political home front, we see similar concerns for holiness in Owen's writings and activities during the 1650s. The short-lived era of the Protectorate had given rise to very real hopes amongst Owen and his contemporaries. Not of least importance was the calling of the Barebones Assembly in July 1653.[21] This was the Assembly of saints which, according to the claims of the Fifth Monarchy men at least, would prepare the way for the return of Christ in 1660 or 1666.[22] In the light of this, eschatological hopes were high – perhaps too idealistic in some quarters – and Owen, alongside Nye and Goodwin, felt constrained in 1654 to write a circular letter to warn of the dangers of Fifth Monarchism. The influence of this sectarian religious group was an affront to holiness in the nation, as the writers were keen to express:

That the Gospell hath been dishonoured, the way of Christ evil spoken of, the power of Magistracy weakened, and the Civil peace of the Nation endangered...is much more evident and naked to the view of all, than that we are able to cover it with that garment of love and forbearance which our soules desire to extend unto all that with us call upon the name of the Lord.[23]

Indeed, it was concern about the idealism of the Fifth Monarchy men that led Owen and the Independents to work closely with the Presbyterians over an issue for which they had no natural inclination, namely the retention of ministerial tithes. Four days after the calling of the Barebones Parliament, a motion put to the House called for the abolition of such tithes. A complex debate raged throughout July that only served to realign loyalties amongst the Puritan politicians and create intractable factions. What became clear was that the debate was not about the validity of tithes alone. The issue cut to the very heart of the social structures concerning land ownership, patronage, the public maintenance of the ministry and ultimately an attack on university learning. Fear of the implications of Fifth Monarchy power inevitably drove the Independents, Owen included, into an alliance with the Presbyterian camp that wholeheartedly opposed such abolition. Philip Nye co-ordinated the opposition in the City of London whilst Owen worked for the same end at the Universities. As well as writing to the City to commend them for their 'exemplary labour which [they] have shewed to his Church and Gospell in this contending for the faith once delivered to the saints',[24] Owen was busy on many other fronts in his efforts to maintain the standards of religion in the face of the Fifth Monarchy threat. This was most notably amongst his Independent contacts in the Army. After a personal intervention from Cromwell, in which Owen and others were called to meet together to find common ground and unity, the divisions became even more pronounced and the Fifth Monarchy plans eventually foundered.

In addition, so did the experiment that had been the Barebones Parliament. The intervention of Owen in the events leading up to its dissolution had been immense and not without personal repercussions for himself, as an anonymous and rather vindictive letter to Owen reveals:

> As for Parliaments, didst thou not preach up and down the Rump? After its resurrection thou calledst them dry Bones breathed into, and in a short time with Lambert and Desborough, &c. help rebury them, and preach their second Funeral Sermon.... When you have answered these Arguments, ile peruse your Book, and if there be anything worthy a farther reply, you shall have it, with that sweetness and gravity as becomes your Person and cause.[25]

Nevertheless, his actions throughout the entire episode had been guided by his zeal for holiness in the nation and the propagation of the gospel. Whilst that had been protected, the demise of this Parliament did signal the end for widespread millenarian expectations in the nation. This is not to suggest that Owen abandoned his own millenarian hopes altogether at this time but, with the failure of the Barebones Assembly, they were certainly dampened quite considerably.

Owen's primary concern for the nation with regard to the relationship between sin and holiness was that the people of God in England were in danger of losing sight of what God had done during the past decade. The threat of a disparate and unruly separatist movement was very real and the danger was that the church would wander from the path of authentic faith. Such was the theme of Owen's address to Parliament in 1656 when he stated that

> The Lord knows how apt even the best of men are to forget *the spring of their mercies,* – the advantages put into their hands, unto the Lord of all mercies; therefore are they in all seasons to be minded of their proper interest and duty.[26]

This theme was close to Owen's heart since he had addressed similar issues in his previous sermon to Parliament, *God's Work in Founding Zion*.[27] God had shown himself faithful to the English nation in the last few years and it was the duty of all, not least those who exercised administrative and religious power, to respond in an appropriate manner. Given his family background, it is not altogether surprising that Owen's concern for the holiness of the nation is made explicit in his desire to see Wales in particular the recipient of evangelical efforts:

> It is for Wales I speak, where the unhappiness of almost all men running into extremes, hath disadvantaged the advancement of the gospel and the progress of it, when we had great ground for the expectation of better things.... The good Lord guide you to somewhat for its relief, that those who are godly may be encouraged, and those that need instruction may not be neglected.[28]

After March 1654, Owen sat on the Board of 'Triers' which was set up to increase the quality of public ministers. On the other extreme, he also sat as an Oxfordshire 'ejector' with his brother William and others. The aim of the 'ejectors' was to rid the congregations of the leadership of inadequate and unlearned pastors. Nothing is known of Owen's work in this capacity other than a desire on his part, cited by Toon,[29] to prevent the ejection of the Laudian Professor of Arabic, Edward Pococke,[30] from his living at Childrey. What is clear with all of Owen's activities listed above, is his desire for corporate holiness in the nation and church.

The polemical intent of many of Owen's writings on holiness is clear. As we have seen, both Socinianism and Quakerism were deemed very real threats to Reformed orthodoxy. Owen therefore felt bound to protect his understanding of sin and his doctrine of God from the perverting influence of these heretical teachings. Owen was concerned for the holiness and spiritual growth of the people of the nation in which he lived. He was concerned lest they become complacent and forget the grace of God that had delivered them from the tyranny of an ungodly monarch and the Romish corruption of the Church he governed. He was concerned, most especially for the Welsh, that they should not be left to wallow in ungodliness and spiritual depravity. He was concerned about the growth in heretical ideas that were sweeping the nation and leading people away from the truth of God.

Paradoxically, it was Owen's desire for the holiness of the

nation and the purity of the Protestant religion that resulted in the beginning of his estrangement from public political life in general and the court of Cromwell in particular. We have already noted in chapter three the controversy surrounding the pressure upon Cromwell to accept monarchical status in May 1657. It is sufficient only to reiterate Owen's concern that the restoration of a monarchy would inevitably lead to a state religion akin to, if not identical with, the type of Church of England that had been so successfully opposed in recent years. Alluding to this political manoeuvring of Cromwell and his cohorts towards monarchical power, Owen spoke of the overwhelming power of temptation into sin:

> Public temptations are usually accompanied with *strong reasons and pretences,* that are too hard for men, or at least insensibly prevail upon them to an undervaluation of the evil whereunto the temptation leads.... He that should see the prevailing party of these nations, many of those in rule, power, favour, with all their adherents, and remember that they were a colony of Puritans, – whose habitation was 'in a low place,' as the prophet speaks of the city of God, – translated by a high hand to the mountains they now possess, cannot but wonder how soon they have forgot the customs, manners, ways, of their own old people, and are cast into the mould of them that went before them in the places whereunto they are translated.[31]

The curtailing of Owen's public ministry after 1660 enabled him to devote his energies to pastoral and academic tasks. Ministering to eclectic congregations in Oxford and London,[32] Owen was presented with the opportunity to ground his theological teachings in an intensely practical manner such as he had not been able to do for many years previously. Many of his writings and sermons from this period reveal his unstinting desire to lead his people in obedience and holiness and the cultivation of a deep sense of the grace of God in their lives. Toon summarises the ethos of his work from this period, in distinction from that which had gone before, when he states, 'The difference between his early writing (e.g. A Display of Arminianism) and later writing (e.g. A Discourse concerning the Holy Spirit) is that the former is primarily polemical whilst the latter aims to be expository and devotional as well.'[33]

On a national level too, Owen felt the pain of uncertainty. The events following the Restoration had been unsettling enough. However, the prospect of having a Catholic king succeeding Charles was utterly abhorrent to Owen. As we noted in the last chapter, one is able to trace through his writings on the sins of the nation, and of the church in particular, a rather profound sense of bitterness that was characteristic of his old age. This, of course, was exacerbated by his experience of the collapse of the Puritan project. Repeatedly, Owen decried the modern state of things in comparison with how they had been when he was younger. People did not pray as they used to. The professors of religion were more sinful than they used to be. There was an apathetic spirit towards things spiritual that far surpassed the atheistic spirit of days gone by, and so on.

Yet, despite his personal sufferings, despite his ageing spirit, despite his increasing sense of melancholy, there was still a fervent spirit within Owen that filled his writings with a sense of urgency and awe for God. If the nation would only repent and reform then England would know a sense of glory deeper and more profound than ever before. Owen remained, until the very end of his days, optimistic about the providential acts of God towards individuals and the nation of England. Yes, sin remained a great problem – but the solution still lay within the grasp of those that would but seek it out.

Owen's final years were characterised by his recognition that the key to understanding and dealing with sin, whether on a personal or corporate level, is experiential faith. It is by experience of the judgements of God in forewarnings that the nation is able to recognise how far short it has fallen.[34] It is by faith and reformation that it will regain its sense of holiness and election.[35] It is by experience of the evils of Catholicism that the church should know the depth of the abyss it faces in not rooting out this atheistic error.[36] It is by faith and reformation that the church will become, again, the glory of God in the nation.[37] It is by experiencing the implications of a crucified Lord that the individual becomes more convicted of personal sin and thereby grows in faith.[38] It is by faith in that glorious God and through repentance that the individual is able to combat the power of sin.[39] Owen stressed the need for experiential faith for the individual, the nation and the church in their continuing battle against sin; for when the experience of faith takes root, the inevitable fruit that grows is holiness and obedience to Christ.

Spiritual Mindedness

The priority of personal experience in the development of holiness to combat sin was central to Owen's teaching. In a work published in 1679 entitled *The Person of Christ*, Owen placed personal sin in the context of what it means for an individual to reflect the image of God.[40] In this work, Owen stated the impossibility for the individual to have any comprehension of the image of God, following the effects of the Fall, other than through the experience of faith in Christ.[41] The life of God in us consists solely in our growing conformity unto Christ, which is achieved through contemplation of him and obedience to his commands. In that context, then, Owen was able to state that

> [he] who doth not loathe every thing that is of the remainder of sin in him and himself for it – who doth not labour after its absolute and universal extirpation – hath no sincere design of conformity unto Christ, nor can so have. He who endeavours to be like him, must 'purify himself, even as he is pure'.[42]

For Owen, the definition of sin is not to participate in our responsibility towards conformity to Christ, namely growth in holiness. For the individual to be unwilling to play a part in this process is not only a denial of our purpose in creation. It is also a grave rejection of the free, unmerited grace of God shown towards us: the ultimate rejection of his love. According to Owen, the nature of man, which results from the loss of the image of God, is more representative of Satan than God. The very purpose of creating man in his image – to make a representation of God's holiness and righteousness amongst his creatures – is frustrated by the Fall and is an affront to the intentions of God:

> He that would learn the divine nature, from the representation
> that is made of it in the present actings of the nature of man, will
> be gradually led unto the devil instead of God. Wherefore no
> greater indignity could be offered unto divine wisdom and
> holiness, than there was in this rejection of the image of God
> wherein we were created.[43]

The world was originally created to contain goodness, love and
righteousness. However, it is now filled with 'envy, malice,
revenge, cruelty, oppression, and all engines of promoting self,
whereunto man is wholly turned, as fallen off from God'.[44]

The combatting of sin, as far as is possible for each individual,
must be centred on the development of a state of spiritual-
mindedness. Owen wrote a treatise on this subject in 1681. The
context for his writing this goes some way towards explaining its
theme: Owen was seriously ill at this point in his life and believed
he was about to die.[45] The treatise he wrote was for himself only.
However, on regaining his health, he considered that a wider
circulation of his thoughts might be of benefit to others. In the
treatise, entitled *The Grace and Duty of Being Spiritually Minded*,
Owen stressed that the activity of the mind is only one aspect of
the process of mortification:

> It is that which is sinful, which ought to be mortified; yet it is not
> absolutely inconsistent with the substance and being of the grace
> inquired after. Some who are really and truly spiritually-minded,
> yet may, for a time at least, be under such an inordinate affection
> unto and care about earthly things, that if not absolutely, yet
> comparatively, as unto what they ought to be and might be, they
> may be justly said to be earthly minded. They are so in respect of
> those degrees in being spiritually minded which they ought to
> aim at and may attain unto.[46]

Owen clearly understood the rooting out of sin through spiritual-
mindedness to be one of process, never fully completed in this
lifetime but only consummated in the next world.

Owen thereby attempted to define the spiritual life of the
individual and the sinfulness of the same, not in terms of actions

but of thoughts. The mind of man is the most accurate barometer
of sin and, conversely, of spirituality. Furthermore, Owen stated
that not all thought processes are equally valid in assessing such
spiritual movement towards God. Involuntary thoughts, which
sometimes are opposed to God, are not controllable by the
individual any more than he is able to contain a storm at sea.
Rather, the voluntary thought processes are the best indicators of
our state of sinfulness or spirituality:

> But ordinarily voluntary thoughts are the best measure and
> indication of the frame of our minds. As the nature of the soil is
> judged by the grass which it brings forth, so may the disposition
> of the heart by the predominancy of voluntary thoughts; they are
> the original actings of the soul, the way whereby the heart puts
> forth and empties the treasure that is in it.... Every man's heart is
> his treasury, and the treasure that is in it is either good or evil.[47]

However, although all men have spiritual thoughts, that does not
necessarily mean that all men are spiritually minded. For those
who are not spiritually minded, spiritual thoughts often arise, not
out of the natural state of their heart, but through the excitation of
their lusts. If there is the prospect of selfish gain in a given situation,
men may be tempted to think spiritually in order to benefit
themselves in these circumstances. Owen categorised such thought
process as being brought about either through the pressure of
inward force (a sense of conviction) or the pressure of outward
occasions.[48] This is an altogether different form of voluntary
thought from that which gives rise to authentic spiritual desire.
That which is authentic is born out of a naturalness of being, a
desire to see God, to know him, and to recognise him at work in
any given situation.

Spiritual-mindedness, then, is the goal towards which all
believers should be striving in their walk with God. Conformity
to Christ is a dynamic principle. Growth into the image of God is
a dynamic principle. To become fully human, to become who we
were created to be, the development of spiritual-mindedness must
necessarily begin with an awareness of our innate sinfulness and
a knowledge of just how far we have fallen from God:

Unless the foundation of [a return to God] be laid in a deep and broken sense of our past miscarriages and present frames.... I shall much despond in this thing. But let us be persuaded that we are to lay this foundation (I desire we may agree upon this), that it is our duty to get a deep sense upon our hearts, as the first thing God aims at his calls, of our past miscarriages, and of our present dead, wretched frame; in comparison of that vigour, liveliness, and activity of grace that ought to be found in us. Ought we not to lay the foundation here? If so, then we ought to apply ourselves unto it.[49]

Once that foundation of awareness has been laid, the believer is ready to embark upon the war that is being raged in the soul against the grand enemy of sin. This is not to suggest, of course, that the raising of such awareness is a 'one-off' event. Owen believed it to be something that needs daily effort; a constant aspect of Christian spirituality. It is to the strategy for that daily battle against the power of sin that we now turn.

The Nature and Practice of Mortification

Owen had a great deal to say about the believer's daily battle against sin, which is properly known as mortification. Published in 1656, an entire treatise was devoted to the topic. This work, *On the Mortification of Sin in Believers*, arose from a series of sermons Owen preached to his students in Oxford as Vice-chancellor.[50] Eighteen years later, a considerable section of his treatise on the Holy Spirit consolidated his published thoughts.[51]

Owen was acutely aware of the need for sound teaching on mortification, for two reasons. First, the practice of mortification was considered by Owen to be essential for all Christians. Unless sin is mortified daily, it will encompass the believer and destroy faith. Furthermore, mortification is the method whereby the believer grows in grace, is perfected and is renewed. Secondly, Owen felt compelled to provide a biblical doctrine founded upon the reality of the covenant of grace, for, as he stated in his primary work, 'true evangelical mortification is nearly lost amongst us.'[52]

Much contemporary teaching on the topic was considered by Owen 'suitable to that of the gospel neither in respect of nature,

subject, causes, means, nor effects; which constantly produces
the deplorable issues of superstition, self-righteousness, and
anxiety of conscience in them who take up the burden which is so
bound for them.'[53] This comment, of course, was aimed as much
towards what he perceived as the Romish corruption of the doctrine
of mortification as it was towards Protestant professors of religion,
most notably the Quaker brethren. Contrary to Gleason's statement
that '[his] works often contain polemics against certain groups
(e.g., Arminians and Papists) but this was not his primary
concern',[54] the contention of this writer is that polemical intent
was indeed at the very heart of Owen's teaching on mortification.
It is almost impossible to separate positive exposition from polemic
in the seventeenth-century theological context. This is clearly
revealed in the preface to *On Mortification*, which begins thus:

> I shall in a few words acquaint thee with the reasons that obtained
> my consent to the publishing of the ensuing discourse. The
> consideration of the present state and condition of the generality
> of professors, the visible evidences of the frame of their hearts
> and spirits, manifesting a great disability of dealing with the
> temptations therewith...holds the chief place amongst them. This
> I am assured is of...great importance.... This was seconded by an
> observation of some men's dangerous mistakes, who of late days
> have taken upon them to give directions for the mortification of
> sin, who, being unacquainted with the mystery of the gospel and
> the efficacy of the death of Christ, have anew imposed the yoke
> of a self-wrought-out mortification on the necks of their disciples,
> which neither they nor their forefathers were ever able to bear.[55]

Owen was indeed dedicated to promoting Christian holiness but
we must not underestimate the degree to which that desire was
motivated by polemical intent.

Owen developed his teaching on mortification within a
comprehensive Trinitarian framework. The atoning work of Christ
was central to Owen's approach to this topic. He insisted that the
believer 'Set faith at work on Christ for the *killing* of thy sin. His
blood is the great sovereign remedy for sin-sick souls. Live in
this, and thou wilt die a conqueror.'[56] Owen beseeched the believer

to consider the weight of sin by viewing it in relation to the death of Christ:

> Say to thy soul, 'What have I done? What love, what mercy, what blood, what grace have I despised and trampled on! Is this the return I make to the Father for his *love,* to the Son for his *blood,* to the Holy Ghost for his *grace?* Do I thus requite the Lord? Have I defiled the heart that Christ died to wash, that the blessed Spirit hath chosen to dwell in?'[57]

In short, Owen understood mortification to be the daily effectuation of the atoning death of Christ. This christological emphasis was of course, common to the approach of many within the Reformed tradition, not least Thomas Brooks when he stated that

> the best means [for mortification] is to meditate on the blood and sufferings of Christ.... If anything under heaven will subdue and bring under darling sins, it will be the daily sight of a bleeding, groaning, dying Saviour...therefore never leave looking up to a crucified Christ, till virtue flow from him to the crucifying of those special sins that do most obstruct and hinder the growth and increase of holiness.[58]

Owen understood the believer's work of mortification to be linked to Christ through the activity of His Spirit: 'This whole work...is effected, carried on, and accomplished by the power of the Spirit, in all the parts and degrees of it.'[59] Because of that christological and pneumatological emphasis, Owen believed that mortification could only be achieved in the life of true believers.[60] Conversion is a pre-requisite to success in mortification, as Owen pointed out with a reference to Acts 2:37:

> When the Jews, upon the conviction of their sin, were cut to the heart... and cried out, 'What shall we do?' what doth Peter direct them to do? Does he bid them go and mortify their pride, wrath, malice, cruelty and the like? No; he knew that was not their present work, but he calls them to conversion and faith in Christ in general.[61]

Owen's primary text for exploring the process of mortification was Romans 8:13. From this verse, he proposed five underlying principles integral to a biblical understanding of the issue. First, mortification is a Christian duty. Second, it is a Christian duty in which all believers are required to participate. Third, it is a duty met by God with the unwavering promise of life. Fourth, mortification is an activity that can only be performed in the power of the Spirit. Fifth, the duty, means and promise are only active within 'the *conditionality* of the whole proposition'.[62]

It is interesting to note that Owen differs from Calvin in his scriptural approach. In the latter's *Institutes*, Romans 8:13 warrants no mention at all. Reference to his *Commentary on the Epistle to the Romans* may lead to an expectation of a developed doctrine but, again, we are left disappointed since little mention is made of mortification:

> Although we may still be subject to sin, nevertheless he still promises us life, provided we strive to mortify the flesh. He does not strictly require the destruction of the flesh, but only bids us make every exertion to subdue its lusts.[63]

Owen would not have argued with Calvin's words but they hardly provide a foundation, in and of themselves, for the intricately developed doctrine that our subject consequently produced. Calvin, without specifically using the term 'mortification', implied that its scriptural root is to be found not in Chapter 8 of Romans but in Chapter 12:1 thus:

> It is the duty of believers to present their 'bodies a living sacrifice, holy and acceptable unto God, which is their reasonable service' (Rom. 7:1). Hence he draws the exhortation: 'Be not conformed to this world: but be ye transformed by the renewing of your mind, that ye may prove what is that good, and acceptable, and perfect will of God'. The great point, then, is; that we are consecrated and dedicated to God, and therefore should not henceforth think, speak, design, or act, without a view to his glory. What he hath made sacred cannot, without signal insult to him, be applied to profane use. But if we are not our own but the Lord's, it is plain

both what error is to be shunned, and to what end the actions of our lives ought to be directed.[64]

In his writings on mortification, Owen did not once refer to Romans 12:1. Certainly there was some overlap of biblical material cited by the two authors on this topic but the fundamental scriptural bias of each writer was different.

Despite this difference in approach, however, the writings of the respective theologians are largely sympathetic. In his publication *John Calvin and John Owen on Mortification*,[65] Gleason provides considerable evidence for the debt that Owen owed Calvin concerning the development of his doctrine. For instance, Owen concurred with Calvin's estimation that mortification involves the whole of man: mind, affection and will. Indeed Calvin, like Owen, placed primary importance on the mind as the controlling factor concerning behavioural processes: 'Let this, then, be the first step, to abandon ourselves, and devote the whole energy of our minds to the service of God,'[66] and again, 'In seeking the convenience or tranquility of the present life, Scripture calls us to resign ourselves, and all we have, to the disposal of the Lord, to give him up the affections of the heart, that he may tame them and subdue them.'[67]

In characteristically rigorous fashion, Owen outlined a working definition of the nature of mortification before examining the way in which it operates in the life of the individual. Crucially, mortification is not the rooting out of all sin such that it has no more power in the life of the believer.[68] Owen held to no doctrine of perfectionism, realising the Pauline implication that such an achievement is beyond the realms of possibility in this earthly life.[69] True mortification therefore offers no pretence about the ultimate removal of sins. Any believer who thinks of sin as having been permanently removed through mortification 'hath added cursed hypocrisy, and is got in a safer path to hell than he was in before'.[70] Quoting the example of Simon Magus, Owen stressed that even temporary abeyance of some particular sin is not necessarily indicative of its complete mortification.[71] The believer may well enjoy the occasional conquest of sin but that pacifying of its effects for a season does not guarantee its mortification.[72]

Mortification is, primarily, 'an *habitual* weakening of [sin]'[73] such that its expression in the behavioural and thought patterns of the believer is diminished. Owen's words, which implied mortification as process, specifically spoke of a weakening of the lusts of the heart. Owen referred to Galatians 5:24 and likened the process of the dying of the old self through mortification to

> a man *nailed to the cross*; he first struggles, and strives, and cries out with great strength and might, but, as his blood and spirits waste, his strivings are faint and seldom, his cries low and hoarse, scarce to be heard...it may have sometimes a dying pang, that makes an appearance of great vigour and strength, but it is quickly over, especially if it be kept from considerable success.[74]

Owen here painted a vivid picture of the disempowerment of sin through mortification. It is a long and painful process but Owen's illustration gives assurance of the outcome in accordance with Romans 6:6.

The actual process of mortification finds its outworking 'in constant *fighting* and *contending* against sin',[75] achieved in two ways. First, there must be recognition of sin, without which the believer is ignorant of his own perilous condition.[76] Owen exhorted believers to '*get a clear and abiding sense upon thy mind and conscience of the guilt, danger, and evil* of that sin wherewith thou art perplexed'.[77]

However, it is not only the contemplation of sin that results in a trembling of the soul. Meditation on the fallen nature of self achieves a similar end and is vital for the process of mortification. Owen did not specify the method but he clarified only the desired end: 'Use and exercise thyself to such meditations as may serve to fill thee at all times with *self-abasement* and thoughts of thy own vileness.'[78] Having '*load*[ed the] *conscience with the guilt of sin* [and] the guilt of its actual eruptions and disturbances',[79] the believer is now well situated to analyse the natural disposition in order to ascertain the impact of that in sinning:

Consider whether the distemper with which thou art perplexed be not rooted in thy *nature,* and cherished, fomented, and heightened from thy *constitution* [since] A proneness to some sins may doubtless lie in the natural temper and disposition of men.[80]

The power of such consideration of one's lowly estate before God was self-evident to Owen: 'Will not a due apprehension of this inconceivable greatness of God, and that infinite distance wherein we stand from him, fill the soul with a holy and awful fear of him, so as to keep it in a frame unsuited to the thriving or flourishing of any lust whatever?'[81]

Second, such recognition must lead to an understanding of the way sin works in the believer: 'To labour to be acquainted with the ways, wiles, methods, advantages, and occasions of its *success,* is the beginning of this warfare. So do men deal with their enemies.'[82] Owen continued with the warfare illustration thus: 'To load it daily with all the things which shall after be mentioned, that are grievous, killing, and destructive to it, is the height of this contest.'[83] It is folly to think of a lust or sin as dead; it only lies dormant, waiting for a fresh opportunity to wage war on the soul. Thus every opportunity must be taken to 'give it new wounds, new blows every day'.[84]

Owen was acutely aware, not least through the example of Paul, of the need to tame the body in order to control a naturally sinful temperament.[85] He was eager however, to warn the reader away from Romish practices which he condemned as being useless for the purposes of mortification: 'Want of a right understanding and due improvement of these and the like considerations, hath raised a mortification among the Papists that may be better applied to horses and other beasts of the field than to believers.'[86] Drawing on the words of Christ to his disciples in Luke 21:34, Owen stressed that watchfulness and self-awareness is the first part of mortification.[87]

It is at this point that Owen reveals the depth and clarity of his thought concerning mortification. The believer is not left to wallow in his own sense of unworthiness and vileness but is encouraged to direct his thoughts towards the holiness and majesty of God. After the example of David in Psalm 42, Owen exhorted the believer to allow a longing for God to determine future behavioural patterns. The impact of such an attitude is immense since 'Longing, breathing, and panting after deliverance is a grace in itself, that hath a mighty power to conform the soul into the likeness of the thing longed after'.[88] God is more than willing to meet the believer's desire for transformation but patience is essential for the completion of this process:

> In case God disquiet the heart about the guilt of its distempers, either in respect of its root and indwelling, or in respect of any eruptions of it, *take heed thou speakest not peace to thyself before God speaks it; but hearken what he says to the soul.*[89]

Discerning the voice of God within is far from easy, yet Owen provided some guidelines. He wrote of the 'secret instinct of faith, whereby it knows the voice of Christ when he speaks indeed', and referred to Jesus' words in John 10:4 that the sheep will know the voice of the shepherd.[90]

Comprehension of the success of mortification is only achievable through the axiom, '*By its fruit shall it be known.*' If victory over a specific sin is won, if that sin is completely conquered in the life of the believer, then mortification has performed its work.[91] Such is the nature of this success that sin no longer hinders the Christian duties of the believer and peace of mind is attained in one's relationship with God. Owen stressed the importance of peace in the conscience to be a tangible outworking of the covenant of grace that stands between men and God.

Owen wrote of mortification as being 'taken from our own natural power or ability, and resolved into the grace of the Spirit'.[92] Far from its being a Pelagian confusion, Owen was stressing the role of the Holy Spirit in the regenerate life of the believer. The regenerated natural powers are a restoration of the image of God in the individual which necessarily result in a desire for obedience of which mortification is a part:

> Although it be a great work in itself, that wherein the renovation of the image of God in us doth consist, yet it is not wrought in any

but with respect unto a farther end in this world; and this end is, that we may live to God. We are made like unto God, that we may live unto God.[93]

Again,

[Being made in the image of God] was, that it might be a means to bring man unto that *eternal enjoyment* of Himself, which he was fitted for and designed unto. For this was to be done in a way of obedience; – 'Do this and live,' was that rule of it which the nature of God and man, with their mutual relation unto one another, did require.[94]

Owen referred to the 'gracious principle of spiritual life' that comes about through regeneration.[95] Against the Socinians, Owen argued that this regeneration is properly a new creation, not merely a moral reformation of character.

We say and believe that regeneration consists *in spirituali renovatione naturæ*, – 'in a spiritual renovation of our nature;' our modern Socinians, that it doth so *in morali reformatione vitæ*, – 'in a moral reformation of life'. Now, as we grant that this spiritual reformation of nature will infallibly produce a moral reformation of life; so if they will grant that this moral reformation of life doth proceed from a spiritual renovation of our nature, this difference will be at an end.[96]

This regeneration is exclusively a work of the Holy Spirit in the life of the individual:

[There is] a *physical* immediate operation of the Spirit, by his power and grace, or his powerful grace, upon the minds or souls of men in their regeneration.... This *internal efficiency* of the Holy Spirit on the minds of men, as to the event, is *infallible,* victorious, irresistible, or always efficacious.[97]

There follows this regeneration, in a very real sense, a new creation:

Wherefore, it is plain in the Scripture that the Spirit of God works internally, immediately, efficiently, in and upon the minds of men in their regeneration. The new birth is the effect of an act of his power and grace; or, no man is born again but it is by the inward efficiency of the Spirit.[98]

It is through this process of sanctification, which is the restoration of the image of God in the life of the believer through regeneration, that mortification becomes possible, even desirable:

In the sanctification of believers, the Holy Ghost doth work in them, in their whole souls, their minds, wills, and affections, a gracious, supernatural habit, principle, and disposition of living unto God; wherein the substance or essence, the life and being, of holiness doth consist.[99]

Union with Christ

Since Owen's understanding of sin was predominantly theocentric rather than anthropocentric, it is not surprising that he linked mortification to his doctrine of God. Owen stood firmly within the mainstream Reformed tradition, reliant upon the teachings of Calvin,[100] in that the predominant principle in this regard was the union between Christ and the believer made effective in the process of sanctification. As was mentioned above, mortification of sin can only be undertaken by true believers, united to Christ. This is a work of the Holy Spirit.

The notion of spiritual union with Christ was axiomatic to Puritan anthropology and was a theme commonly taken up by Owen's contemporaries. David Clarkson, who later preached at Owen's funeral, wrote that union 'is the basis of communion',[101] an idea expounded further by Matthew Barker[102] :

[Communion with God] consisteth of the Divine Operations of our Souls towards God, when the faculties of the Soul are tending towards him, and terminated upon him; when the Mind is exercised in the contemplation of him, the Will in chusing and embracing him, when the Affections are fixt upon him, and center in him, when by our Desires we pursue after him, by our Love we cleave to him, and by Delight we acquiesce and solace ourselves in him.[103]

The Larger Catechism of the Westminster Assembly considered union with Christ to be co-incidental with the effectual calling of the believer and thus logically to precede justification, adoption and sanctification. Richard Baxter took a similar approach when he stated that 'the first and great work of faith is to receive and close with the person of Christ.... He is the vine, and we are the branches; we must be planted into him, and live in him, or else we can have nothing further from God.'[104]

Many mainstream Puritan writers pursued this theme and any differences we find tend to be of detail rather than substance.[105] Thomas Goodwin, for example, wrote of union with Christ in a three-fold progression in his *Commentary on Ephesians*. First, there is union with Christ from eternity. Second, there is union through the incarnation. The third type of union is that achieved when the work of redemption is applied to the soul of the believer. Thus 'A man, before he is called, is justified *in* Christ, but not *with* Christ; that is, it is not actually applied to the man's person.'[106] However, as Tudur Jones comments in his article 'Union with Christ: The Existential Nerve of Puritan Piety',[107] we note that this is a curious reversal of Eastern patristic theology. Primarily through the writings of Gregory of Nyssa, union with Christ was understood to be the goal of the Christian life, not the beginning of it. Owen's doctrine concerning union with Christ, whilst following a familiar approach to that of his contemporaries, was reliant upon three particular themes, all of which deserve further comment.

First, Owen placed the union between Christ and the believer within his framework of federalism, most especially the covenant of grace:

Now, this covenant is made us under this formal consideration, that we are the children and seed of Abraham, which we are not but by our union with Christ, the one seed, to whom the promises of it were originally made...the condition of the covenant should certainly, by free grace, be wrought and accomplished in all that are taken into covenant.[108]

There is, therefore, a guarantee of God's promises to the believers inherent in this covenant that, through Christ Jesus, they should share in the benefits of salvation. On more than one occasion Owen referred to the parable of the vine in John 15[109] to show that progress in holiness, and therefore by implication mortification included, is wholly reliant upon our union with Christ, for example

> We must be in Christ as the branch is in the vine, or we can derive nothing from him: John 15: 4, 'As the branch cannot bear fruit of itself, except it abide in the vine; no more can ye, except ye abide in me.' Whatever any way belongeth unto holiness is our fruit, and nothing else is fruit but what belongeth thereunto. Now this our Saviour affirms that we can bring forth nothing of, unless we are in him and do abide in him. Now, our being in Christ and abiding in him is by faith, without which we can derive nothing from him, and consequently never be partakers of holiness in the least degree.[110]

Secondly, Owen wrote of union with Christ in terms of a spiritual marriage.[111] This marriage, which demands obedience from the believer, has clear ramifications for the process of holiness in general and mortification in particular. Calvin, like Owen after him, had written about this union in Pauline terminology with an analogy of marriage, again stressing the role of the Spirit in the consummation of the union:

> To this union alone it is owing that, in regard to us, the Saviour has not come in vain. To this is to be referred that sacred marriage, by which we become bone of his bone, and flesh of his flesh, and so one with him (Eph. 5:30), for it is by the Spirit alone that he unites himself to us.[112]

Comparing this with Owen's words, we note the similarity of thought:

> Christ makes himself over to the soul, to be his, as to all the love, care, and tenderness of a husband; and the soul gives up itself wholly unto the Lord Christ, to be his, as to all loving, tender

obedience...the souls of his saints are very beautiful, even perfect, through his comeliness, which he puts upon them...particularly, that their spiritual light is very excellent and glorious; like the eyes of a dove, tender, discerning, clear, and shining.[113]

However, we must not claim too much for Owen in terms of originality since this was a common metaphor amongst the Puritan writers which, as Tudur Jones states, 'reveals the appealing and tender aspect of Puritan preaching'.[114] Indeed, many of Owen's contemporaries used the analogy with greater skill and sensitivity than Owen ever managed. There is great consideration, for example, of the Song of Songs in this regard with no apology offered for erotic spirituality. Hence Rutherford on that union: 'We cannot rest till we be in other's arms – and o, how sweet is a fresh kiss from his holy mouth: His breathing that goeth before a kiss upon my poor soul, is sweet, and hath no fault, but that it is too short.'[115]

Third, this union with Christ becomes effective through the indwelling of the Holy Spirit in the believer. This is achieved in two ways, the first being related to the act of incarnation by which the work of redemption was achieved through the participation of the human element. Owen considered this vital for making sanctification possible:

One end of God in filling the human nature of Christ with all grace, in implanting his glorious image upon it, was, that he might in him propose *an example* of what he would by the same grace renew us unto, and what we ought in a way of duty to labour after.... He is in the eye of God as the idea of what he intends in us, in the communication of grace and glory; and he ought to be so in ours, as unto all that we aim at in a way of duty.[116]

However, union with Christ is more than by just example; there is a real and actual union operable that makes mortification possible. This is not achieved through self-effort but by the vivifying power of the Holy Spirit:

I say, then, this is that which gives us union with Christ, and that wherein it consists, even that the one and self-same Spirit dwells

in him and us.... Their quickening is everywhere ascribed to the
Spirit that is given unto them; there is not a quickening, a life-
giving power, in a quality, a created thing...in the first bestowing
of the Spirit we have union with Christ; the carrying on whereof
consists in the farther manifestation and operations of the
indwelling Spirit, which is called communion.[117]

Owen was careful to maintain the orthodox understanding of the
nature and boundaries of that union with Christ, never hinting at a
mix of natures.

The first signal issue and effect which is ascribed to this indwelling
of the Spirit is *union;* not a personal union with himself, which is
impossible. He doth not assume our nature, and so prevent our
personality, which would make us one person with him, but dwells
in our persons, keeping his own and leaving us our personality
infinitely distinct. But it is a *spiritual union,* – the great union
mentioned so often in the gospel, that is the sole fountain of our
blessedness, – our union with the Lord Christ, which we have
thereby.[118]

However, in another context, he did stress the fact that the
believers' union makes real the benefits of Christ through actual
participation:

Because being in him, and members of him, *we* are accounted to
have done, *in him* and *with him,* whatsoever *he* hath done *for us:*
We are 'dead with him,' Romans 6:8; 'buried with him,' verse 4;
...'risen with him,' Colossians 3:1...wherefore we, having an
interest in their performance, by reason of that heavenly
participation derived from them unto us.[119]

Thus, for Owen, mortification is made possible through a real
union with Christ made effectual in the life of the believer through
the work of the Holy Spirit who is the cause of all participation in
God's grace.[120]

It is undeniable that Owen's teaching on the believer's union
with Christ, as with his teaching on the whole topic of

mortification, was profoundly scriptural. Owen referred to a phenomenal amount of texts to validate his line of argument. However, what is also noticeable is the sheer quantity of allusions made to various Greek and Latin philosophers and poets from an earlier age. We are left in no doubt as to the depth and breadth of his learning as Owen takes recourse in these writers to illuminate his own ideas. Owen was never guilty of using such writings indiscriminately; he was well aware that the writers of antiquity had set many erroneous doctrines forth. These he made plain in the 'Epistle to the Reader' which prefaced his *Biblical Theology*. However, he was wise enough – perhaps we may even say broadminded enough – to recognise the benefit of immersing oneself in such writings:

> The great foundation of the literature of the past was Classical poetry and, even now, this is the usual starting point for a liberal education. Its garlands and ivy-leaved crowns it can keep without any opposition from me. Classical poetry has been adapted by the saints of old to sing the praises of God and, besides, the very fact of an antiquity itself carries with it a certain authority and reverence.[121]

With specific regard to our present inquiry, however, Owen was as discerning as ever in his treatment of these early sources. His objectivity enabled him to draw on the thoughts of a particular individual, sometimes to add weight to his own argument and then again to dispute some erroneous idea. With the Emperor Hadrian, for example, Owen was happy to allude to one of his favourite poems to reveal the frailty of human existence and the need to look beyond this material world towards a greater security.[122] Yet, Owen's acceptance of Hadrian was not all-embracing. Elsewhere he criticised the Emperor for worshipping idols and lying about Constantine's cure from leprosy.[123] Again, Owen was happy to concur with Aristotle's words, 'Η σοφια εστι των τιμιωτατων,' that the second part of wisdom is self-knowledge.[124] Yet, only a few paragraphs before, he had criticised the philosopher for having too vague a notion of mercy to be effectual in our regenerating unity with Christ.[125]

What emerges is a distinct pattern in Owen's use of these writers concerning the believer's union with Christ. He was willing to draw on, or allude to, sayings and thoughts from the philosophers and poets when they accorded with scriptural teaching. Hence Owen referred to or made allusions to the writings of Arrian, Cicero, Lactantius, Homer, Hieron, Virgil, Mercerus and Lombard, amongst others, in this way.[126] However, he was quick to refute their teachings when the human spirit is exalted to such a level that Pelagian optimism is suggested. Therefore, Owen condemned Socrates, Plato and Aristotle for becoming fools.[127] Likewise Xenophanes, who 'bears the *crown* of reputation for wisdom from them all, with whom to have lived was counted an inestimable happiness, died like a fool',[128] whilst Cicero exemplifies 'the proud conceits and expressions of the philosophers'.[129] Certainly, Owen stood firmly in the mainstream of the Reformed tradition regarding his understanding of the believer's union with Christ. However, he was no slave to it. Owen was willing to engage in debate with the past masters of philosophy and literature, affirming their teachings when they accorded with Christian belief. Nevertheless, he used them as a foil when he desired to uncover more of the uniqueness of this central and fundamental Christian doctrine.

Conclusion

For many years, Owen suffered from ill health. He never forsook his childhood habit of 'burning the candle at both ends' which, over the years, weakened his constitution considerably. As early as 1663 Owen was under the doctor for meliceris, a disease of the eyes and eyelids.[130] Within a few years, Owen was feeling the pressure of failing health, as he insinuated in a letter to his dear friend, Mr. Nichols: 'I have daily warnings from my age, being now about fifty four and many infirmities to be preparing for my dissolution.'[131] The exact nature of these infirmities is difficult to discern. However, from 1670 onwards, the severity of them brought Owen to the point of death on a number of occasions.[132] In January 1683, Owen was to receive the diagnosis for the illness that would take his life seven months later, the news broken to him by his physician Dr. Edmund King:

Honoured Sir, have received your viol tach that came in it, and I doe believe you have a stone too bigg to pass which galls the internal superficies of your kidney...its the safest way to suspect the worst.[133]

As Owen drew near to the end of his life, it was his thoughts on the glory of Christ and his eternal prize of salvation that sustained him. Asty testifies that this was the case, right until his end on 24 August 1683: 'From Kensington he went to Ealing...where he finished his course. During which time he employed his thoughts in the contemplation of the other world, as one that was drawing near to it every day.'[134] This concern for the next world led, naturally enough, to his distancing of himself from the theological debates that he would soon leave behind. As Owen commented in one of his final written passages,

In the continual prospect hereof do I yet live, and rejoice; which, among other advantages unspeakable, hath already given me an inconcernment in those oppositions which the passions or interests of men engage them in, of a very near alliance unto, and scarcely distinguishable from, that which the grave will afford.[135]

Such a process of distancing oneself from relationships and matters of this world is a natural stage that every individual goes through in preparing for death. This process may be long or short, depending upon the given circumstances. However, it would seem that Owen was still concerned with earthly matters – or at least the impact of the faith upon earthly matters – until the final stages of his life. The late dates of his sermons and letters and published treatises give full evidence of this fact. Just a little over a year before his final diagnosis, Owen had apologised to his friend Thomas Whitaker for not keeping up to date with his correspondence since 'I have scarce leisure time to write a line'.[136] Indeed, on the very morning of the day on which he died, 24th August 1683, Owen was visited by William Payne from Saffron Walden to inform him that his *Meditations on the Glory of Christ* had just gone to press. Without doubt, Owen was committed to the propagation of the gospel and the teaching of the faith almost until his dying breath.

Primary amongst this effort was his work *On Indwelling Sin*.[137] This highly developed systematic approach to this most intriguing of topics has rarely, if ever, been equalled. Revealed therein is a profound understanding of the biblical material and its appropriate application in the life of the individual. This pastoral approach is mirrored in the sermons he preached at the time and the various *Discourses*, most of which were posthumously published. These works, short in nature but profound in terms of theology and understanding, are devoted to Owen's responses to various pastoral and ethical dilemmas.[138] Owen's writings during this final period of his life reveal a deep concern for the spirituality of his congregations and readers. The opportunity to express that had been largely denied him since his time as a minister at both Fordham and Coggeshall in the 1640s. A freshness and relevancy in Owen's approach here surpasses almost all of his other writings in this regard.

Perhaps most of all, his later writings on the relationship between sin and holiness are hallmarked by the paradoxical nature of Owen's realism intertwined with his Christian hope. An acknowledgement of the perilous state of the nation, the church and the individual was matched by Owen's fervent belief that the glory of God could still be sought and won for each of these groups. Half a century of engagement in some of the most complex and tumultuous theological, ecclesiological and political battles known to modern man had given Owen a profound wisdom and sense of God's providence that was to infuse his writings with a vitality and sense of optimism that could only draw his readers away from sin and towards the light of Christ. In the final analysis, that was all John Owen, the pastor, ever hoped to achieve.

CONCLUSION

David Clarkson anticipated the Owenian legacy in his funeral oration when he stated that 'The account that is due to the world, requires a volume, and a better hand than mine, which I hope it will meet with in time'.[1] It is encouraging to see the continuing fulfilment of that aspiration in recent years with renewed scholarly interest in Owen. His importance and influence is unquestionable, not only for the purposes of historical study, but also for contemporary theological debate.

It has been the aim of this book to make a further contribution to this field of research. The Introduction outlined three primary objectives for the work. First, to explore the claim that the doctrine of sin was foundational to the writings of John Owen.[2] Second, to undertake Owenian research outside the restrictive boundaries of the 'Calvin versus the Calvinists' debate.[3] Third, to locate Owen's doctrine of sin within his pastoral ministry.[4] By way of conclusion, we can now analyse to what extent these three objectives have been met and their importance in the study of this topic.

First, to assert the foundational importance of the doctrine of sin in Owen's thought may seem a little bold, given the extent and sheer breadth of his literary output. Owen's system of thought evolved to become a masterful construction of intertwined and interdependent ideas. When one consides his writings in their totality, it is difficult to claim any one specific idea as the foundation upon which all else is built. Far more difficult would it be to claim that for his understanding of sin. However, that is not our intent in describing his teaching on this topic as foundational.

In examining the nature of this claim, we must first be clear that asserting the foundational position of Owen's doctrine of sin does not compromise the intensely theocentric nature of his thought. It is certainly the case that Owen developed his doctrine of sin within the context of his doctrine of God. To re-iterate the point that his approach never displaced theocentric centrality, we note Owen's comment that

Sin opposes the divine nature and existence; it is enmity against God, and it is not an idle enemy; it has even engaged in a mortal war with all the attributes of God.... He hath often and heavily complained, in his word, that by sin he is robbed of his glory and honour, affronted, exposed to calumny and blasphemy; that neither his holiness, nor his justice, nor name, nor right, nor dominion, is preserved pure and untainted.... Let sinners, then, be informed that every the least transgression abounds so much with hatred against God.[5]

Rather, the doctrine of sin was foundational to Owen's thought inasmuch as he understood the effects of the Fall to render impossible any effective theological work through human endeavour. Epistemological clarity had been lost in Eden. Any subsequent discourse about God must begin with the realisation that 'no one can grasp or rightly understand evangelical theology by human power or reliance on intellect, apply what outside assistance he will'.[6] The fundamental importance of this is in the fact that, for Owen, epistemology was essentially linked to the teleological aim of humanity. He stated that 'the primary purpose and end of all knowledge [is] how to live acceptably before God'.[7] Again, the 'end of all true theology is the cultivation of a most holy and sweet communion with God, wherein lies the true happiness of mankind'.[8] If the epistemological endeavour is rendered impossible through sin, the very purpose of existence is thwarted.

It is not just the case that, in a post-Edenic epoch, sin precedes theological activity. For Owen, a *doctrine* of sin must precede theological activity. The reason for that is clear. The foundational reality of the corrupting influence of sin, far from replacing theocentric centrality, actually makes it a necessity. In short, if there can be no theological endeavour other than that which originates from – and relies exclusively upon – God, Owen could claim with confidence that 'the Holy Spirit leads us into all truth, by giving us that understanding of it which of ourselves we are not able to attain'.[9] As Ferguson rightly observes, 'If believers are to know the Father through the Son, they must first experience the Spirit and know his influences on their lives leading them to the fountain of grace.'[10] The utterly depraved nature of humanity is the greatest justification for a theocentric and Trinitarian scheme. The '*economical* or dispensatory proceeding [of the Spirit], for the carrying on of the work of grace'[11] was vital for Owen in his polemical debates concerning sin. This was most notable, for instance, in his interaction with the Arminians, Quakers and the Cambridge Platonists, all of whom claimed some degree of human ability in spiritual matters.

Second, our stated intention was to avoid intensive interaction with the 'Calvin versus the Calvinists' debate. This is a controversy which, as Gleason commented, 'has provoked lively discussion on a variety of topics ranging from differences in methodology to issues central to the doctrine of salvation.'[12] Continuity and disparity between Owen and Calvin concerning the doctrine of sin has been noted throughout this book. Gleason also addressed this issue, in summary form at least, in his work, *John Calvin and John Owen on Mortification.*[13] Our conclusion is that their writings were largely sympathetic concerning the themes explored in this work. For our purposes, the extent to which Owen remained faithful or departed from Calvin has not proved to be of great importance, for two reasons.

The first reason is that Owen has been located throughout this work within the Reformed tradition. He has not been described as a Calvinist. What has become obvious is that the Reformed tradition is broad indeed. Owen's writings were dependent upon many great thinkers alongside Calvin. Augustine was undoubtedly Owen's primary source. Aquinas' influence is obvious, as is that of Aristotle. His free use of the Fathers was extraordinary and the assimilation of contemporary political and economic theories creative. Therefore, to speak of continuity with Calvin as the benchmark for loyalty is to misinterpret the nature of the Reformed tradition. The genius of Owen was to absorb ideas from a wide range of thinkers and disciplines and then channel that into contemporary teaching of his own. Owen was able to distil truth from many sources and construct one coherent system.

The second reason for avoiding the 'Calvin versus the Calvinists' debate is that the story of salvation is integrally linked to history and thus should be applied in its particularity. Barth made this point in *Church Dogmatics*, when he stated that 'The history of salvation is both a history between God and man and also a history between man and man. It is the second as and because it is the first'.[14] If the context of history is vital for an understanding of salvation, the same must necessarily be true for the doctrine of sin which is, in essence, an understanding of that from which humanity is saved. However, the 'Calvin versus the Calvinists' debate has diminished the historical dimension at best and destroyed it at worst. An example of the historical dislocation that has often accompanied an endorsement of the debate is that of Clifford's work, *Atonement and Justification*, in which the author compared the writings of Owen with Baxter, Tillotson and Wesley. In the Preface, Clifford states: 'The fact that Wesley was not a contemporary of the others in no way affects the investigation, which is concerned primarily with their convictions rather than their careers.'[15] To suppose that it is possible to divorce the convictions from the careers of Owen, Wesley or, indeed, any other theologian, is a gross methodological error. Conviction, career and context inform each other in the complex interaction of life experience out of which theological thought is developed. Owen's doctrine of sin illustrates this idea well, to use Barth's idea, in the sense of both 'God to man' and 'man to man'.

An example of the importance of historical context in the 'God-man' dimension is Owen's attitude towards the implications of eternal justification on his doctrine of sin. We recognise that this debate 'is not correctly proposed in the antithesis *justification in time vs. justification from eternity*'.[16] However, the doctrine does impinge on the truth of justification as a historical act between God and man. Crucial to our purpose is the implication that eternal justification holds true for the elect before their conversion, whilst still in a state of unregeneracy and unbelief. The qualitative difference of faith is only in the appropriation of justification in the believer's consciousness.

Owen utterly refuted this doctrine. Responding to the animadversions of Baxter against *The Death of Death* in 1650, Owen stated that 'For pactional justification, evangelical justification, whereby a sinner is completely justified, that it should precede believing, I have not only not asserted but positively denied.'[17] It was vital for Owen to take that stance, not only due to the unbiblical nature of the doctrine itself but also because of its consequences for his doctrine of sin. The doctrine of eternal justification inevitably diminishes a sense of the seriousness of sin itself since the unregenerate predestined for conversion enjoys a state of eternal grace. The idea of living under the curse of the law becomes irrelevant, giving rise to doctrinal Antinomianism. As Berkouwer has argued, the doctrine of eternal justification led the Antinomian party to conclude 'that all sin and guilt, all taint and impurity were swept away and were now not merely disallowed, but impossible. Sin as guilt before God could no longer exist in the believer'.[18] Most important of all, the doctrine of eternal justification has grave ramifications for the actual achievement of Christ's atoning death, as Owen was keen to recognise.[19]

Owen was convinced that the process of justification is a historical act; Trinitarian in nature but integrally linked to the work of Christ:

> This, therefore, is that which herein I affirm: – *The righteousness of Christ* (in his obedience and suffering for us) *imputed unto believers, as they are united unto him by his Spirit, is that righteousness whereon they are justified before God, on the account whereof their sins are pardoned, and a right is granted them unto the heavenly inheritance.*[20]

It is appropriate to note that, in this, Owen remained faithful to the Westminster Confession: 'God did, from all eternity, decree to justify all the elect, and Christ did, in the fulness of time, die for their sins, and rise again for their justification: nevertheless, they are not justified, until the Holy Spirit doth, in due time, actually apply Christ unto them.'[21]

What is clear is the dual historical element in the process of justification and, by inference, the conquering of the dominion of sin. The means of justification is located in a historical act – the death and resurrection of Jesus Christ. The ensuing application of justification is located in a historical event – the work of the Spirit in the heart of the believer. To think of this gracious act of God in the abstract terminology of eternal justification is to deny the very essence of it. Owen perceived the message of salvation and the doctrine of sin to be eternal truths but applicable to particular people at a particular time. Salvation from sin is linked to history in the 'God-man' dimension and must be considered in that context.

It is also the case that salvation and the overthrow of sin have a historical dimension, using Barthian terminology, between man and man. A considerable part of this book has focused on the notion that God is working his purposes out in history. Owen clearly believed that God had called his people to be instruments of his will. He understood God's purposes to be wider than just individual salvation. The establishment of a holy community and a godly state that would bring glory to his name was an integral part of Christian salvific activity.

Owen's beliefs in this regard were in keeping with the wider Reformed community. Walzer has suggested that an integral aspect of Calvin's legacy was to inspire a tradition

> committed...to the literal reforming of human society, to the creation of a Holy Commonwealth.... The saints saw themselves as divine *instruments* and theirs was the politics of wreckers, architects, and builders – hard at work upon the political world.... They treated every obstacle as another example of the devil's resourcefulness and they summoned all their energy, imagination, and craft to overcome it.[22]

The practical outworking of this tradition was diverse indeed. Geneva was the original model, being the handwork of Calvin himself,[23] but others were inspired by the same ideal. The Separatists who boarded *The Mayflower* in September 1620 – and the 21,000 who followed during the 1630s – were motivated, at least in part, by the desire to create a godly society under the authority of God. Reverend John Norton, for example, described New England as 'holding forth a pregnant demonstration of the consistency of Civil-Government with a Congregational-Way'.[24] Back in England, Stephen Marshall stated that the Civil War concerned but one issue: 'Should Christ or Antichrist rule?'[25] The Fifth Monarchy movement of the early 1650s was concerned to link the Kingdom of God with political and military developments. We could cite many more examples, given Baskerville's comment that 'the Protestant Reformation created not only a new kind of piety but also a new kind of politics, and English Puritanism created a new kind of person: the citizen, the activist, the "ideologically committed political radical".'[26]

It is not surprising, then, that Owen should have devoted so much energy to political activity. For him, involvement in matters of State was never a diversion from Christian ministry. Rather, it was *of the very essence* of Christian ministry as interpreted within the Reformed tradition. Sadly, the historical dislocation resulting from the 'Calvin versus the Calvinists' debate has obscured this integral focus of Owen's life and thought. Those who have written on Owen from purely theological perspectives, in the context of that debate, offer only a partial analysis at best. They turn Owen the pastor into an abstract theologian or philosopher. What is needed, most of all, is Owenian research that takes seriously his historical context, focusing not least on his thought as it relates to both Church and State.

Finally, and in the light of the above, this thesis has attempted to locate Owen's doctrine of sin within his pastoral ministry. We have noted that Owen's desire was never to develop a new doctrine. Rather, his aim was to apply the received Reformed Orthodox teaching to his present day context in practical, everyday Christian service.[27] During the forty years of his ministry, Owen devoted himself to propagating the message of God's grace and attempted to lead Christians into a deeper experience of holiness. His teaching on sin was a vital aspect of that pastoral intent and any historical consideration demands that focus.

Owen's pastoral concern was, of course, in keeping with a society keenly aware of the reality of sin and its consequences for the individual. Baird Tipson suggests that 'the historian of late sixteenth- and seventeenth-century English Protestantism encounters the testimony of terrified men and women who suspected that they themselves had sinned against the Holy Spirit and were beyond forgiveness.'[28] John Bunyan is perhaps the best known of all seventeenth-century writers who felt the crushing weight of personal sin. His 1666 spiritual autobiography, *Grace Abounding to the Chief of Sinners* is testimony to what Wakefield calls his 'lone trail with constant hazards'.[29] However, his was by no means an isolated case or even the most dramatic. His Bedford colleague, John Child, depressed by his own sinfulness, hanged himself. Another such example is the story of Joan Drake; a wealthy and influential Surrey woman who was convinced that she had committed the sin of blasphemy against the Holy Spirit. Suffering depression for many years, she was ministered to by a succession of renowned clergymen, including John Dod, Thomas Hooker, James Ussher and John Preston, only receiving assurance of salvation shortly before her death in 1625.[30] Church records from around the country reveal many similar cases.[31]

There is no reason to believe that Owen succumbed to such a melancholic spirit upon reflection of his own sinfulness. Nevertheless, he did have a profound experience, not unlike Bunyan, that was to convince him of the gravity of sin, as Packer relates:

> In his early twenties...God showed him his sins, and the torment of conviction threw him into such a turmoil that for three months he avoided the company of others and, when addressed, could scarcely utter a coherent sentence. Slowly he learned to trust Christ, and so found peace.[32]

Given that personal experience, it is not surprising that Owen should conceive of sin in pastoral and highly experiential terms. Indeed, he believed a profound awareness of sin to be a prerequisite to effective Christian ministry: 'The man that understands the evil of his own heart, how vile it is, is the only useful, fruitful, and solid believing and obedient person.'[33]

Owen's concern was always to produce 'useful, fruitful, and solid believing and obedient' people. That was the case in his parochial duties at Fordham and Coggeshall.[34] That was the case in his chaplaincy role to Cromwell and his preaching to the armies.[35] That was the case in his dealings at Christ Church, Oxford, despite opposition from Convocation,[36] as well as in his parliamentary activities.[37] That was the case, too, in his nurturing of gathered congregations during his final years in London and Stadham.[38] Owen was convinced that awareness of the gravity of sin was essential for Christian growth:

> There are two things that are suited to humble the souls of men, and they are, first, a due consideration of God, and then of themselves; – of God, in his greatness, glory, holiness, power, majesty, and authority; of ourselves, in our mean, abject and sinful condition.[39]

The development of a doctrine of sin was, for Owen, of profound pastoral importance. The good news of salvation is incomplete without a thorough apprehension of that from which we have been saved:

> Most men love to hear of the doctrine of grace, of the pardon of sin, of free love, and suppose they find food therein.... But to be breaking up the fallow ground of their hearts, to be inquiring after the weeds and briars that grow in them, they delight not so much, though this be no less necessary than the other.[40]

Owen was not morbidly obsessed with sin. He understood with great clarity that, to appreciate the grace of God, the believer must first comprehend the depravity of man.

The final words to the Preface of his 1668 treatise, *The Nature, Power, Deceit, and Prevalency of the Remainders of Indwelling Sin in Believers* indicates the pastoral intent of his doctrine. Indeed, these final words seem to encapsulate the very motivation for his whole ministry: to build up a community of believers whose experience of grace would inspire them into a life of service, both to God and to one another:

> And if the reader receive any advantage by these weak endeavours, let him know that it is his duty, as to give glory unto God, so to help them by his prayers who in many temptations and afflictions are willing to labour in the vineyard of the Lord, unto which work they are called.[41]

Surely, the context of that statement is final proof, if any more were required, of the foundational importance of Owen's doctrine of sin.

'His intimate knowledge of the Word of God, [and] his profound acquaintance with the heart of man, [and] the skill with which he brings the one into vigorous and healing action upon the other' has long been recognised as Owen's genius.[42] Theology and hamartology are inextricably linked. It is our hope that this book has gone some way in exploring this relationship and will provide impetus for further research that takes seriously John Owen's historical and pastoral context.

BIBLIOGRAPHY

I. PRIMARY SOURCES

Allsop, V. *Melius Inquirendum: Or, A Sober Inquiry into the Reasonings of the Serious Inquiry.* London, 1681

Annesley, A. *England's Confusion.* London, 1659

>*The truth unvailed [sic] in behalf of the Church of England.* London, 1676

Anonymous, *Two Captains, two Camps. Their Fatall and Finall Warres.* n.p. Probably London, 1642

>*The Break-neck of Presumptuousnesse in Sinning.* London, 1644

>*The Copy of a Most Pithy and Pious Letter.* London, 1645

>*The Plain Case of the Commonweal Neer the Desperate Gulf of the Common-woe.* London, 1658

>*A Seasonable Speech Concerning the Other House.* London, 1659

Aquinas, T. *Nature and Grace: Selections from the Summa Theologica of Thomas Aquinas.* London: SCM, 1954

>*Summa Theologiae.* London: Blackfriars: Eyre and Spottiswoode, 1964

>*Summa Contra Gentiles.* "Book One: God", Notre Dame and London: University of Notre Dame, 1975

Aristotle, *The Nicomachean Ethics.* London, 1893

>*The Nicomachean Ethics.* London: Methuen, 1900

>*The Ethics of Aristotle: The Nicomachean Ethics Translated.* Harmondsworth: Penguin, 1955

Arminius, J. *The Works of Arminius.* trans. J & W. Nichols, 3 vols. Grand Rapids, Michigan: Eerdmans, 1986

Asty, J. 'Memoirs of the Life of Dr. Owen'. in *A Complete Collection of the Sermons of John Owen.* n.p., 1721

Athenagoras, *The Resurrection of the Dead.* in "Ante-Nicene Fathers vol. 2" Edinburgh: T & T Clark, 1989

Augustine, *Confessions.* London: Collins, 1923

>*The City of God.* New York: Random House, 1950

>*On Free Will.* in "Earlier Writings" London: Westminster, 1953

>*The Problem of Free Choice.* London: Longmans, Green & Co. 1955

>*The Nature of the Good.* in "Earlier Writings" London: Westminster, 1953

>*The Soliloquies.* in "Earlier Writings" London: Westminster, 1953

>*The Trinity.* Washington: Catholic University of America Press, 1963

>*On the Nature and Origin of the Soul.* Book III as an Appendix of "Eloquence and Ignorance in Augustine's 'On the Nature and Origin of the Soul'", M.C. Preus, New York: Scholars Press, 1985

Ball, J. *A Treatise of the Covenant of Grace.* London, 1645

Baxter, R. *Two disputations of original sin.* London, 1675

>*The Saints' Everlasting Rest.* London, n.d.

>*A Christian Directory.* in "The Practical Works of Richard Baxter" vol. 1. Ligonier, PA: Soli Deo Gloria Publications, 1990

>*The Reformed Pastor.* Edinburgh: Banner of Truth, 1974

Baylie, R. *Satan the Leader in Chief to all who resist the reparation of Sion.* London, 1643

Bedford, T. *Of the Sinne unto Death.* London, 1621

Benn, W. *Soul Prosperity, in Several Sermons.* London, 1683

Bowles, E. *The Mystery of Iniquity.* London, 1643

Brooks, T. *The Works of Thomas Brooks*. ed. A. Grosart, 6 vols. Edinburgh: Banner of Truth, 1980

Burgesse, A. *Vindiciæ Legis: Or, A Vindication of the Morall Law and the Covenants, From the Errours of Papists, Arminians, Socinians and more especially, Antinomians*. London, 1646
The Doctrine of Original Sin, Asserted and Vindicated Against the old and new Adversaries thereof, both Socinians, Papists, Arminians and Anabaptists. London, 1658

Calvin, J. *The Gospel according to St. John 11-21 and the First Epistle of John*. Edinburgh: St. Andrew's Press, 1961
The Epistles of Paul to the Romans and Thessalonians. Grand Rapids, Michigan: Eerdmans, 1961
The Institutes of Christian Religion. 2 vols. Grand Rapids, Michigan: Eerdmans, 1962
Hebrews and 1 and 2 Peter. Grand Rapids, Michigan: Eerdmans, 1963
A Commentary on Genesis. London: Banner of Truth, 1965
The Epistles of Paul to the Galatians, Ephesians, Philippians and Colossians. Edinburgh: St. Andrew's Press, 1965
John Calvin's Sermons on Ephesians. Edinburgh: Banner of Truth, 1973
Sermons on Deuteronomy. Edinburgh: Banner of Truth, 1987
A Commentary on Jeremiah. Edinburgh: Banner of Truth, 1989
Sermons on Jeremiah by Jean Calvin. Lampeter: Edwin Mellen Press, 1990
Sermons on Job. Edinburgh: Banner of Truth, 1993

Camfield, B. *A Serious Examination of the Independent's Catechism*. London, 1668

Carlyle, T. ed. *The Letters and Speeches of Oliver Cromwell*. Vol. III. London: Methuen, 1904

Carter, T. *Non-Conformists No Schismaticks, No Rebels*. London, 1670

Caryl, J. *The Saints Thankful Acclamation*. London, 1644
The Present Duty and Endeavour of the Saints. London, 1645
A Sermon Preached upon Revel. 3 Ver 4. London, 1662

Chamberlayne, E. *Angliæ Novitiæ: or The Present State of England*. London, 1674

Charles I, *The Kings Cabinet Opened*. London, 1645
His Speech Made Upon the Scaffold. London, 1649

Charles II, *His Majesties Gracious Speech to Both Houses of Parliament*. London, 1660

Cheynell, F. *The Rise, Growth and Danger of Socinianisme*. London, 1643

Clarkson, D. *A Discourse of the Saving Grace of God*. London, 1688

Corbett, J. *An enquiry into the oath required of non-conformists by an Act made at Oxford, wherein the true meaning of it, and the warrantableness of taking it, is considered*. London, 1682

Crispe, T. *Christ alone exalted*. London, 1644

Crook, S. *The Guide unto True Blessedness; or, A Body of the Doctrine of the Scriptures, Directing Man to the saving Knowledg [sic] of God*. London, 1650

Davenant, J. *Animadversions on a Treatise entitled Gods Love to Mankind*. Cambridge, 1641

Digges, D. *The Unlawfulnesse of Subjects taking up Arms*. London, 1643

Ellwood, T. *A Discourse Concerning Riots*. London, 1683

Falkner, W. *Christian Loyalty*. London, 1679

Fenner, W. *A Treatise of the Affections*. London, 1642
Hidden Manna. London, 1652

Gataker, T. *Antinomianism Discovered and Confuted: And Free-Grace As it is held forth in Gods Word*. London, 1652

Giffard, F. *The Wicked Petition, or Israels Sinfulness in Asking a King.* London, 1681

Glanvill, J. *A Loyal Tear Dropt on the Vault.* London, 1667

Goodwin, J. *Redemption Redeemed.* London, 1657

Goodwin, T. *The Vanity of Thoughts Discovered: With their Danger and Cure.* London, 1643

Gower, S. *Things Now-a-Doing.* London, 1644

Green, W. *Abyssus Mali: or, the Corruption of Man's Nature.* London, 1676

Harrington, J. *Oceana.* Cambridge: CUP, 1992

Hartlib, S. *Clavis Apocaliptica.* London, 1651

Hill, T. *The Season for Englands Selfe-Reflection, And Advancing Temple-Work.* London, 1644

Hoard, S. *The Souls Misery and Recovery.* London, 1658

Hobbes, T. *Leviathan.* Cambridge: CUP, 1991

Humfrey, J. *The Obligations of Human Laws Discussed.* London, 1671
    Peaceable Disquisitions On a Discourse writ against Dr. Owen's Book of the Holy Spirit. London, 1678

Iamblichus, *The Exhortation to Philosophy.* Grand Rapids, Michigan: Phanes Press, 1988

Jenkins, D. *Lex Terrae.* London, 1647

Jones, T. *Of the Heart. And its Right Soveraign: And Rome no Mother- Church to England.* London, 1678

King, D. *Self, the Grand Enemy of Christ.* London, 1660

Lane, S. *A Vindication of free Grace, in Opposition to an Arminian Position of John Goodwin.* London, 1645

Laud, W. *The Archbishop of Canterbury's Speech: or, His Funeral Sermon, preached by himself.* London, 1644

L'Evesque de Burigny, J. *The Life of the truly Eminent and Learned Hugo Grotius.* London, 1754

Lilly, W. *The Starry Messenger.* London, 1645

Lloyd, W. *A Seasonable Discourse Shewing the Necessity of Maintaining the Established Religion, In opposition to Popery.* London, 1673

Love, C. *Englands Distemper, having Division and Error, as its Cause.* London, 1645

Marshall, S. *A Sacred Record to be made of Gods Mercies to Zion.* London, 1645

Martyr, Justin *On the Resurrection, Fragments.* in "Ante-Nicene Fathers vol.1", Edinburgh: T & T Clark, 1989

Ministers of London, *A Seasonable Exhortation of Sundry Ministers of London to the People of their Respective Congregations.* London, 1660

Morton, T. *The Threefold State of Man.* London, 1613

Osborn, F. *A Perswasive to a Mutuall Compliance under the Present Government.* London, 1652

Overton, R. *Mans Mortalitie.* Amsterdam, 1644

Owen, J. *The Works of John Owen, DD.* ed. W.H. Goold, 24 vols. London, 1850-53
    The Correspondence of John Owen. ed. P. Toon, Cambridge: James Clarke & Co., 1970

Perkins, W. *The Work of William Perkins.* ed. I. Breward, Appleford: The Sutton Courtenay Press, 1970

Perrinchief, R. *Indulgence not Justified.* London, 1668

Perrot, R. *The Scriptures Stability. Or, The Scripture cannot be Broken.* London, 1658

Pierce, T. *The Signal Diagnostick Whereby We are to judge of our own Affections.* London, 1670

Plato, *The Apology.* in "The Last Days of Socrates", London: Penguin, 1954

240

Redeem the Time

Crito. in "The Last Days of Socrates" London: Penguin, 1954

Euthyphro. in "The Last Days of Socrates", London: Penguin, 1954

Phaedo. in "The Last Days of Socrates", London: Penguin, 1954

The Republic. London: Penguin, 1955

Thaetetus. Indianapolis: Hackett, 1992

Euthydemus. Indianapolis: Hackett, 1993

Plotinus, *The Enneads*. London: Penguin, 1991

Prynne, W. *The Popish Royal Favourite*. London, 1643

A looking-glasse for all lordly prelates. London, 1636

A Moderate Apology. London, 1644

A Gagge for Long-hair'd Rattleheads. London, 1646

Canterburies Doome. London, 1646

Reeve, T. *Englands Beauty in seeing Charles the Second Restored in Majesty*. London, 1661

A Dead Man Speaking, or the Famous Memory of King Charles I. London, 1661

Resbury, R. *Some stop to the Gangrene of Arminianism, Lately promoted by M. John Goodwin in his Book entituled Redemption Redeemed*. London, 1651

The Lightless-Starre: or, Mr. John Goodwin discovered a Pelagio-Socinian. London, 1651

Reyner, W. *Babylons Ruining-Earthquake and the Restauration of Zion*. London, 1644

Roborough, H. *The Doctrine of Justification cleared and vindicated from Arminian, Socinian, and Popish Errors*. London, 1650

Rowe, J. *The Saints Temptations*. London, 1675

Rutherford, S. *The Covenant of Life Opened*. Edinburgh, 1655

Sibbes, R. *The Souls Conflict with It selfe and Victory over It selfe by Faith*. London, 1658

Strong, W. *A Treatise Shewing the Subordination of the Will of Man Unto the Will of God*. London, 1657

Symmons, E. *A Vindication of King Charles*. n.p., 1648

Teate, F. *A Scripture-Map of the Wilderness of Sin, and way to Canaan. Or the Sinners Way to the Saints Rest*. London, 1655

Tertullian, *A Treatise On the Soul*. in "Ante-Nicene Fathers, vol.3" Edinburgh: T & T Clark, 1989

On the Resurrection of the Flesh. in "Ante-Nicene Fathers vol.3" Edinburgh: T & T Clark, 1989

Tickell, J. *A Sober Enquiry About the New Oath Enjoyned on Non-Conformists According to Act of Parliament*. Oxford, 1665

Tomkins, T. *The Inconveniences of Toleration*. London, 1667

Tuckney, A. *The Balme of Gilead for the Wounds of England*. London, 1643

Twisse, W. *The Riches of Gods Love unto the Vessells of Mercy, Consistent with His Absolute Hatred or Reprobation of the Vessells of Wrath*. Oxford, 1653

Tyndale, W. *The Parable of the Wicked Mammon*. 1527 in *Writings of Tindal, Frith, and Barnes*. London: Religious Tract Society, n.d.

Unknown, *The Charge of the Commons of England*. London, 1649

Various, *A Declaration of the Faith and Order Owned and practised in the Congregational Churches in England*. London, 1658

Venning, R. *The Sinfulness of Sin*. Edinburgh: Banner of Truth, 1965

Wall, T. *A Comment on the Times*. London, 1657

God's Revenge Against the Enemies of the Church. London, 1658

Watson, T. *A Body of Divinity*. Edinburgh: Banner of Truth, 1958

The Lord's Prayer. Edinburgh: Banner of Truth, 1960
The Beatitudes. Edinburgh: Banner of Truth, 1971
Whitefeild T. *The Doctrines of the Arminians & Pelagians Truly stated and clearly Answered*. London, 1652
Wild, R. *Oliver Cromwells Ghost: or Old Noll Newly Revived*. London, 1679
Wilkinson, H. *Babylons Ruine, Jerusalems Rising*. London, 1643
Wood, A. *Athenae Oxonienses*. ed. P. Bliss, 4 vols., Oxford, 1813-18
Woodhouse, J. *A Catalogue of Sins*. London, 1699
Young, S. *An Apology for Congregational Divines*. London, 1698
A New-Year's Gift for the Antinomians. London, 1699

2. SECONDARY SOURCES

Allan, D.J. *The Philosophy of Aristotle*. Oxford: OUP, 1952
Armstrong, A. ed. *The Cambridge History of Later Greek and Early Medieval Philosophy*. Cambridge: CUP, 1967
Ashley, M. *England in the Seventeenth Century (1603-1714)* Harmondsworth: Penguin, c.1961
Aylmer, G. *The Interregnum: The Quest for Settlement 1646-1660*. London and New York: MacMillan, 1972
Ball, B.W. *A Great Expectation: Eschatological Thought in English Protestantism to 1660*. Leiden: E.J. Brill, 1975
The English Connection. The Puritan Roots of Seventh-day Adventist Belief. Cambridge: James Clarke, 1981
Bangs, C. *Arminius - A Study in the Dutch Reformation*. Grand Rapids, Michigan: Francis Asbury Press, 1985
Barnes, J. *Aristotle*. Oxford: OUP, 1982
Barth, K. *Church Dogmatics vols. 1.1 - 4.4*. Edinburgh: T & T Clark, 1960
Baskerville, S. *Not Peace But a Sword*. London: Routledge, 1993
Beeke, J.R. *Assurance of Faith*. New York: Peter Lang, 1991
Berkouwer, G.C. *Faith and Justification*. Grand Rapids, Michigan: Eerdmans, 1954
Bethune-Baker, J. *The Early History of Christian Doctrine*. London: Methuen, 1903
Bourke, V.J. *The Essential Augustine*. London: Mentor, 1964
Boyer, R. ed. *Oliver Cromwell and the Puritan Revolt*. Boston: Heath, 1966
Brailsford, H.N. *The Levellers and the English Revolution*. Nottingham: Spokesman, 1983
Braithwaite, W.C. *The Beginnings of Quakerism*. London: MacMillan, 1912
The Second Period of Quakerism. London: MacMillan, 1919
Bratt, J.H. *The Heritage of John Calvin*. Grand Rapids, Michigan: Eerdmans, 1973
Bremer, F.J. *The Puritan Experiment*. Hanover: University Press of New England, 1995
Brown, P. *Augustine of Hippo – a Biography*. London: Faber, 1967
Burrell, D. *Aquinas – God and Action*. London: Routledge, Kegan and Paul, 1979
Campbell, I.D. *The Doctrine of Sin*. Fearn: Mentor, 1999
Capp, B.S. *The Fifth Monarchy Men*. New Jersey: Rowman & Littlefield, 1972
Carey, G. *I Believe in Man*. London: Hodder and Stoughton, 1977
Chadwick, H. *Augustine*. Oxford: Clarendon, 1991
Christianson, P. *Reformers and Babylon*. Toronto: University of Toronto,1978
Cliffe, J.T. *The Puritan Gentry*. London: Routledge, 1984
Clifford, A. *Atonement and Justification*. Oxford: Clarendon, 1990
Collinson, P. *The Elizabethan Puritan Movement*. Oxford: Clarendon, 1990
Coolidge, J.S. *The Pauline Renaissance in England*. Oxford: Clarendon, 1970
Copleston, F. *History of Philosophy vol.1*. London: Bellarmine, 1946

History of Philosophy vol. 2. London: Bellarmine, 1950

Aquinas. Harmondsworth: Penguin, 1955

History of Philosophy vol. 5. London: Bellarmine, 1959

A History of Medieval Philosophy. London: Bellarmine, 1972

Corns, T.N. and Loewenstein, D. eds. *The Emergence of Quaker Writing: Dissenting Literature in Seventeenth-Century England*. London: Frank Cass, 1995

Cragg, G.R. ed. *The Church and the Age of Reason 1648-1789*. Harmondsworth: Penguin, 1960

The Cambridge Platonists. Oxford: OUP, 1968

Davie, M. *British Quaker Theology since 1895*. Lampeter: Edwin Mellen Press, 1997

Davies, B. *The Thought of Thomas Aquinas*. Oxford: Clarendon, 1992

Davies, G. *The Restoration of Charles II, 1658-1660*. Oxford: OUP, 1955

Dickinson, G.L. *Plato and His Dialogues*. Edinburgh: Penguin, 1931

Dillon, J. *The Middle Platonists*. London: Duckworth, 1977

Donnelly, J. *Calvinism and Scholasticism in Vermigli's Doctrine of Man*. Leiden: E.J. Brill, 1976

Doran, S. and Durston, C. *Princes, Pastors and People*. London: Routledge, 1991.

Evans, G.R. *Augustine On Evil*. Cambridge: CUP, 1982

Feibleman, J.K. *Religious Platonism*. London: Greenwood, 1959

Ferguson, S. *John Owen on the Christian Life*. Edinburgh: Banner of Truth, 1987

Fox, A. *Plato and the Christians*. London: SCM, 1957

Fraser, A. *Cromwell our Chief of Men*. London: Weidenfield and Nicolson, 1973

Gamble, R. ed. *An Elaboration of the Theology of Calvin*. New York: Garland, 1992

Gilson, E. *History of Christian Philosophy in the Middle Ages*. London: Sheed and Ward, 1955

The Christian Philosophy of St. Thomas Aquinas. London: Victor Gollancz, 1957

The Christian Philosophy of Saint Augustine. London: Victor Gollancz, 1961

St. Thomas Aquinas. London: Victor Gollancz, 1961

Gleason, R.C. *John Calvin and John Owen on Mortification*. New York: Peter Lang, 1995

Greaves, R. *Deliver Us from Evil*. New York: OUP, 1986

Enemies Under His Feet. Stanford: SUP, 1990

Gregory, J. *The Neoplatonists*. London: Kyle Cathie, 1991

Gunary, M. *The Story of Fordham*. Colchester, 1954 n.p.

Hare, R.M. *Plato*. Oxford: OUP, 1991

Harris, E. *Man's Ontological Predicament*. Uppsala: Academia Upsaliensis, 1984

Harrison, A. *Arminianism*. London: Duckworth, 1937

Hayes, C.J.H. *The Historical Evolution of Modern Nationalism*. New York: MacMillan, 1931

Helm, P. *Calvin and the Calvinists*. Edinburgh: Banner of Truth, 1982.

Hendriksen, W. *Matthew*. Edinburgh: Banner of Truth, 1973

Hick, J. *Evil and the God of Love*. London: MacMillan, 1966

Hill, C. *Society and Puritanism in Pre-Revolutionary England*. London: Panther, 1969

Intellectual Origins of the English Revolution. Oxford: Clarendon, 1965

Puritanism and Revolution. London: Secker & Warburg, 1965

God's Englishman. London: Weidenfeld and Nicolson, 1970

Change and Continuity in Seventeenth Century England. London : Weidenfeld & Nicolson, 1974

The Century of Revolution 1603-1714. London: Routledge, 1980

The Experience of Defeat. London: Faber and Faber, 1984

Antichrist in Seventeenth-Century England. London: Verso, 1990
    The World Turned Upside Down. London: Penguin, 1991
Hill, C. & Dell, E., *The Good Old Cause*. London: Frank Cass, 1969
Hill, C., Reay, B and Lamont, W. *The World of the Muggletonians*. London: Temple Smith, 1983
Hoekema, A. *Created in God's Image*. Grand Rapids, Michigan: Eerdmans, 1986
Holmes, G. *The Making of a Great Power*. London: Longman, 1993
Hopfl, H. *The Christian Polity of John Calvin*. Cambridge: Cambridge University Press, 1982
Horrocks, J.W. *A Short History of Mercantilism*. London: Methuen & Co. Ltd., 1925
Hubbard, G. *Quaker by Convincement*. Harmondsworth: Penguin, 1974
Hutton, R. *The Restoration*. Oxford: Clarendon, 1985
Inge, W.R. *Christian Mysticism*. London: Methuen, 1913
    The Philosophy of Plotinus vol 1. London: Longmans, 1929
    The Philosophy of Plotinus vol 2. London: Longmans, 1929
Jensen, P. *Using the Shield of Faith: Puritan Attitudes to Combat with Satan*. St. Antolin's Lectureship Charity, November 1995
Johnston, W. *The Mystical Way*. London: Harper Collins, 1993
Jones, J.R. ed. *The Restored Monarchy 1660-1688*. London: MacMillan, 1979
    Charles II: Royal Politician. London: Allen & Unwin, 1987
Jones, R.T. *Congregationalism in England 1662-1692*. Independent Press: London, 1962
Katz, D.S. *Philo-Semitism and the Readmission of the Jews to England 1603-1655*. Oxford: Clarendon, 1982
Kelly, J.N.D. *Early Christian Doctrines*. London: A & C Black, 1958
Kendall, R.T. *Calvin and English Calvinism to 1649*. Oxford: OUP, 1979
Kenny, A. *Reason and Religion - Essays in Philosophical Theology*. Oxford: Blackwell, 1987
    Aquinas on Mind. London: Routledge, 1993
Kenyon, J.P. ed. *The Stuart Constitution 1603-1688*. Cambridge: CUP, 1986
Kevan, E.F. *The Grace of Law*. London: Carey Kingsgate, 1964
Kistler, D. ed. *Justification by Faith Alone*. Morgan: Soli Deo Gloria, 1995
Knappen, M.M. *Tudor Puritanism*. Chicago and London: University of Chicago Press, 1939
Kyle, R. *Awaiting the Millennium*. Leicester: IVP, 1998
Lamont, W. *Richard Baxter and the Millennium: Protestant Imperialism and the English Revolution*. London: Croom Helm,1979
Lewis, P. *The Genius of Puritanism*. Sussex: Carey 1975
Lewis, P. *All Saints Church Fordham – A Guide*. Fordham, 1984 n.p.
Lindsay, T.M. *History of the Reformation vol. 2*. Edinburgh: T & T Clark, 1908
Liu, T. *Discord in Zion: The Puritan Divines and the Puritan Revolution 1640-1660*. The Hague: Martinus Nijhoff, 1973
Lloyd-Jones, D.M. *The Puritans: Their Origins and Successors*. Edinburgh: Banner of Truth, 1987
Louth, A. ed. *Early Christian Writings*. London: Penguin, 1968
MacPherson, C.B. *The Political Theory of Possessive Individualism: Hobbes to Locke*. Oxford: OUP, 1962
Manning, B. *Politics, Religion and the English Civil War*. London: Edward Arnold, 1973
Martin, H. *Puritanism and Richard Baxter*. London: SCM, 1954
Matthews, A. *Calamy Revised*. Oxford: Clarendon, 1934
Matthews, A.G. ed. *The Savoy Declaration of Faith and Order 1658*. Letchworth:

Independent Press Ltd., 1959

McGregor, J.F. & Reay, B (eds.), *Radical Religion in the English Revolution.* Oxford: OUP, 1984

McKim, D.K. ed. *Major Themes in the Reformed Tradition.* Grand Rapids, Michigan: William B. Eerdmans, 1992

McLachlan, H. *Socinianism in Seventeenth-Century England.* London: OUP, 1951

Melling, D.J. *Understanding Plato.* Oxford: OUP, 1987

Merton, R.K. *Science, Technology & Society in Seventeenth Century England.* New York: H. Fertig, 1970

Miller, J. *Popery and Politics in England 1660-1688.* Cambridge: CUP, 1973

Morant, P. *The History and Antiquities of the County of Essex, vol. II.* London, 1768

Moravcsik, J. ed. *Aristotle.* London: MacMillan, 1968

Morgan, J. *The Psychological Teaching of St. Augustine.* London: Elliot Stock n.d.

Moxon, R.S. *The Doctrine of Sin.* London : Allen & Unwin, 1922

Muller, R.A. *Christ and the Decree: Christology and Predestination in Reformed Theology from Calvin to Perkins.* Grand Rapids, Michigan: Baker Book House, 1986
   Post-Reformation Dogmatics. 2 vols. Grand Rapids, Michigan: Baker Book House, 1993

Murray, I.H., *The Puritan Hope.* Edinburgh: Banner of Truth, 1971

Niesel, W. *The Theology of Calvin.* London: Lutterworth, 1956

Nuttall, G.F. *Visible Saints 1640-60.* Oxford: Blackwell, 1957
   Richard Baxter. London: Nelson, 1965
   The Puritan Spirit. London: Epworth, 1967

Oberman, H.A. *The Dawn of the Reformation.* Edinburgh: T & T Clark, 1992

O'Brien, E. *The Essential Plotinus.* Indianapolis: Hackett, 1964

Packer, J.I. *Among God's Giants.* Eastbourne: Kingsway, 1991

Packer, J.W. *The Transformation of Anglicanism 1643-1660.* Manchester: MUP, 1969

Partee, C. *Calvin and Classical Philosophy.* Leiden: E.J. Brill, 1977

Patrides, C.A. *The Cambridge Platonists.* Cambridge: CUP, 1969

Pennington, D. and Thomas, K. eds. *Puritans and Revolutionaries - Essays in Seventeenth-Century History Presented to Christopher Hill.* Oxford: Clarendon, 1978

Pettit, N. *The Heart Prepared: Grace and Conversion in Puritan Spiritual Life.* New Haven: Yale University Press, 1966

Popkin, R.J. ed. *Millenarianism and Messianism in English Literature and Thought 1650-1800.* Leiden: E.J. Brill, 1988

Portalie, E. *A Guide to the Thought of St. Augustine.* London: Burns & Oates, 1960

Porter, H.C. ed. *Puritanism in Tudor England.* London and Basingstoke: MacMillan, 1970

Powell, H.T. *The Fall of Man.* London: SPCK, 1934

Powicke, F.J. *The Cambridge Platonists.* London: J.M. Dent, 1926

Preus, M.C. *Eloquence and Ignorance in Augustine's 'On the Nature and Origin of the Soul'.* Scholars Press, 1985 n.p.

Raitt, J. ed. *Shapers of Religious Traditions in Germany, Switzerland and Poland, 1560-1600.* New Haven and London: Yale University Press, 1981

Ricoeur, P. *The Conflict of Interpretations.* Evanston: NUP, 1974

Rist, J.M. *Plotinus – the Road to Reality.* Cambridge: CUP, 1967

Rowe, T. *St. Augustine – Pastoral Theologian.* London : Epworth, 1974

Russell, C. ed. *The Origins of the English Civil War.* Basingstoke: MacMillan 1973
   The Causes of the English Civil War. Oxford: Clarendon, 1990

Schneider, H. *The Puritan Mind.* Michigan: Ann Arbor, 1958

Bibliography 245

Seaward, P. *The Cavalier Parliament and the Reconstruction of the Old Regime, 1661-1667.* Cambridge: CUP, 1989

Shaw, W.A. *A History of the English Church During the Civil Wars and under the Commonwealth.* London, 1900

Smeaton, G. *The Doctrine of the Holy Spirit.* London: Banner of Truth, 1958

Smith, A. *The Emergence of a Nation State: The Commonwealth of England 1529-1660.* London: Longman, 1984

Solt, L.F. *Saints in Arms.* London: OUP, 1959

Stephens, W. *The Holy Spirit in the Theology of Martin Bucer.* London: CUP, 1970

Stone, L. *The Causes of the English Revolution 1529-1642.* London: Routledge & Kegan Paul, 1972

Sullivan, J.E. *The Image of God: The Doctrine of St. Augustine and its Influence.* Dubuque, Iowa: The Priory Press, 1963

Tamburello, D.E. *Union with Christ - John Calvin and the Mysticism of St. Bernard.* Westminster: John Knox, 1994

Thomas, K. *Religion and the Decline of Magic.* London: Peregrine, 1978

Thompson, A. *John Owen – Prince of the Puritans.* Fearn: Christian Focus, 1996

Todd. M. *Christian Humanism and the Puritan Social Order.* Cambridge: CUP, 1987

Tomlinson, H. & Greeg, D. *Politics, Religion and Society in Revolutionary England, 1640-60.* London: MacMillan, 1989

Toon, P. *The Emergence of Hyper-Calvinism in English Nonconformity, 1689-1765.* London: Olive Tree, 1967

  ed, *Puritans, the Millennium and the Future of Israel.* Cambridge: James Clarke, 1970

  God's Statesman – The Life and Work of John Owen. Exeter: Paternoster, 1971

  Puritans and Calvinism. Swengel, Pennsylvania: Reiner Publications, 1973

Torrance, T. *Calvin's Doctrine of Man.* London: Lutterworth, 1949

Trinterud, L.J. ed. *Elizabethan Puritanism.* New York: OUP, 1971

Trueman, C.R. *Luther's Legacy: Salvation and the English Reformers 1525-1556.* Oxford: Clarendon, 1994

  The Claims of Truth. Carlisle: Paternoster, 1998

Tyacke, N. *Anti-Calvinists – The Rise of English Arminianism c.1590-1640.* Oxford: Clarendon, 1987

Underdown, D. *Pride's Purge.* Oxford: Clarendon, 1971

Underwood, T.L. *Primitivism, Radicalism, and the Lamb's War.* Oxford: OUP, 1997

Wakefield, G. *Puritan Devotion. Its Place in the Development of Christian Piety.* London: Epworth, 1957

  Bunyan the Christian. London: Harper Collins, 1992

Wallace, D.D. *Puritans and Predestination: Grace in English Protestant Theology 1525-1695.* Chapel Hill: University of North Carolina, 1982

Wallace, R.S. *Calvin's Doctrine of the Christian Life.* Edinburgh: Oliver and Boyd, 1959

Wallis, R.T., *Neoplatonism.* London: Duckworth, 1972

Walzer, M. *The Revolution of the Saints.* New York: Atheneum, 1972

Watkins, D. *The Puritan Experience.* London: Routledge Kegan & Paul, 1972

Watts, M. *The Dissenters* Vol. 1. Oxford: Clarendon, 1978

Wendel, F. *Calvin: the Origins and Development of his Religious Thought.* London: Collins, 1963

Western, J. *Monarchy and Revolution.* London: Blandford, 1972

Westfall, R.S. *Science and Religion in Seventeenth-Century England.* New Haven and London: Yale University Press, 1958

Wilbur, E.M. *A History of Unitarianism*. Cambridge, Massachusetts: Harvard
    University Press, 1946
Williams, N.P. *The Ideas of the Fall and of Original Sin*. London: Longmans, 1927
Wink, W. *Naming the Powers*. Philadelphia: Fortress, 1984
    Unmasking the Powers. Philadelphia, Fortress, 1986
    Engaging the Powers. Philadelphia: Fortress, 1992
Wood, A. Harold, *Church Unity Without Uniformity*. London: Epworth, 1963
Wright, C.J. *The People of God and the State: An Old Testament Perspective*. Nottingham:
    Grove, 1990
Zagorin, P. *A History of Political Thought in the English Revolution*. London: Routledge
    Kegan and Paul, 1954

3. PUBLISHED ARTICLES

Babcock, W. "Augustine on Sin and Moral Agency." *Journal of Religious Ethics* (Spring
    1988) 28-55
Barbour, H. "Ranters, Diggers and Quakers Reborn." *Quaker History* 6 (Spring 1975)
    60-65
Bierma, L. D. "Federal Theology in the Sixteenth Century: Two Traditions?" *Westminster
    Theological Journal* 45 (1983) 304-321
Bloesch, D.G. "Law and Gospel in Reformed Perspective." *Grace Theological Journal*
    V12 #2:179-188 - Fall 91
Boughton, L. "Supralapsarianism and the Role of Metaphysics in Sixteenth-Century
    Reformed Theology." *Westminster Theological Journal* 48 (1986) 63-96
Brauer, J.C. "Reflections on the Nature of English Puritanism." *Church History* 23 (1954),
    99-108
Brown, R. F. "The First Evil Will Must be Incomprehensible: A Critique of Augustine."
    Journal of the American Academy (Sep. 1978) 315-329
Burns, J.P. "Augustine on the Origin and Progress of Evil." *Journal of Religious Ethics*
    (Spring 1988) 18-27
Clowney, E. "The Politics of the Kingdom." *Westminster Theological Journal* 41 (1978-
    79): 291-310
Elmen, P. "The Theological Basis of Digger Communism." *Church History* 23 (Sep.
    1954): 207-218
Gamble, R. C. "Brevitas et Facilitas: Toward an Understanding of Calvin's Hermeneutic."
    Westminster Theological Journal 47 (1985) 1-17
    "Exposition and Method in Calvin." *Westminster Theological Journal* 49 (1987)
    153-165
Godfrey, W. "Reformed Thought on the Extent of the Atonement to 1618." *Westminster
    Theological Journal* 37 (1974) 133-171
Greenhough, G. H. "The Reformers' Attitude to the Law of God." *Westminster
    Theological Journal* 39 (1976) 81-99
Harper, G. W. "'Calvin and English Calvinism to 1649': A Review Article." *Calvin
    Theological Journal* 20 (1985): 255-262
Helm, P. "'Calvin, English Calvinism and the Logic of Doctrinal Development." *Scottish
    Journal of Theology* 34 (1981): 179-185
Hicks, J.M. "The Righteousness of Saving Faith: Arminian versus Remonstrant Grace."
    Evangelical Journal 9 (Spring 1991): 27-39
Ingle, H.L. "From Mysticism to Radicalism: Recent Historiography of Quaker
    Beginnings." *Quaker History* 76 (Fall 1987) 79-94
Johnston, O.R. "Growth in Grace in Puritan Theology." *Evangelical Quarterly* 25 (July
    1953) 131-141

Jones, R. T. "Union with Christ: the existential nerve of Puritan piety." *Tyndale Bulletin* 41 (Nov.1990) 186-208

Klauber, M. I. "Continuity and Discontinuity in Post-Reformed Theology – an evaluation of the Muller thesis." *Journal of the Evangelical Theological Society* 33 (1990): 467-475

"Reason, revelation, and Cartesianism: Louis Tronchin and Enlightened Orthodoxy in Late Seventeenth-Century Geneva." *Church History* 59 (1990)

"Between Protestant Orthodoxy and Rationalism: Fundamental Articles in the Early Career of Jean LeClerc." *Journal of the History of Ideas* (1993) 611-636

Kline, M. G. "Law Covenant." *Westminster Theological Journal* 27 (1964) 1-20

Mayor, S. "The Teaching of John Owen Concerning the Lord's Supper." *Scottish Journal of Theology* (1965): 170-181

McKim, D. K. "John Owen's Doctrine of Scripture in Historical Perspective." *Evangelical Quarterly* 45:4 (1973): 195-207

Miles, M.R. "Theology, Anthropology and the Human Body in Calvin's 'Institutes of the Christian Religion'." *Harvard Theological Review* (July 1981)

Moo, D. "'Law,' 'Works of Law,' and Legalism in Paul." *Westminster Theological Journal* 45 (1983) 73-100

Muller, R. "Covenant and Conscience in English Reformed Theology: Three Variations on a 17th Century Theme." *Westminster Theological Journal* 42 (1980): 308-334

"'Vera philosophia cum sacra theologia nusquam pugnat': Keckerman on Philosophy, Theology and the Problem of Double Truth." *Sixteenth-Century Journal* 15 (1984): 341-365

"The Priority of the Intellect in the Soteriology of Jacob Arminius." *Westminster Theological Journal* 55 (1993): 55-72

Nicole, R. "John Calvin's View of the Extent of the Atonement." *Westminster Theological Journal* 47 (1985) 197-225

Payne, G. R. "Augustinianism in Calvin and Bonadventure." *Westminster Theological Journal* 44 (1982) 1-30

Probes, C.M. "Calvin on Astrology." *Westminster Theological Journal* 37 (1974-75): 24-33

Reid, W.S. "Justification by Faith According to John Calvin." *Westminster Theological Journal* 42 (1979-80): 290-307

"Review of Kendall 'Calvin and English Calvinism to 1649'." *Westminster Theological Journal* 42 (1980): 155-164

Robertson, O. P. "Current Reformed Thinking on the Nature of the Divine Covenants." *Westminster Theological Journal* 40 (1977) 63-76

Scheffler, J. "Prison Writings of Early Quaker Women: 'We Were Stronger Than Before'." *Quaker History* 73 (Fall 1984) 25-37

Shaw, M. R. "Drama in the Meeting House: The Concept of Conversion in the Theology of William Perkins." *Westminster Theological Journal* 45 (1983) 41-72

Simpson, A. "Saints in Arms: English Puritanism as Political Utopianism." *Church History* 23 (June 1954) 119-125

Smith C. R. "'Up and be doing': The Pragmatic Puritan Eschatology of John Owen." *Evangelical Quarterly* 61:4 (Oct. 1989)

Solt, L.F. "Anti-Intellectualism in the Puritan Revolt." *Church History* 25 (Dec. 1956): 306-316

Spence, A. "John Owen and Trinitarian Agency." *Scottish Journal of Theology* 43 (1990) 157-173

Taylor, T.F. "Richard Farnworth and Thomas Atkinson: The Earliest Quaker Writings on Sacred Music." *Quaker History* 75 (Fall 1986) 83-101

Tipson, B. "A Dark Side of English Protestantism: The Sin Against The Holy Spirit." *Harvard Theological Review* 77:3-4 (1984) 301-330

Trinterud. L.J. "The Origins of Puritanism." *Church History* 20 (1951) 37-57

Wells, P. "Covenant, Humanity and Scripture: Some Theological Reflections." *Westminster Theological Journal* 48 (1986) 17-45

Young, W. "Historic Calvinism and Neo-Calvinism." *Westminster Theological Journal* 36 (1973) 48-64 and 156-173

4. UNPUBLISHED THESIS

Rolston III, H. "The Understanding of Sin and Responsibility in the teaching of John Calvin." PhD. Edinburgh (1958)

5. ARTICLES AND EXTRACTS FROM THE INTERNET

Baxter, R. *Richard Baxter and the Army.* website 'Richard Baxter Society'

Godfrey, W.R. *Who was Arminius?* website 'Alliance of Confessing Evangelicals'

Origen, *Commentary on St. Matthew* www.newadvent.org/fathers

Sibbes, R. *Extracts from "A Description of Christ"* www.puritansermons.com

Watson, T. *Mystic Union between Christ and the Saints* www.puritansermons.com

6. MISCELLANEOUS SOURCES

Blackman, M. *Walton & Weybridge Local History Society Paper no. 28 - A Short History of Walton-On-Thames*, n.d., n.p.

Chambers Encyclopaedia. London: International Learning Systems Corporation Limited, 1973

The Civil War 1642-51. A Pitkin Guide. Andover: Pitkin Unichrome Ltd., 1993

Dictionary of National Biography. OUP, 1995, CD-Rom.

Parish Registers for All Saints, Fordham 1643-1646. Essex County Council Public Records Office, microfiche D/P 372/1/1

Parish Registers for St. Peter's, Coggeshall 1646-1652. Essex County Council Public Records Office, microfiche D/P 36/1/1

The Catalogue containing the Library of the Reverend and Learned Dr. JOHN OWEN, deceased. *Published prior to the sale on Monday 26th May, 1684 at the Auction-House in Ave-Mary-Lane, London.*

The New Schaff-Herzog Encyclopaedia of Religious Knowledge. New York and London: Funk and Wagnells, 1909

NOTES

Introduction

1. Peter Toon is notable in this regard for his biography of Owen, entitled *God's Statesman – The Life and Work of John Owen* (Exeter: Paternoster, 1971). However, other notable works, which will be mentioned in this book, are the following: J.I. Packer, *Among God's Giants* (Eastbourne: Kingsway, 1991), C. Trueman, *The Claims of Truth* (Carlisle: Paternoster, 1998), S. Ferguson, *John Owen on the Christian Life* (Edinburgh: Banner of Truth, 1987), A. Clifford, *Atonement and Justification* (Oxford: Clarendon Press, 1990) and R. Gleason, *John Calvin and John Owen on Mortification* (New York: Peter Lang, 1995). Some of these have made a good contribution to Owenian research whilst others, arguably, have rather muddied the waters. Adequate critique will be given to the views of these authors in the main body of the book.

2. The following is only a brief biographical outline, as all the events mentioned will be considered more fully in later chapters.

3. Stadham is now known as Stadhampton, a small village five miles from Oxford.

4. *The Correspondence of John Owen (1616-1683),* ed. P. Toon (Cambridge: James Clarke & Co. Ltd., 1970), p.14.

5. Mary and Roger Kynaston are mentioned as beneficiaries in Owen's Will. *The Correspondence of John Owen*, p.181.

6. Judith died whilst the Owen family were living in Stoke Newington in the mid-1660s. *The Correspondence of John Owen*, p.125.

7. Mathew died in April 1665. Reference to his love of melons is made in a letter Owen wrote to John Thornton: 'Our musk melons are ripe, witnes that I have sent you, I would have sent more but you know Mathew.' *The Correspondence of John Owen*, p.135.

8. Toon, *God's Statesman*, p.63. The letter is recorded in *The Report of the Manuscripts of the Earl of Egmont*, 1905, I, Pt. II, p.576.

9. The baptism of John, as Toon states, is recorded as December 20th 1644. It would appear that he died in the Spring of 1649 (Essex County Records Office, Microfiche D/P 372/1/1). Owen's first daughter was Mary. She was buried 18th July 1647. Another daughter, Elizah, was buried in August 1647. Thomas was buried in March (1648?) and Elizabeth was baptised on February 10th 1650. (Essex County Records Office, Microfiche D/P 36/1/1). Naturally, the condition of these

documents has deteriorated over the years but the information above is believed to be accurate.

10. The sermon was later published as *A Vision of Unchangeable Free Mercy, In Sending the Means of Grace to Undeserving Sinners*, VIII.1ff.

11. His views were published in *Eshcol; A Cluster of the Fruit of Canaan* (1647) XIII.51ff.

12. Owen, *The Death of Death in the Death of Christ*, X.139ff.

13. Owen, *A Vindication of the Animadversions on "Fiat Lux"*, XIV.190.

14. The invitation came in a letter from John Endecott, Governor of New England colony, dated 20th October 1663, *The Correspondence of John Owen*, No. 71, p.135f.

15. In January 1664, Owen was unsuccessful in his attempts to persuade Thomas Gilbert to leave St. Ebbe's, Oxford and take the Presidency of Harvard. The approach of the College to Owen was made in August 1671 in a letter addressed to him and eighteen others (*The Correspondence of John Owen*, No.77 p.149f). The following February, one of the recipients – Dr. Leonard Hoare – accepted the post. He was President from 1672 until 1675.

16. Owen, *Animadversions on A Treatise Entitled 'Fiat Lux'*, XIV.1ff.

17. Edward Hyde, Lord Clarendon (1608-74). Clarendon was a defender of Charles I and episcopacy against Parliamentary attack. From 1661 to 1667 he was Charles II's chief minister until the debacle of the Dutch invasion of Medway forced his exile to France. He died in Rouen.

18. Owen, *A Discourse Concerning Liturgies, and Their Imposition*, XV.1ff.

19. Joseph Caryl (1602-73) was born in London and educated at Exeter College, Oxford. After ordination, he became preacher to Lincoln's Inn and a regular preacher for Parliament. Caryl sat at the Westminster Assembly in 1643. After the Restoration, he was ejected from St. Magnus in the City of London, where he had been the minister since 1645. He gathered a congregation in Leadenhall Street, which amalgamated with Owen's congregation after Caryl's death. Caryl is best remembered for his exhaustive *Commentary on the Book of Job* (1651-66) in 12 volumes.

20. Owen, *Pneumatalogia or, A Discourse Concerning the Holy Spirit*, III.1ff.

21. Owen, *Exposition of the Epistle to the Hebrews*, XVIII.1-XXIV.485.

22. David Clarkson (1622-86) was educated at Clare Hall, Cambridge

and became fellow there in 1645. One of his pupils was John Tillotson, the future Archbishop of Canterbury. He was ejected from his Curacy at Mortlake, Surrey, in 1662 and eventually joined Owen in London in 1682. He succeeded Owen as sole pastor the next year.

23. After lying in a house in St. James, Westminster, Owen was buried in Bunhill Fields on 4th September. Toon, *God's Statesman*, p.171f.

24. An enormous quantity of works have been published in an attempt to define Puritanism, of which the following are nothing more than a representative sample: J.C. Brauer, 'Reflections on the Nature of English Puritanism,' *Church History* 23 (1954), 99-108; B. Hall, 'Puritanism: The Problem of Definition' *Studies in Church History* 2 (London: Nelson, 1965) ed. G.J. Cumming, pp.283-96; L.J. Trinterud, 'The Origins of Puritanism,' *Church History* 20 (1951), 37-57; P. Collinson, *The Elizabethan Puritan Movement* (Oxford: Clarendon, 1990) and C. Hill, *Society and Puritanism in Pre-Revolutionary England* (London: Panther Books, 1969).

25. N. Tyacke, *Anti-Calvinists – The Rise of English Arminianism c.1590-1640* (Oxford: Clarendon Press, 1987), p.186.

26. William Laud (1573-1645). After ordination in 1601, Laud enjoyed a privileged rise to Archbishop of Canterbury in 1633. He was impeached for treason in December 1640. Four years later he was found guilty of 'endeavouring to subvert the laws, to overthrow the protestant religion and to act as an enemy to parliament'. Whilst this was not treason, he was executed at Tower Hill on 10th January 1645.

27. Tyacke explores this issue in his book *Anti-Calvinists - The Rise of English Arminianism c.1590-1640*, most especially pp.7f. and pp.137-139.

28. P. Collinson, *The Elizabethan Puritan Movement*, p.13.

29. M.M. Knappen, *Tudor Puritanism* (Chicago and London: University of Chicago Press, 1939), *passim* especially p.494ff.

30. L.J. Trinterud ed., *Elizabethan Puritanism* (New York: OUP,1971), p.10f: (1) the original, anti-vestment party; (2) the passive-resistance party; (3) the Presbyterians.

31. H.C. Porter, *Puritanism in Tudor England* (London and Basingstoke: MacMillan, 1970), p.9f: (1) the English Separatists; (2) the 'evangelical Puritans'; (3) the radical dissenters; (4) the Presbyterians.

32. P. Wiburn, *A Checke or Reproofe of M. Howlett's untimely schreeching*, 1581, fol.15, *verso*, quoted by Collinson, *The Elizabethan Puritan Movement*.

33. H.G. Wood, 'Puritanism', 1918, *Encyclopaedia of Religion and*

Ethics X.507, quoted by Kevan, *The Grace of Law*, p.17.

34. Trinterud, *Elizabethan Puritanism*, p.9.

35. William Perkins (1558-1602). Perkins, a Fellow of Christ's College, Cambridge, was one of the most prolific Puritan authors.

36. Perkins, Introduction to *The Work of William Perkins*, ed. I. Breward (Appleford: the Sutton Courtenay Press, 1970), p.15.

37. Perkins is listed amongst delegates from London, the Midlands and East Anglia to a presbyterian conference held in the Master's Lodge of St. John's College, Cambridge in September 1589. This conference, the last of its type, was for the purpose of discussing the Book of Discipline. Details of the conference proceedings are given by Collinson in *The Elizabethan Puritan Movement*, p.401f.

38. A.F. Mitchell, *Westminster Assembly*, 1883, pp.6,7, quoted by Kevan, *The Grace of Law*, p.19.

39. For an excellent overview of the history of caricaturing Puritans, see Hill's first chapter, 'The Definition of a Puritan' in *Society and Puritanism in Pre-Revolutionary England*, p.15f.

40. Owen, *Of Schism: The True Nature Of It Discovered and Considered With Reference to the Present Differences in Religion*, XIII.94 (italics his).

41. In G.E. Duffield, ed., *John Calvin* (Appleford:Abingdon, 1966).

42. R.T. Kendall, *Calvin and English Calvinism to 1649* (Oxford: OUP, 1979).

43. *Scottish Journal of Theology*, 34 (1981) 179-185. See also Helm's book, *Calvin and the Calvinists* (Edinburgh: Banner of Truth, 1982).

44. *Westminster Theological Journal* 42 (1980) 155-164.

45. Toon, *God's Statesman*, p.176.

Chapter One: Owen's Theological Framework

1. The secondary literature for this period is vast. The following are a representative example of books carrying information pertinent to our thesis: G.R. Cragg, *The Church and the Age of Reason 1648-1789* (Harmondsworth: Penguin, 1960), M. Ashley, *England in the Seventeenth Century (1603-1714)* (Harmondsworth: Penguin, c.1961), C. Hill, *Intellectual Origins of the English Revolution* (Oxford: Clarendon, 1965), C.Hill, *Change and Continuity in Seventeenth-Century England* (London: Weidenfeld & Nicolson, 1974), A.G.R. Smith, *The Emergence of a Nation State: The Commonwealth of England 1529-1660* (London: Longman, 1984), and L. Stone, *The Causes of the English Revolution 1529-1642* (London: Routledge, Kegan & Paul, 1972).

2. The influence of Richard Simon, Spinoza, Hugo Grotius and Pierre Bayle in this regard is examined by Cragg, *The Church and the Age of Reason 1648-1715*, p.47f.

3. Owen, *On the Holy Spirit*, III.285

4. Owen, *A Vision of Unchangeable, Free Mercy*, VIII.20

5. Ball, *A Treatise of the Covenant of Grace*, p.6

6. Owen, *The Doctrine of Justification by Faith, Through the Imputation of the Righteousness of Christ; Explained, Confirmed, and Vindicated*, V.275

7. Owen, *A Practical Exposition Upon Psalm CXXX*, VI.470; *The Death of Death*, X.168; *The Doctrine of the Saints' Perseverance Explained and Confirmed*, XI.210; *The Epistle to the Hebrews*, XIX.77, 78, 82; XXIII.55

8. For an excellent treatment of this topic, see C. Hill's chapter 'Masterless Men' in *The World Turned Upside Down* (London: Penguin, 1991), p.39ff

9. S. Doran and C. Durston analyse the role of the church in this regard in their chapter 'The Church and Social Control', *Princes, Pastors and People* (London: Routledge, 1991), p.174ff

10. Owen, *A Brief Instruction in the Worship of God and Discipline of the Churches of the New Testament*, XV.467 (italics his).

11. Owen, *A Discourse of Spiritual Gifts*, IV.496

12. Owen, *On the Holy Spirit*, III.251

13. Owen, *Of Communion with God the Father, Son, and Holy Ghost, Each person Distinctly, In Love, Grace, and Consolation*, II.75f

14. R. A. Muller, 'Covenant and Conscience in English Reformed Theology,' *Westminster Theological Journal* (1980) 42 309

15. Tyndale, *The Parable of the Wicked Mammon*, in *Writings of Tindal, Frith, and Barnes* (London: The Religious Tract Society, n.d.) p.64f.

16. C.R. Trueman, *Luther's Legacy: Salvation and the English Reformers 1525-1556* (Oxford: Clarendon, 1994), p.115f.

17. Leonard J. Trinterud, 'The Origins of Puritanism' *Church History* 20 (1951) 37-57.

18. For an excellent treatment of this debate, see L.D. Bierma, 'Federal Theology in the Sixteenth Century: Two Traditions?' *Westminster Theological Journal*, 45 (1983) 304-321.

19. G.H. Greenhough, 'The Reformers' Attitude to the Law of God,' *Westminster Theological Journal*, 39 (1976) 86

20. L.D. Bierma, 'Federal Theology in the Sixteenth Century: Two Traditions?' p.321 (italic his).

21. Anthony A. Hoekema has analysed this aspect of Calvin's writings in his article, 'The Covenant of Grace in Calvin's Teachings' *Calvin Theological Journal*. See also Bierma, 'Federal Theology in the Sixteenth Century: Two Traditions?' p.313f.

22. Calvin, *Commentary on Jeremiah* (Edinburgh: Banner of Truth, 1989), 31:31-34.

23. *Westminster Confession of Faith*, Chapter Seven.

24. The place of Gomarus in the development of federal theology is considered by Lynne Courter Boughton in her article 'Supralapsarianism and the Role of Metaphysics in Sixteenth-Century Reformed Theology', *Westminster Theological Journal* 48 (1986) 63-96 and also by K. Barth in *Church Dogmatics* IV.1 (Edinburgh: T & T Clark, 1956), p.59

25. See D. J. Bruggink's contribution to *An Elaboration of the Theology of Calvin*, ed. R. Gamble (New York: Garland, 1992), p.37f.

26. Barth, *Church Dogmatics*, IV.1 p.59

27. *Larger Catechism*, question 93

28. See Bruggink, *An Elaboration of the Theology of Calvin*, p.41. See also Packer's comments on the historical impact of Baxter's neonomianism in *Among God's Giants*, p.398.

29. Baxter, *Aphorisms of Justification*, p.47f.

30. Calvin, *Institutes of the Christian Religion* (2 vols. Grand Rapids, Michigan: Eerdmans, 1963), III.17.5, p.107f.

31. Owen, *The Epistle to the Hebrews*, XIX.388; XXIII.62

32. Owen, *The Epistle to the Hebrews*, XIX.337

33. Owen, *The Epistle to the Hebrews*, XIX.337

34. Owen, *Christologia: or, A Declaration of the Glorious Mystery of The Person of Christ - God and Man*, I.183 (italics his).

35. L.D. Bierma, 'Federal Theology in the Sixteenth Century: Two Traditions?' p.320 (italics his).

36. Owen, *The Epistle to the Hebrews*, XIX.337

37. Owen, *The Death of Death*, X.354

38. Owen, *The Epistle to the Hebrews*, XXIV.475

39. Owen, *The Doctrine of the Saints' Perseverance*, XI.210

40. *Westminster Confession*, VII.III

41. Owen, *The Epistle to the Hebrews*, XIX.77

42. Owen, *Vindiciæ Evangelicæ* XII.496f.

43. The scriptural basis for this is indicated by the Father/Son relationship within the Trinity; Psalm 16:2; 22:1; 40:8; 45:7; Micah 5:4; John 20:27; Revelation 3:13 are all cited by Owen in this regard.

44. Ferguson, *John Owen on the Christian Life*, p.27

45. Owen, *The Epistle to the Hebrews*, XIX.387

46. Owen, *The Epistle to the Hebrews*, XIX.388; cf. VIII.293, XXIII.215

47. Owen, *The Epistle to the Hebrews*, XIX.389

48. Ferguson, *John Owen on the Christian Life*, p.29

49. Whitefeild, *The Doctrines of the Arminians & Pelagians Truly stated and clearly Answered*, 1652, p.86

50. Johannes Cocceius (1603-69) was a Dutch theologian with extraordinary abilities in ancient languages. He studied in Hamburg, specialising in Hebrew and rabbinic studies. From there, he went in 1629 to Franeker to study. His return to Bremen in 1630 brought with it the professorship of biblical philology. Six years later, he accepted the chair of Hebrew at Franeker. Cocceius moved to Leyden in 1650 and continued his work as a prolific writer.

51. Cocceius, *Commentarius in Jobum, continens Expositionem Verborum ex Hebraismi proprietate, &c.* (1644), *Examinatio Apologiæ Equitis Poloni de Sociniana Smal &c.* (1656), *Ejusd. Consideratio Princip. Evang. Joh. Ch. V.19. contra Socinum, Smal &c.* (1654), *Ejusd. Compendiolum Socinianismi confutatem* (1651) and *Ejusd. Explicatio in Epistolam ad Hebraos & Veritat Demonstratio* (1659).

52. Owen, *The Epistle to the Hebrews*, XX.III.185

53. Owen, *Vindiciæ Evangelicæ*, XII.503

54. Owen, *Vindiciæ Evangelicæ*, XII.503

55. Barth, *Church Dogmatics* IV.1 p.60 (italics his).

56. It is regrettable that inclusive language will not always be used in this book, for two reasons. First, Owen himself uses the word 'man' which primarily denotes inclusivity for him. It would be awkward to speak of 'man' in his quotations whilst using an alternative word in the main body of the text. Second, it is difficult to find a word which could replace 'man' in a consistent way in the light of the topic being discussed: 'humanity' is a corporate term whilst 'individual' or 'person' will, at times, be too individualistic. It is hoped that the reader will not take offence at the lack of inclusive language in this chapter by accepting that the writer is at least aware of the sensitivity of the issue.

57. Owen, *On the Holy Spirit*, III.468f

58. Ferguson, *John Owen on the Christian Life*, p.65

59. Owen, *A Display of Arminianism*, X.85

60. Owen, *On the Holy Spirit*, III.102

61. William Benn (1600-80) was educated at Queen's College, Oxford. He left without a degree to share a living in Berkshire. He moved on to become chaplain to the Marchioness of Northampton before moving to Dorchester in 1629. Benn was ejected in 1662 but remained

in Dorchester until his death.

62. Benn, *Soul Prosperity, in Several Sermons*, p.318f

63. Aristotle, *The Ethics of Aristotle: The Nichomachean Ethics Translated* (Harmondsworth: Penguin, 1955), 1.2, p.26f.

64. Aristotle, *The Ethics of Aristotle*, 1.7, 36f.

65. Aristotle, *The Ethics of Aristotle*, 1.10, p.48.

66. Owen, *On the Holy Spirit*, III.284

67. Owen, *On the Holy Spirit*, III.285

68. Owen, *On the Holy Spirit*, III.482

69. Owen, *A Vision of Unchangeable, Free Mercy*, VIII.36

70. Owen, *Of the Mortification of Sin in Believers; the Necessity, Nature and Means of it*, VI.40,43 (italics his).

71. Owen, *The Grace and Duty of Being Spiritually Minded Declared and Practically Improved*, VII.332 (italics his).

72. Owen, *The Person of Christ*, I.182 (italics his).

73. Owen, *The Person of Christ*, I.183

74. Owen, *The Person of Christ*, I.183 (italics his).

75. Owen, *The Person of Christ*, I.181f.

76. Owen, *The Person of Christ*, I.181f.

77. Augustine, *The City of God* (New York: Random House, 1950), XI.26, p.370f

78. Augustine, *The Trinity* (New York: New City Press, 1991), IX.1.1-XII.4.25, p.270ff.

79. Augustine, *The Trinity*, IX.1.6, p.274

80. Augustine, *The Trinity*, IX.1.8, p.275

81. Augustine, *The Trinity*, X.4.17-19, p.298f.

82. Augustine, *The Trinity*, X..4.18, p.298f.

83. Augustine, *The Trinity*, XII.4.22, 25, p.334, 336

84. Augustine, *The Trinity*, XII.1.4, p.324

85. Augustine, *City of God*, XI.26, p.370

86. Aquinas, *De veritate*, 10.

87. Aquinas, *Summa Theologiæ* (London: Blackfriars: Eyre and Spottiswoode, 1964), 1a.93, p.49ff.

88. Aquinas, *Summa Theologiæ*, 1a.93.1, p.51

89. Aquinas, *Summa Theologiæ*, 1a.93.1, p.51

90. Aquinas, *Summa Theologiæ*, 1a.93.2, p.53ff.

91. Aquinas, *Summa Theologiæ*, 1a.93.4, p.59 (italics his).

92. Aquinas, *Summa Theologiæ*, 1a.93.4, p.61

93. Aquinas, *Summa Theologiæ*, 1a.93.4, p.61 (italics his).

94. Calvin, *Institutes*, 1.15.4, p.165

95. Calvin, *Institutes*, 3.2.6, p.474

96. Owen, *Vindiciæ Evangelicæ*, XII.143

97. Owen, *On the Holy Spirit*, III.101

98. Owen, *On the Holy Spirit*, III.417f.(italics his).

99. Calvin, *Institutes*, 1.15.3, p.162

100. Owen, *A Display of Arminianism*, X.85

101. Calvin, *Institutes*, 1.15.4, p.164

102. Owen, *A Display of Arminianism*, X.85, 84

103. Owen, *On the Holy Spirit*, III.101 (italics his).

104. Owen, *On the Holy Spirit*, III.101f (italics his).

105. e.g. Owen, *A Display of Arminianism*, X.85, 87; *On the Holy Spirit*, III.101; *Vindiciæ Evangelicæ*, XII.143, 152

106. Owen, *Vindiciæ Evangelicæ*, XII.143

107. Owen, *Vindiciæ Evangelicæ*, XII.156, 157

108. Owen, *On the Holy Spirit*, III.102 (italics his).

109. Owen, *The Person of Christ*, 1.75

110. Owen, *The Person of Christ*, I.169, 170 (italics his).

111. Owen, *The Person of Christ*, I.169ff

112. Owen, *The Person of Christ*, I.169 (italics his).

113. Owen, *The Person of Christ*, I.173

114. Owen, *The Person of Christ*, I.175 (italics his).

115. Owen, *The Person of Christ*, I.176

116. Owen, *The Person of Christ*, I.170, 171

117. Calvin, *Institutes*, 1.15.4, p.164

118. Owen, Preface to *The Nature, Power, Deceit, and Prevalency of the Remainders of Indwelling Sin in Believers*, VI.155

119. Owen, *On the Holy Spirit*, III.290

120. Owen, *On the Holy Spirit*, III.287 (italics his).

121. Owen, *On the Holy Spirit*, III.287

122. Augustine, *The City of God*, XI.21, p.364f. Augustine refers the reader to Plato's comment in *Timaeus*, p.29 D: 'Let us say what was the cause of the Creator's forming this universe. He was good; and in the good no envy is ever generated about anything whatever. Therefore, being free from envy, He desired that all things should, as much as possible, resemble Himself.'

123. Augustine, *Enchiridion*, 11

124. Augustine, *City of God*, XII.7, p.387

125. E. Gilson, *The Christian Philosophy of St. Augustine* (London: Victor Gollancz, 1961), p.144

126. Augustine, *Enchiridion*, 12

127. Owen, *On the Holy Spirit*, III.289 (italics his).

128. Augustine, *The City of God*, XIV.13, p.460.

129. Augustine, *The City of God*, XII.7, p.387. The quotation is a biblical reference to Psalm 19:12.

130. Owen, *On the Holy Spirit*, III.291

131. Augustine, *On Free Will*, in *Augustine: Earlier Writings* (Philadelphia: Westminster, 1953),_I.i.2, p.114

132. Owen, *The Person of Christ*, I.208 (italics his).

133. Augustine, *City of God*, XI.17, p.361

134. Owen, *On the Holy Spirit*, III.295

135. Owen, *On the Holy Spirit*, III.295

136. Owen, *On the Holy Spirit*, III.295f.

137. Owen, *On the Holy Spirit*, III.286

138. Owen, *On the Holy Spirit*, III.287

139. G. Evans, *Augustine on Evil* (Cambridge: CUP, 1982), p.29

140. Owen, *On Indwelling Sin*, VI.221

141. Owen, *On Indwelling Sin*, VI.199

142. Owen, *On Indwelling Sin*, VI.252

143. Owen, *On the Holy Spirit*, IV.475

144. Owen, *On Indwelling Sin*, VI.163ff

145. Owen, *On Indwelling Sin*, VI.163f

146. Owen, *On Indwelling Sin*, VI.164 (italics his).

147. Owen, *On Indwelling Sin*, VI.164

148. Owen, *On Indwelling Sin*, VI.165 (italics his).

149. Owen, *On Indwelling Sin*, VI.165 (italics his).

150. Owen, *On Indwelling Sin*, VI.166

151. Owen, *On Indwelling Sin*. VI.167

152. Owen, *On the Holy Spirit*, III.270 (italics his).

153. Augustine, *The City of God*, XII.3, p.382f.

154. Evans, *Augustine on Evil*, p.99

155. Owen, *On Indwelling Sin*, VI.169

156. Barth, *Church Dogmatics* IV.1 p.65f

157. Owen, *Vindiciæ Evangelicæ*, XII.497

Chapter Two: Sin and the Individual

1. Perkins, *The Calling of the Ministerie*, part 1, *Works* III, p.438

2. For the pre-1640 notion that Antichrist was the Pope or, at the very least, the Church of Rome, see C. Hill, *Antichrist in Seventeenth-Century England* (London: Verso, 1990), p1f.

3. Owen, *The Duty of a Pastor*, IX.460f (italics his).

4. Baxter, *A Christian Directory, Works I*, p.581

5. Such instances of this understanding are numerous, e.g. T. Morton, *A Treatise of the Three-Fold Division of Man* (1613), D. Dyke, *The*

mystery of selfe (1620) and W. Fenner, *A Treatise of the Affections* (1642)

6. Calvin, *Institutes*, 1.15.7, p.168

7. Calvin, *Institutes*, 1.15.7, p.169

8. Calvin's phraseology in *Institutes* 1.15.7 (p.168f.) reveals this intent, for example: 'Let us therefore hold, for the purpose of this present work'; 'We dwell not on the subtlety of Aristotle'; 'Not to lose ourselves in superfluous questions', and 'it will be seen in another place'.

9. Owen, *On Indwelling Sin*, VI.222

10. Owen, *On the Holy Spirit*, III.285

11. Owen, *On the Holy Spirit*, IV.83 (italics his).

12. Owen, *On the Holy Spirit*, III.537f.

13. Aquinas informs the reader of *Summa Contra Gentiles* that 'according to Aristotle "what a thing is" is the principle of demonstration, it is necessary that the way in which we understand the substance of a thing determines the way in which we know what belongs to it.' *Summa Contra Gentiles* (Notre Dame and London: University of Notre Dame, 1975), 'Book One: God', 1.1.3, p.63. The reference given to Aristotle's works is *The Nicomachean Ethics*, 1.3 1094b 24.

14. Aquinas, *Summa Contra Gentiles*, 1.1.3, p.63f.

15. Aquinas, *Nature and Grace: Selections from the Summa Theologica of Thomas Aquinas* (London: SCM, 1954), 22ae, Q.2, Art. 3.

16. Augustine, *On Free Will*, I.viii.18, p.123

17. Augustine, *On Free Will*, II.vi.13, p.143

18. Augustine, *The Soliloquies*, in *Augustine: Earlier Writings*, I.vi.12, p.30

19. Calvin, *Institutes*, 1.15.2, p.161

20. Benjamin Whichcote (1609-83) entered Emmanuel College, Cambridge in 1626 and became a Fellow in 1633. He became Provost of King's College in 1644 but was deprived at the time of the Restoration. After that, he held various livings in London.

21. John Smith (1618-1652) was educated at Emmanuel College where he was admitted as pensioner in 1636. He was tutored by Whichcote and probably Cudworth. He was appointed Fellow of Queen's in 1644. His *Select Discourses* were posthumously published.

22. Ralph Cudworth (1617-88) was the leading figure amongst the Cambridge Platonists. From being a Pensioner of Emmanuel College (1632) and a Fellow (1639), he became Master of Clare Hall in 1644, and then Regius Professor of Hebrew in 1645. In 1654, he became Master of Christ's College.

23. Henry More (1614-87) was a Fellow of Christ's College from 1639 and he remained there until his death.

24. Nathaniel Culverwell (1618?-51?) entered Emmanuel College in 1633 and became a Fellow there in 1642.

25. Quoted by G.R. Cragg in his Introduction to *The Cambridge Platonists* (Oxford: OUP, 1968), p.26 (italics his).

26. Among the books in his library at the time of his death were the following: Peter Sterry, *Discourse of the Freedom of the Will* (1675); John Smith, *Plea for Christianity against Scepticks* (1679); Henry More, *Conjectura Cabbalitica interpreting the Mind of Moses* (1653), *Grand Mystery of Godliness* (1660), *Philosophical Writings* (1662), *Modest Inquiry into the Mystery of Iniquity* (1664); Ralph Cudworth, *The True Notion of the Lord's Supper* (1642), *Discourse Concerning the Lord's Supper* (1670), *Intellectual System of the Universe* (1678); and Nathaniel Culverwel *Elegant Discourse of the Light of Nature* (1650). These were all key texts by the Cambridge Platonists.

27. Owen, *The Doctrine of the Saints' Perseverance*, XI.487

28. Owen, *The Death of Death*, X.221, 222. See also pp.230 and 247

29. Copleston, *A History of Philosophy*, vol.5 (London: Bellarmine, 1959), p.56

30. Whichcote, *Aphorisms*, No. 40

31. F.J. Powicke, *The Cambridge Platonists* (London: J.M. Dent, 1926), p.33f

32. Powicke, *The Cambridge Platonists*, p.35f

33. Owen, *On the Holy Spirit*, III.244f. (italics his).

34. Whichcote affirmed the credibility and sufficiency of Scripture in his second letter to Antony Tuckney (G. Cragg ed., *The Cambridge Platonists*, p.40).

35. Quoted by Powicke, *The Cambridge Platonists*, p.30

36. Owen, *On the Holy Spirit*, III.248f.

37. Owen, *On the Holy Spirit*, III.251 (italics his).

38. Owen, *On Indwelling Sin*, VI.173

39. Calvin, *Institutes*, II.2.12, p.233

40. Owen, *The Reason of Faith*, IV.55 (italics his).

41. Owen, *On Indwelling Sin*, VI.213

42. 'But exhort one another every day, as long as it is called "today," that none of you may be hardened by the deceitfulness of sin' (RSV). Owen uses this verse in *On Indwelling Sin*, VI.211

43. Owen, *On Indwelling Sin*, VI.212

44. Owen, *On Indwelling Sin*, VI.213

45. Owen, of course, was not the only writer to make this analysis. In his work, *The Signal Diagnostick*, Thomas Pierce made the same observation: 'In this very mire men of swinish affections delight to

wallow. For whatsoever 'tis we love, be it as ugly as the Devil, we paint it hansom in our thoughts, and blot out all its deformities with our Imaginations; and so we love it not as it is, but rather as it is disguis'd and fancyed by us...we look upon it with a Fleshly, that is to say, with a Lovers eye. And sure the Eye of a Lover sees no defect in its Beloved' (p.56).

46. Owen, *On Indwelling Sin*, VI.215
47. Genesis 22:1-19
48. Owen, *Of Temptation*, VI.94
49. Owen, *Of Temptation*, VI.95 (italics his).
50. Owen, *On Indwelling Sin*, VI.214
51. Owen, *On Indwelling Sin*, VI.218 (italics his).
52. Owen, *On Indwelling Sin*, VI.219
53. Owen, *On Indwelling Sin*, VI.219
54. Owen, *On Indwelling Sin*, VI.219
55. Owen, *On Indwelling Sin*, VI.221
56. Owen, *On Indwelling Sin*, VI.221
57. 'I remember the kindness of thy youth, the love of thine espousals,' Owen, *On Indwelling Sin*, VI.221f.
58. Owen, *On Indwelling Sin*, VI.222
59. Owen, *On Indwelling Sin*, VI.223
60. Owen, *On Indwelling Sin*, VI.236
61. Owen, *On Indwelling Sin*, VI.238
62. Mk.13:37; Hag.1:5,7; Deut.32:29; Heb.5:11; 6:11-12; 2 Pet.1:5
63. Owen, *On Indwelling Sin*, VI.242f
64. Owen, *On Indwelling Sin*, VI.229
65. Owen, *On Indwelling Sin*, VI.229
66. Owen, *On Indwelling Sin*, VI.230 (italics his).
67. Owen, *On Indwelling Sin*, VI.230
68. So Saul said, 'Bring the burnt offering here to me, and the peace offerings,' And he offered the burnt offering.... And Samuel said to Saul, 'You have done foolishly; you have not kept the commandment of the Lord your God which he commanded you' (1 Sam.13: 9,13, RSV).
69. Owen, *On Indwelling Sin*, VI.230
70. Owen, *Of Temptation*, VI.99 (italics his).
71. Owen, *Of Temptation*, VI.109 (italics his).
72. Owen, *Of Temptation*, VI.109
73. Owen, *Of Temptation*, VI.109
74. Owen's analysis of the Quakers will be dealt with in more detail in Chapter Four.
75. An extract from William Dewsbury, *The New Birth*, 'Works',

pp.44-57. Quoted by W.C. Braithwaite in the Introduction to *The Beginnings of Quakerism* (London: MacMillan, 1912), p.xxxv.

76. Owen, *A Brief Declaration and Vindication of the Doctrine of the Trinity*, II.399

77. Owen, *On the Holy Spirit*, III.66

78. Owen, Preface to *Vindiciæ Evangelicæ*, XII.12

79. Owen, The Epistle Dedicatory to *Of the Divine Original, Authority Self-Evidencing Light, and Power of the Scriptures*, XVI.292

80. John Eaton (fl. 1619) was educated at Trinity College, Oxford. He took the living at Wickham Market in 1604 and stayed there for fifteen years. Despite his Antinomianism, he was respected as an excellent minister.

81. For details of this polemical interaction see Kevan, *The Grace of Law*, especially Chapter 5, 'The Continuance of Moral Obligation', p.167ff.

82. Owen, *Meditations and Discourses on the Glory of Christ*, I.341; *The Death of Death*, X.283

83. For an analysis of the Antinomian tradition with regard to the issues of justification and sanctification, see Kevan, *The Grace of Law*, p.94f.

84. Kevan, *The Grace of Law*, p.26.

85. Arthur Annesley, first Earl of Anglesey (1614-86) was an Irishman educated at Magdalen College, Oxford. In 1634, he joined Lincoln's Inn and returned to Ireland in 1640. He was a parliamentary man but not a republican. He was on friendly terms with the Royalist party and was respected for his moderacy. In April 1661, he became Lord Annesley of Newport-Pagnell and Earl of Anglesey. He retired to Blechingdon in Oxfordshire in 1682 and died of quinsy four years later.

86. Annesley, *The truth unvailed in behalf of the Church of England*, p.31

87. Young, *An Apology for Congregational Divines*, 1698, p.7

88. Thomas Gataker (1574-1654) was a Fellow of Sidney Sussex College, Cambridge in 1596. He became a Lecturer at Lincoln's Inn in 1601 before becoming Rector of Rotherhithe ten years later. He was an influential member of the Westminster Assembly and later condemned the trial of Charles I.

89. Gataker, *Antinomianism Discovered and Confuted*, 1652, p.26f

90. Owen, *Of the Death of Christ*, X.449

91. Owen, *On Justification*, V.145.

92. For an excellent overview of this topic, see Packer's chapter 'The Puritan Conscience' in *Among God's Giants*, p.140ff.

93. Owen, *Of Temptation*, VI.124

94. Owen, *Of Temptation*, VI.121 (italics his).

95. Revelation 3:1f. Owen draws the parallel in *Of Temptation*, VI.121

96. Owen, *Of Temptation*, VI.132 (italics his).

97. Owen, *Of Temptation*, VI.132

98. Owen, *Of Temptation*, VI.124

99. Owen, *Of Temptation*, VI.126

100. Owen, *Of Temptation*, VI.134

101. Owen, *A Discourse of Spiritual Gifts*, IV.437 (italics his).

102. Ferguson, *John Owen on the Christian Life*, p.204

103. Owen, *Of Spiritual Gifts*, IV.454

104. Owen, *Of Spiritual Gifts*, IV.473f (italics his).

105. Owen, *Of Spiritual Gifts*, IV.475 (italics his).

106. Ferguson, *John Owen on the Christian Life*, p.208

107. Owen, *Grace and Duty*, VII.397

108. Owen, *Grace and Duty*, VII.396 (italics his).

109. Owen, *Grace and Duty*, VII.395

110. Packer, *Among God's Giants*, p.255f

111. William Fenner (1600-40) was educated at Pembroke College, Cambridge. After being ordained in 1622, he became chaplain to the Earl of Warwick and ministered at Sedgley, Staffordshire. In 1629, he took the living of Rochford in Essex, where he stayed until his death in 1640. Fenner was greatly appreciated as a preacher.

112. Fenner, *A Treatise of the Affections*, pp.3,9

113. Morton, *Of the Three-Fold State of Man*, p.480

114. Owen, *A Display of Arminianism*, X.84, 85

115. Owen, *Of Communion with God*, II.118

116. Owen, *Of Communion with God*, II.118 cf. *Eth., lib.* vii., cap.14

117. Owen, *On the Holy Spirit*, III.496 (italics his). Anthony Burgesse expressed the same idea more poetically when he referred to the affections as 'wild horses' in *The Doctrine of Original Sin, Asserted and Vindicated Against the old and new Adversaries thereof, both Socinians, Papists, Arminians and Anabaptists,* 1658, p.114

118. Thomas Pierce (1622-91) was educated at Magdalen College, Oxford and was well famed for his musical skills. Pierce was loyal to the royalist cause and spent some time on the Continent in the 1650s. Pierce had been a Calvinist until 1644 and, thereafter, spent much energy on attacking that system of doctrine. At the Restoration, Pierce was appointed chaplain-in-ordinary to Charles II. He became canon of Canterbury in 1660, and prebendary at Lincoln in 1662, holding both preferments until his death. In 1675, Pierce was installed as dean of

Salisbury where he would be best remembered for his fierce temper and controversial spirit.

119. Pierce, *The Signal Diagnostick Whereby We are to judge of our own Affections*, p.112

120. Owen, *On Indwelling Sin*, VI.199

121. Owen, *Of Temptation*, VI.109 and *On Indwelling Sin*, VI.200

122. Owen, *On the Holy Spirit*, IV.177

123. Thomas Morton (1564-1659) was educated at St. John's College, Cambridge after having been schooled in York with fellow pupil, Guy Fawkes. He was ordained in 1592 and lectured in logic at the University until 1598. Morton was well respected for his sacrificial ministry in York during the 1602 plague. After holding several livings, Morton became bishop of Chester in 1616 and thereafter bishop of Lichfield and Coventry. Under Charles I, Morton was translated to the see of Durham, where he stayed until his death. He held little sympathy with the theological leanings of Laud and was well respected for his sincerity by Baxter.

124. Morton, *On the Three-fold State of Man*, p.490f

125. Owen, *On Psalm CXXX*, VI.579

126. Owen, *On the Holy Spirit*, III.80

127. Owen, *On the Holy Spirit*, III.334

128. Owen, *On Indwelling Sin*, VI.254 (italics his).

129. Owen, *On Indwelling Sin*, VI.252

130. Calvin, *Institutes*, 2.2.26, p.245 (italics his).

131. Owen, *On Indwelling Sin*, VI.254

132. Owen, *On the Holy Spirit*, III.334 (italics his).

133. Owen, *On the Holy Spirit*, III.334

134. Owen, *On the Holy Spirit*, III.335

135. This definition of the freedom of the will is reliant upon Rist's analysis in 'Augustine on Free Will and Predestination', *Journal of Theological Studies*, 1969.

136. Owen, *On the Holy Spirit*, III.281(italics his).

137. Owen, *On the Holy Spirit*, III.335

138. Owen, *On the Holy Spirit*, III.238

139. Owen, *On the Holy Spirit*, III.238

140. Owen, *On the Holy Spirit*, III.238

141. Owen, *On the Holy Spirit*, III.319

142. Owen, *On Indwelling Sin*, VI.252

143. I Kings 21

144. Luke 22:54-62

145. Owen, *On Indwelling Sin*, VI.252

146. Owen, *On the Holy Spirit*, III.494 (italics his).

147. Owen, *On the Holy Spirit*, III.495

148. Owen, *On Indwelling Sin*, VI.160

149. Owen, *On Indwelling Sin*, VI.160

150. Owen, *On the Holy Spirit*, III.430

151. Calvin, *John Calvin's Sermons on Ephesians* (Edinburgh: Banner of Truth), 2:1, p.129.

152. Calvin, *Sermons on Job* (Edinburgh: Banner of Truth, 1993), 15:11f

153. Calvin, *Sermons on Deuteronomy* (Edinburgh: Banner of Truth, 1987), 24:19f

154. Calvin, *Institutes*, 1.15.4, p.164. See also his *A Commentary on Genesis* (London: Banner of Truth, 1965), 9:6, p.295f.

155. Calvin, *Institutes*, 3.3.9, p.515.

156. Calvin, *Institutes*, 2.2.12, p.233

157. Calvin, *Commentary on Job*, 14:13

158. Calvin, *Institutes*, 2.1.11, p.220

159. Calvin, *The Gospel According to St. John and the First Epistle of John* (Edinburgh: St. Andrew's Press, 1961), 11:25, p.9.

160. Owen, *On the Holy Spirit*, III.248f., 286

161. Young, *A New-Year's Gift for the Antinominans*, 1699, p.15

162. Owen, *On the Holy Spirit*, III.289 (italics his).

163. Owen, *On the Holy Spirit*, III.287 (italics his).

164. Calvin, *Institutes*, 1.15.2, p.160f.

165. Owen, *A Dissertation on Divine Justice*, X.519

166. Owen, *The Person of Christ*, I.229 (italics his). The link between body and soul is more poetically exemplified by William Benn: '[The body] is but the Case, the Cabinet: The Soul is the Jewel that is in it: If that be as the Ring, this is the Diamond in the Ring' (*The Signal Diagnostick*, p.27).

167. Owen, *Vindiciae Evangelicae*, XII.150

168. Owen, *A Display of Arminianism*, X.79

169. Owen, *On the Holy Spirit*, III.418 cf. Pierce's description of the body in relation to the soul in his work, *The Signal Diagnostick*: 'the Part which is material is arrant Rottenness, and Corruption, not only not lovely, but loathsom [sic] too, when abstracted from the part which is immaterial...and for this reason it is, that the zealoulest Lover of what is worldly, and who hath nothing in him of Christ whereby to qualifie and inable him for Spiritual love, He (I say) would not be able to love the Body above the Soul, if the Beauty of the Soul did not shine through the Body' (p.110).

170. Owen, *The Nature and Causes of Apostasy from the Profession of the Gospel and the Punishment of Apostates Declared, in an Exposition of Heb. VI. 4-6,* VII.143

171. Teate, *A Scripture-Map of the Wilderness of Sin, and way to Canaan. Or the Sinners Way to the Saints Rest,* 1655 p.67

172. Owen, *Nature and Causes of Apostasy,* VII.139

173. Owen, *The Person of Christ,* I.216

174. Owen, *The Person of Christ,* I.216 (italics his).

175. Owen, *Nature and Causes of Apostasy,* VII.140 cf. John Rowe, who writes that 'Satans usual and ordinary way of tempting is, by suiting his Temptations to our corrupt nature. Satan observes which way our corrupt nature bends, and inclines, and suits his Temptations accordingly.' (*The Saints' Temptations,* 1675).

176. Owen, *Of Temptation,* VI.95 (italics his).

177. Owen, *Of Temptation,* VI.95 (italics his).

178. Owen, *Of Temptation,* VI.95 (italics his).

Chapter Three: Sin and Society

1. The evangelical writer Walter Wink is especially notable in this regard with his theories about how sin operates within institutions, outlined in his series of books known collectively as 'The Powers': *Naming the Powers* (Philadelphia: Fortress 1984). *Unmasking the Powers* (Philadelphia: Fortress 1986) and *Engaging the Powers* (Philadelphia: Fortress 1992).

2. Hugh Peter (1598-1660) was Lecturer at St. Sepulchre's in London before becoming Minister to an English church in Rotterdam. In 1635, he went to New England for six years before returning and taking up the responsibilities of Army chaplain and parliamentary preacher. He was executed after the Restoration.

3. Philip Nye (1596?-1672) was educated at Brasenose College, Oxford and Magdalen Hall. Under pressure for his nonconformity, Nye went to Holland, where he stayed until 1640. On returning, he spent a great deal of time in Yorkshire. Nye was numbered amongst the Westminster divines and, a decade later, took the living of St. Bartholomew, Exchange. He was active in the Savoy Conference and declared a republican interest in 1659. He lost his preferments at the Restoration and left London in 1663. Returning three years later, he ministered to various congregations before his death.

4. Thomas Goodwin (1600-80) was President of Magdalen College, Oxford. In 1633, he was converted to Independency by John Cotton

and subsequently ministered in both London and Holland. A participant in the Savoy Conference, he was deprived at the Restoration and formed an Independent congregation in London.

5. Cromwell's expedition to Ireland began in mid-August 1649. Owen was chaplain, alongside Rev. Hugh Peter. Owen travelled to Scotland in 1650. He left London with Cromwell on 28 June and crossed the Tweed on 22 July. The second chaplain on this occasion was Rev. William Good (Toon, *God's Statesman*, pp.39, 43f).

6. Toon, *God's Statesman*, p.36

7. Ferguson, *John Owen on the Christian Life*, p.7

8. Owen commented on his time in Dublin in the work he wrote there entitled *Of the Death of Christ*: 'For the present, being by God's providence removed for a season from my native soil, attended with more than ordinary weaknesses and infirmities, separated from my library, burdened with manifold employments, with constant preaching to a numerous multitude of as thirsting a people after the gospel as ever yet I conversed withal' (Owen, *Works* X.479).

9. Toon makes it clear that Owen would have been too busy in Dublin to travel with the army to Drogheda. Apart from his preaching duties mentioned above, Owen found time to make a survey of Trinity College, engage in administrative duties as well as write a small book, *Of the Death of Christ*, X.429f. (Toon, *God's Statesman*, p.40). Furthermore, it is clear that Rev. Hugh Peter was with Cromwell's armies at the Wexford massacre, which happened immediately after Drogheda. It is unlikely that both chaplains would have been together at that time (Hill, *God's Englishman*, p.113).

10. 'For mine house shall be called a house of prayer for all people.'

11. Owen, *The Branch of the Lord the Beauty of Zion*, VIII.290

12. It would be impossible to offer a comprehensive list of valuable publications that focus on this period. Of particular importance for this thesis, see C. Hill, *The World Turned Upside Down* (London: Penguin, 1991), K. Thomas, *Religion and the Decline of Magic* (London: Peregrine, 1978), A. Fraser, *Cromwell Our Chief of Men* (London: Weidenfeld and Nicolson, 1973), B. Manning, *Politics, Religion and the English Civil War* (London: Edward Arnold, 1973), R.K. Merton, *Science, Technology and Society in Seventeenth Century England* (New York: H.Fertig, 1970) and A. Smith, *The Emergence of a Nation State: The Commonwealth of England 1529-1660* (London: Longman, 1984).

13. Statistical information is provided by Professor Hoskins, quoted by Smith, *The Emergence of a Nation State 1529-1660*, p.433f.

14. For analysis of the impact of both the Diggers and the Levellers

see Hill, *The World Turned Upside Down*, p.107ff; L.F. Solt, 'Anti-Intellectualism in the Puritan Revolt,' *Church History* 25 (Dec. 1956): 306-316 and 'The Theological Basis of Digger Communism,' *Church History* 23 (Sep. 1954): 207-218

15. Hill, *The World Turned Upside Down*, p.21f

16. For details of Leveller influence in the Army during this period, see C. Hill, *The Century of Revolution 1603-1714* (London: Routledge, 1980), p.109f. See also H.N. Brailsford, *The Levellers and the English Revolution* (Nottingham: Spokesman, 1983).

17. Brailsford, *The Levellers and the English Revolution*, p.456.

18. Brailsford, *The Levellers and the English Revolution*, p.457f.

19. Quoted by Thomas, *Religion and the Decline of Magic*, p.80. For further examples of anticlericalism during this period, see Thomas, p.79f. and p.85f.

20. Thomas Hobbes (1588-1679) was educated at Magdalen Hall, Oxford. Taking up tutoring roles with the sons of both the Earl of Devonshire and, later, Sir Gervase Clinton (1629), Hobbes' life was spent variously in England, France and Italy. He fled to Paris in 1640 as a result of the political turmoil at home. After the Restoration, despite denunciation by the church, Hobbes received a pension from Charles II.

21. Thomas gives an excellent overview of religious scepticism during this period in *Religion and the Decline of Magic*, p.198-206.

22. Cragg, *The Church and the Age of Reason, 1648-1660*, p.13

23. For an analysis of the impact of astrology in the seventeenth-century, see Hill, *The World Turned Upside Down*, p.87-91

24. Hill, *The World Turned Upside Down*, p.89. For details on the contents of almanacs, see Thomas, *Religion and the Decline of Magic*, p.347f.

25. Quoted by Hill, *The World Turned Upside Down*, p.411

26. C.B. MacPherson, *The Political Theory of Possessive Individualism: Hobbes to Locke* (Oxford: OUP, 1962), p.270

27. James Harrington (1611-77) was educated at Trinity College, Oxford before entering the Middle Temple in 1631. He travelled on the Continent and his experiences, most especially in Venice, confirmed his Republican ideals. He enjoyed a warm personal relationship with Charles I and disapproved of his execution. He did not take an active role in politics under Cromwell and was imprisoned at the Restoration.

28. John Locke (1632-1704) was born in Somerset. He studied at Christ Church, Oxford during Owen's time there but did not seem to enjoy the experience. Despite that, by 1660 he was a Senior Student

and occasionally lectured there. Like Harrington and Hobbes, Locke too travelled extensively throughout the Continent before retiring to France in 1675. Four years later, he returned to England but was exiled to Holland in 1683. Six years later, he returned once more and carried on publishing his writings until 1700.

29. Locke was placed by Owen into the care of Thomas Cole (Toon, *God's Statesman*, p.62).

30 Quoted by Driver in *The Social and Political Ideas of Some English Thinkers of the Augustan Age*, F.J.C. Hearnshaw ed. (London: Dawsons, 1967), p.82.

31. See Brian Manning's essay 'The Levellers and Religion' in *Radical Religion in the English Revolution*, J.F. McGregor & B. Reay eds. (Oxford: OUP, 1984), p.65f.

32. J.W. Horrocks provides an excellent overview of this topic in his book, *A Short History of Mercantilism* (London: Methuen and Co. Ltd., 1925).

33. Fraser explores the relationship between trade in the Spanish West Indies and the military expedition of December 1654 in *Cromwell Our Chief of Men*, p.521f.

34. C.J.H. Hayes, *The Historical Evolution of Modern Nationalism* (New York: MacMillan, 1931), p.6

35. Hayes, *The Historical Evolution of Modern Nationalism*, p.7f

36. Although born in England, Owen had relatives in Wales. His uncle, the benefactor for Owen's education at Oxford, was Welsh. In addition, John Owen's father, Henry Owen, was born about 1586 in Merionethshire (*The Correspondence of John Owen*, p.3).

37. Brailsford, *The Levellers and the English Revolution, passim*

38. Dudley Digges (1613-43) was educated at University College, Oxford. A passionate royalist, he was involved in providing for Oxford against parliamentary attacks during the Civil War.

39. Digges, *The Unlawfulnesse of Subjects Taking up Arms*, London, 1643 p.20

40. Digges, *The Unlawfulnesse of Subjects Taking up Arms*, p.66

41. James Ussher (1581-1656) was ordained in 1601. Five years later he became Chancellor of St. Patrick's before accepting the Professorship of Divinity in Dublin. He was translated to Archbishop in 1625 before moving to England in 1640. Despite his Royalist persuasions, Cromwell gave Ussher a State funeral in Westminster Abbey.

42. Anonymous, *The Copy of a Most Pious and Pithy Letter*, p.5.

43. Christopher Love (1618-1651) was a Welshman, educated at

Oxford. He stood against Laud's canons at the University and left to take a chaplaincy in London. He was a controversial preacher at Windsor Castle during the Civil War and received Presbyteral ordination before becoming pastor of St. Lawrence Jewry in London. As a leading Presbyterian agitating in favour of Charles II, he was arrested on 7 May 1651 and beheaded on Tower Hill on 22 August the same year.

44. Love, *Englands Distemper, having Division and Error, as its Cause*, p.7, 1645

45. *The Works of John Owen*, VIII.1ff.

46. The sermon is dated 29 April 1646. The war, which had begun at Nottingham in August 1642, was all but over when Owen received the summons to preach before Parliament. The King left Oxford during the last week of April and surrendered himself to the Scots in May.

47. Owen, *A Vision of Unchangeable, Free Mercy*, VIII.6 (italics his).

48. Owen, *A Vision of Unchangeable, Free Mercy*, VIII.6f

49. Owen, *A Vision of Unchangeable, Free Mercy*, VIII.24f

50. Owen, *A Vision of Unchangeable, Free Mercy*, VIII.29

51. *The Works of John Owen*, VIII.128ff.

52. Goold, 'The Life of Dr. Owen', in *The Works of John Owen*, I.40

53. 2 Kings 21:1-18

54. Owen, *Righteous Zeal Encouraged by Divine Protection*, VIII.135f

55. Owen, *Righteous Zeal Encouraged*, VIII.136

56. Owen, Introduction to *Righteous Zeal Encouraged*, VIII.129

57. Owen, Introduction to *Righteous Zeal Encouraged*, VIII.129

58. The most comprehensive of these works are the following: B. Ball's *The English Connection. The Puritan Roots of Seventh-day Adventist Belief* (Cambridge: James Clarke, 1981) and *A Great Expectation: Eschatological Thought in English Protestantism to 1660* (Leiden: E.J. Brill, 1975), P. Toon's *Puritans, the Millennium and the Future of Israel* (Cambridge: James Clarke, 1970) and Hill's *Antichrist in Seventeenth Century England*.

59. Haller, quoted by C.R. Smith in his article, ' "Up and be Doing": The Pragmatic Puritan Eschatology of John Owen', *Evangelical Quarterly* 61:4 (1989), 343

60. Owen, *A Vision of Unchangeable, Free Mercy*, VIII.39

61. Owen, *A Vision of Unchangeable, Free Mercy*, VIII.15

62. 'Post-millennialism' is broadly that category of beliefs which endorse a 'thousand year' period (literal or non-literal) which can be distinguished from the rest of history by the prevailing of good over

evil, both spiritual advancement and social improvements. After that will come the Parousia, the return of Christ. Owen believed that the generation in which he lived was either to be interpreted as that period of history or, at the very least, as a time that would prepare the way and usher in that period. Whilst giving Owen the label of a 'post-millennialist', it is necessary to remember that this definition would have been anathema to the man himself; such terminology and differentiation of millennial views was not current in theological debate until the nineteenth century. I.H. Murray is helpful in categorising mainstream Puritan millennial beliefs in *The Puritan Hope* (Edinburgh: Banner of Truth, 1971), p.52f.

63. Owen, *Righteous Zeal Encouraged*, VIII.147.

64. Johannes Alsted (1588-1638) became professor of philosophy at Herborn in 1610. In 1629, he went to the new University of Weissenburg after having represented the Church of Nassau at the Synod of Dort. Alsted was one of the most prolific authors of his time, covering a vast range of philosophical topics.

65. Sterry based his idea on the text from Matthew 24:37: 'As were the days of Noah, so will be the coming of the Son of Man' (RSV). See Hill 'Till the Conversion of the Jews' in *Millenarianism and Messianism* ed. R.H. Popkin (Leiden: E.J. Brill, 1988), p.15. cf. Z. Crofton, *Bethshemesh Clouded* (London, 1653), p.3-4, cited by David S. Katz, *Philo-Semitism and the Readmission of the Jews to England 1603-1655* (Oxford: Clarendon Press 1982), p.89: 'It was in 1656, the flood came on the old world, and lasted fourty daies: Ergo in that year 1656, fire must come on this world and last fourty years.'

66. John Napier (1550-1617) was a Scottish mathematician, educated at St. Andrews. A strict Presbyterian, Napier is best known not for his theological views but for discovering logarithms in 1614. Three years later, he published a work that improved the notation for writing decimals.

67. Samuel Hartlib (died 1670?) was a half-Polish educationist and a prolific pamphleteer. He was to have a great influence on the work and writings of Milton and received a pension from Cromwell. Very little is known of him after the Restoration.

68. Hartlib, *Clavis Apocaliptica*, p.156f

69. William Lilly (1602-81) came from a farming family in the Midlands. Receiving little by way of education, he was nevertheless able to learn some classical languages at a tender age. In 1620, he moved to London and earned a living as a domestic servant. Lilly became interested in astrology in 1632 but, suffering from depression in 1637,

was forced to leave his pupils and move to Hersham in Surrey. He continued to write on astrology until his move back to London five years later. His annual almanacs sold very well, as did the other writings that came from his prolific pen. During the 1640s, Lilly served parliament and received a pension. The next decade saw Lilly coming to prominence throughout the Continent for his astrological predictions. Although arrested at the Restoration, Lilly was soon set free. After 1666, he lived at Hersham and studied medicine. He died of paralysis in 1681.

70. Lilly, *The Starry Messenger*, p.11

71. Lilly, *The Starry Messenger*, p.24

72. Lilly, *The Starry Messenger*, p.20

73. Lilly, *The Starry Messenger*, p.24

74. Owen, *Seasonable Words for English Protestants*, IX.10f (italics his).

75. Owen, Preface to *The Duties of Pastors and People Distinguished*, XIII.5

76. 'All men know who he is that saith he can shut up heaven and open it at his pleasure, and took upon him to be Lord and Master above all kings and princes, before whom kings and princes fall down and worship, honouring that Antichrist as a God.' Quoted by Hill, *Antichrist in Seventeenth-Century England*, p.4.

77. Hill gives many examples of this in *Antichrist in the Seventeenth Century*, p.7f. The following are just some: Gregory VII, Gregory IX, and Sylvester I.

78. Thomas Brightman (1562-1607) was educated at Queen's College, Cambridge. An early Presbyterian, he was famous for his expositions on Revelation and Daniel. His collected works became available in 1644.

79. Hill, *Antichrist in the Seventeenth-Century*, p.27.

80. Owen, *The Use and Advantage of Faith in a Time of Public Calamity*, IX.510 (italics his).

81. Quoted by Toon in his book *Puritans, the Millennium and the Future of Israel*, p.37

82. 'And this word, Yet once more, signifieth the removing of those things that are shaken, as of things that are made, that those things which cannot be shaken may remain.'

83. Owen, *The Shaking and Translating of Heaven and Earth*, VIII.253

84. Owen, *The Shaking and Translating*, VIII.253

85. Owen, *The Shaking and Translating*, VIII.257

86. Most pertinent to Owen's exposition are the following texts:

Daniel 2:44; 7:27; 12:10; Rev. 17:12-16; 18:2; 19:13. Owen, *The Shaking and Translating*, VIII.261-263.

87. Whilst not limiting itself to those writing exclusively on Daniel and Revelation, Dr. Bernard Capp's research gives some idea of the extent of published millennial interest. Of those people who published three or more works between 1640 and 1653, no less than 77 expressed millenarian ideas compared with only 34 who did not. B.S. Capp, *The Fifth Monarchy Men* (New Jersey: Rowman & Littlefield, 1972), p. 46f.

88. The *preterist* view interprets the Scriptures as written for the people of that time. All the events described were relevant to the first hearers and readers. The *futurist* view regards the apocalyptic writings in Scripture as describing events that will happen in the future with direct reference to the Second Coming of Jesus. The *historicist* view interprets these passages as being prophetic readings of history; some of the events have already happened whilst others are still to come. For an analysis of the Book of Revelation in the light of these three approaches, see R. Kyle, *Awaiting the Millennium* (Leicester: IVP, 1998), p.33.

89. Owen's sermon is littered with such references and it would be useful to cite only one example to show his historicist perspective: 'The great river Euphrates, the strength and fulness of whose streams doth yet rage so high that there is no passage for the kings of the east to come over. Wherefore this must be dried up...Rev.xvi.12. Doubtless this is spoken in allusion to Abraham's coming over that river into Canaan...and then it may well enough denote the Turkish power; which, proud as it is at this day, possessing in peace all those regions of the east, yet God can quickly make it wither and be dried up.' Owen, *The Shaking and Translating*, VIII.267

90. Owen, *The Shaking and Translating*, VIII.278, 279

91. Owen, *A Vision of Unchangeable, Free Mercy*, VIII.16

92. Owen, *A Vision of Unchangeable, Free Mercy*, VIII.19

93. Owen was not alone in his concern for the lack Christian faith in Wales. See Hill's comments in *The World Turned Upside Down*, p.73ff.

94. Owen, *A Vision of Unchangeable, Free Mercy*, VIII.19. Augustine used the phrase in *De Ordine*, I.iv.11. For the story behind Augustine's allusion, see Evans, *Augustine on Evil*, p.93f.

95. Owen, *A Vision of Unchangeable, Free Mercy*, VIII.23

96. Owen, *Ebenezer: A Memorial of the Deliverance of Essex County, and Committee*, VIII.97

97. Smith explores this co-dependent relationship in his article, '"Up

and be Doing": The Pragmatic Puritan Eschatology of John Owen' *Evangelical Quarterly*, 61:4 (1989), 335-349.

98. Owen, *Righteous Zeal Encouraged*, VIII.133f

99. Owen, *Righteous Zeal Encouraged*, VIII.152

100. Owen, *Righteous Zeal Encouraged*, VIII.135

101. Owen, *Righteous Zeal Encouraged*, VIII.137

102. See Katz, *Philo-Semitism and the Readmission of the Jews to England 1603-1655*, p.2f.

103. Quoted by Katz in *Philo-Semitism and the Readmission of the Jews to England 1603-1655*, p.194

104. Katz, *Philo-Semitism and the Readmission of the Jews to England, 1603-1655*, p.195.

105. Katz, *Philo-Semitism and the Readmission of the Jews to England, 1603-1655*, p.202.

106. Katz, *Philo-Semitism and the Readmission of the Jews to England, 1603-1655*, p.204.

107. The Conference met on the following dates in 1655: 4, 7, 12, 14 and 18 December.

108. Katz, *Philo-Semitism and the Readmission of the Jews to England, 1603-1655*, p.209.

109. The letter sent to Owen by Lawrence the following day is copied in *The Correspondence of John Owen*, No. 38, p.88

110. Owen, *The Correspondence of John Owen*, No. 39, p88

111. Quoted by Katz, *Philo-Semitism and the Readmission of the Jews to England 1603-1655*, p. 215

112. Owen, *Christ's Kingdom and the Magistrate's Power*, VIII.375 (italics his).

113. Owen, *Christ's Kingdom*, VIII.375f

114. Owen, *Christ's Kingdom*, VIII.376

115. Katz examines the impact of radical millenarianism on the Jewish question in Chapter 3 of his book *Philo-Semitism and the Readmission of the Jews to England 1603-1655*, p.89ff.

116. A.G. Matthews ed., *The Savoy Declaration of Faith and Order 1658* (Letchworth: Independent Press, 1959), p.42f.

117. Matthews, *The Savoy Declaration of Faith and Order 1658*, p.43

118. Toon, *God's Statesman*, p.106

119. Toon, *God's Statesman*, p.106 (italics mine).

120. Owen, *A Vision of Unchangeable, Free Mercy*, VIII.26

121. Owen, *A Vision of Unchangeable, Free Mercy*, VIII.26 (italics his).

122. Owen, *A Vision of Unchangeable, Free Mercy*, VIII.24

123. Respectfully acknowledging, but refuting, the crucial research produced by R.S. Paul in *The Lord Protector*, M. Watts considers the mystery surrounding Cromwell's church allegiance in *the Dissenters* Vol. 1 (Oxford: Clarendon, 1978), p.107f.

124. Thomas Fairfax (1612-71) studied at St. John's College, Cambridge, before serving as a volunteer in Holland in 1629. In 1642, he was appointed General of Horse under his father before gaining supreme command of the New Model Army three years later. He was one of the judges at the trial of Charles I but did not want to issue the death sentence. In 1650, he refused to march against the Scots and, consequently, Cromwell was appointed Commander-in-chief. After Cromwell's death, he worked hard for the Restoration.

125. An account of this meeting is given by Toon in *God's Statesman*, p.36

126. Owen, *The Steadfastness of the Promises, and the Sinfulness of Staggering*, VIII.235 [Capitals his].

127. Hill, *God's Englishman* (London: Weidenfield & Nicolson, 1970), p.171ff

128. Fraser, *Cromwell Our Chief of Men*, p.589.

129. Roger Boyle, Lord Broghill (1621-79), as well as enjoying no small fame as a playwright, served under Cromwell in Ireland. He had received an education at Trinity College, Dublin and at Oxford. Switching allegiance in the 1640s between parliamentary and royalist persuasions, he enjoyed Cromwell's confidence during the Commonwealth and, after the Lord Protector's death, prepared Ireland for the Restoration.

130. It was, however, John Ashe who raised the issue before Parliament, supported by George Downing and Sir Christopher Packe. Hill, *God's Englishman*, p.173

131. Charles Fleetwood (d. 1692) began his military career as a life-guard of the Earl of Essex. By the Battle of Naseby, he was Commander of Horse. In 1646, he entered Parliament but played no part in the trial of the king. In 1650, he accompanied Cromwell to Scotland. Fleetwood's influence increased when he married Cromwell's daughter, Henry Ireton's widow. He enjoyed a leading role in Cromwell's court as a member of the Council. An unsubstantiated, though plausible, story from the time is that Cromwell wanted Fleetwood to be his successor. He escaped exactions at the Restoration because he was not guilty of regicide. His only punishment was permanent removal from public office. He retired to Stoke Newington with his third wife and was a member of Owen's congregation. He was buried in Bunhill Fields, near Owen.

132. John Lambert (1619-84) was a Captain under Fairfax at the outbreak of the Civil War. He rose rapidly through the ranks and achieved his greatest notoriety after Cromwell's death by dispelling the Rump Parliament in October 1659. He was put on trial in 1662 and remained in prison until his death, twenty-two years later.

133. John Desborough (1608-80) was married to Oliver Cromwell's sister, Jane. By 1642, he was Captain in the regiment of horse and was renowned for his bravery in the Civil War. Desborough took no part in the trial of the king. As major-general, he fought at Worcester and later became a member of Cromwell's Council of State. At the Restoration, Desborough was arrested and he was permanently removed from public office. After being falsely arrested for plotting to kill Charles II, he left England and went to Holland. Declared a traitor in 1666, he was forced to return to England to be imprisoned in the Tower. After his release, Desborough fell into obscurity and died in Hackney.

134. Quoted by Fraser in *Cromwell Our Chief of Men*, p.605

135. Fraser, *Cromwell Our Chief of Men*, p. 611f.

136. Fraser, *Cromwell Our Chief of Men*, p.611.

137. Thomas Pride, who died in 1658, began life as a drayman and brewer in London. He rose to the rank of Colonel during the war and is most famous for his Purge of Presbyterian Royalists from Parliament in December 1648. His signature was on Charles I's death warrant.

138. Hill notes that a majority of Army officers in London signed the petition; at least two out of each regiment. Hill, *God's Englishman*, p.173.

139. For details of Cromwell's funeral see Fraser, *Cromwell Our Chief of Men*, p.683f.

140. Toon, *God's Statesman*, p.102. Toon cites as his sources for this information the *Public Intelligencer*, Nov 22-29, 1658, and the *Diary of Thomas Barton*, II, p.529.

141. Owen, *Reflections on a Slanderous Libel against Dr. Owen*, XVI.273f.

142. Toon, *God's Statesman*, p.106

143. Edmund Ludlow (1617-92) studied at Trinity College, Oxford. After the Restoration, he lived in France and died at Vevey.

144. Sir Henry Vane the Younger (1613-62) was educated at Oxford but, despite his privileged background, opposed the Royalist cause. He entered Parliament in 1640 as member for Hull and, within five years, was the leading parliamentarian. His particular skills lay in the field of foreign policy. Vane was executed in 1662.

145. Wallingford House was the home of General Fleetwood. Owen

gathered a church of army officers of varying factions and persuasions which became based there. This became known as the Wallingford House Party which, in March 1657, began discussions with Republicans in the House of Commons (Toon, *God's Statesman*, p.109f).

146. Owen, *The Glory and Interest of Nations Professing the Gospel*, VIII.458

147. Owen, *The Glory and Interest of Nations*, VIII.453ff

148. Owen, *The Glory and Interest of Nations*, VIII.457

149. Owen, *The Glory and Interest of Nations*, VIII.458

150. Owen, *The Glory and Interest of Nations*, VIII.466

151. Owen, *The Glory and Interest of Nations*, VIII.467 (italics his).

152. Owen, *The Glory and Interest of Nations*, VIII.467f

153. Marchamont Needham (1620-78) was educated at St. John's College, Oxford. He was admitted a member of Gray's Inn in 1652 and studied medicine for a time before turning to journalism. His *Mercurius Britannicus* newspaper was pro-parliamentary and was first issued in August 1643. Needham was a bold writer who soon became notorious, to the point of suffering imprisonment for his views in 1645. In 1647, he took up the royalist cause and began to refer to Cromwell as 'Copper-Nose,' 'Nose Almighty,' and 'The Town-bull of Ely.' His satirical wit was not appreciated and Needham was forced to leave London for a time. In 1650, he transferred his allegiances yet again and was gifted with an annual pension. Needham suffered great unpopularity after Cromwell's death and he fled to Holland in 1660. There, he practised medicine with occasional pamphleteering.

154. The irony of this statement appears to be lost on Toon when he mentions the episode in *God's Statesman*, p.99. Toon suggests that Owen would have been angry at such 'gossip', but this surely overstates something that was meant as a joke not an expected turn of events.

155. Love, *Englands Distemper*, p. 20f

156. Marshall, *A Sacred Record to be made of Gods Mercies to Zion*, 1645.

157. Love, *Englands Distemper*, p. 16,17

158. Anthony Tuckney (1599-1670) was educated at Emmanuel College, Cambridge. He became a household chaplain in 1619 before returning to the University as a tutor. Benjamin Whichote was one of his pupils. In 1633, Tuckney succeeded John Cotton as vicar at Boston. His brave ministry was well respected during the plague of 1637 and he became one of the Westminster divines in 1643. Three years later, he became Lady Margaret professor of divinity and moved back to Cambridge. After the Restoration, his positions were taken from him

and he moved to London. He died of jaundice and scurvy.

159. Tuckney, *The Balme of Gilead for the Wounds of England* (1643) p. 23f

160. Matthews, *The Savoy Declaration of Faith and Order 1658*, p.42

161. Thomas Reeve (1594-1672) was educated at Caius College, Cambridge. A staunch royalist, he was presented with the living at Waltham Abbey, Essex immediately after taking orders. He remained there until his death. Reeve seems to have been much admired as a preacher.

162. Joseph Glanvill (1636-80) was educated at Exeter College, Oxford. He was a Latitudinarian, taking his livings in the West Country until 1678 when he was installed as prebendary of Worcester. Glanvill was an admirer of and regular correspondent with the Cambridge Platonist, Henry More.

163. Reeve, Epistle Dedicatory of *Englands Beauty in seeing Charles the Second Restored in Majesty*.

164. Owen, *The Correspondence of John Owen*, No. 70, p.132f

165. Glanvill, *A Loyal Tear Dropt on the Vault*, 1667, p.6f

166. Toon, *God's Statesman*, p.122

167. The *Declaration* was issued by Charles II on 4th April 1660: 'Because the passion and uncharitableness of the times have produced several opinions in religion...we do declare a liberty to tender consciences, and that no man shall be disquieted or called in question for differences of opinion in matters of religion, which do not disturb the peace of the Kingdom.' Cited by A. Harold Wood, *Church Unity Without Uniformity* (London: Epworth Press, 1963), p.122.

168. The beliefs and activities of the Fifth Monarchists and the Quakers are dealt with elsewhere in this thesis. For details about the history and ideology of the Muggletonians, see C. Hill, B. Reay and W. Lamont, *The World of the Muggletonians* (London: Temple Smith, 1983).

169. This Act, passed on 19 May 1662, is properly known as *The Act for the Uniformity of Public Prayers, and Administration of Sacraments.*

170. R. Tudur Jones gives excellent, and exhaustive, details concerning those ejected in *Congregationalism in England 1662-1962* (London: Independent Press, 1962) p.46-62. He does acknowledge the research of A.G. Matthews, produced in *Calamy Revised* (Oxford: Clarendon, 1934), in this regard.

171. For details, see Tudur Jones, *Congregationalism in England 1662-1962*, p.57.

172. On 10 January, a Royal proclamation outlawed meetings of Quakers, Anabaptists and Fifth Monarchists. Within a matter of weeks, 4,230 Quakers were languishing in prison. In May 1662, a law was passed outlawing the meeting together for worship of five or more Quakers. Watts, *The Dissenters* Vol. 1, p.223f.

173. The full title was *The Act to prevent and suppress Seditious Conventicles.* Passed on 17 May 1664, those convening unlawful religious gatherings could be fined £5 or imprisoned for three months in the first instance. The second offence doubled both penalties and a third conviction could result in either transportation or a fine of £100. For details, see Tudur Jones, *Congregationalism in England 1662-1962*, p.66.

174. Tudur Jones details the impact of the Five Mile Act, properly known as *An Act for Restraining Nonconformists from Inhabiting in Corporations*, in *Congregationalism in England 1662-1962*, p.67.

175. For individual examples, see Tudur Jones *Congregationalism in England 1662-1962*, p.63f. See also Watts, *The Dissenters* Vol. 1, p.227f.

176. J. Asty, 'Memoirs of the Life of Dr. Owen', in *A Complete Collection of the Sermons of John Owen* (London, 1721), p.xxix. Toon supplies brief biographical details of these men in *God's Statesman*, p.126f.

177. The last Will and Testament of John Owen would suggest that he was indeed a man of means. In that Will, he left instructions for two properties that he owned; one in Stadham, Oxfordshire and the other in Eaton, Berkshire. As well as providing for his immediate family, Owen saw fit to distribute more than £685 among more distant relatives and friends. There is also mention made of a Bond for the sum of £1,332 (Owen, *The Correspondence of John Owen*, p.181f).

178. Toon suggests that, whilst Owen spent considerable time at Stadham, his family resided variously at Hanslope in Buckinghamshire and with the Fleetwood family at Stoke Newington on the outskirts of London (*God's Statesman*, p.129f).

179. Owen, *Indulgence and Toleration Considered: in a Letter unto a Person of Honour*, XIII.526 (capitals his).

180. Owen, *An Account of the Grounds and Reasons on which Protestant Dissenters Desire Their Liberty*, XIII.578.

181. Camfield, *A Serious Examination of the Independent's Catechism*, p.1f

182. Tompkins, *The Inconveniences of Toleration*, p.2

183. Owen, *The Present Distresses on Nonconformists Examined*, XIII.579

184. Owen, *The Present Distresses on Nonconformists Examined*, XIII.580f.

185. Owen, *Indulgence and Toleration Considered*, XIII.529f

186. Owen, *Indulgence and Toleration Considered*, XIII.530

187. Owen, *A Dissertation on Divine Justice*, X.545

188. Owen, *Of Indwelling Sin*, VI.261 (italics his).

189. Owen, *A Memorial of the Deliverance of Essex County*, VIII.85f

190. Owen, *Of Walking Humbly with God*, IX.103, 116f

191. Owen, *Seasonable Words*, IX.10f

192. Thomas Brooks (1608-80) matriculated as pensioner of Emmanuel in 1625 and was ordained in the 1640s. He was a parliamentary preacher and minister of St. Margaret's, Fish-street Hill, London. He was ejected in 1662 but continued his ministry in Moorfields. He remained in London throughout the Plague of 1665.

193. Brooks, *London's Lamentations on the Late Fiery Dispensation*, in the *Complete Works of Thomas Brooks* ed. A. Grosart, 6 vols. (Edinburgh: Banner of Truth, 1980), VI.151f

194. Edward Chamberlayne (1616-1703) was educated at St. Edmund Hall, Oxford. At the outset of the Civil War, he moved to the Continent and returned at the Restoration. In 1679, he tutored Charles II's illegitimate son, Henry. Chamberlayne was one of the original members of the Royal Society.

195. Chamberlayne, *Angliæ Novitiæ: or The Present State of England*, p.199f

196. Owen, *A Word of Advice to the Citizens of London*, XIII.589

197. Owen, *An Humble Testimony unto the Goodness and Severity of God in His Dealing with Sinful Churches and Nations*, VIII.610, 611 (italics his).

198. Owen, *Seasonable Words*, IX.9

199. Owen, *An Humble Testimony*, VIII.597 (italics his).

200. Owen, *An Humble Testimony*, VIII.604f. (italics his).

201. Owen, *An Humble Testimony*, VIII.620, 621 (italics his).

202. Owen, *An Humble Testimony*, VIII.621f.

203. Owen, *Discourse III*, IX.366

Chapter Four: Sin and the Church

1. Owen, *A Display of Arminianism*, X.54 (italics his).

2. Owen, *Justification by Faith*, V.133

3. Owen, *On the Holy Spirit*, III.592

4. Owen, *On the Holy Spirit*, III.592

5. Owen, *A Display of Arminianism*, X.11ff

6. Owen, *On the Holy Spirit*, III.596

7. Owen, *Two Short Catechisms: Wherein the Principles of the Doctrine of Christ are Unfolded and Explained*, I.485

8. Owen, *The Branch of the Lord*, VIII.286

9. Owen, *A Brief Instruction*, XV.479

10. Ferguson, *John Owen on the Christian Life*, p.159

11. Owen, *An Inquiry into the Original*, XV.228 (italics his).

12. Owen, *An Inquiry into the Original*, XV.228

13. Owen, *True Nature of a Gospel Church and Its Government*, XVI.27

14. Owen, *True Nature of a Gospel Church*, XVI.25, 26

15. Owen, *True Nature of a Gospel Church*, XVI.29

16. Owen, *True Nature of a Gospel Church*, XVI.29f

17. Owen, *True Nature of a Gospel Church*, XVI.30

18. Owen, *True Nature of a Gospel Church*, XVI.27 (italics his).

19. Owen, *True Nature of a Gospel Church*, XVI.30

20. Owen, *True Nature of a Gospel Church*, XVI.27f.

21. G.F. Nuttall, *Visible Saints 1640-60* (Oxford: Blackwell, 1957), p.78f

22. For a brief history of the Independent church at Bury St. Edmunds, and the controversy concerning their covenants, see M. Watts, *The Dissenters*, Vol. 1, p.157f.

23. Owen, *True Nature of a Gospel Church*, XVI.27 (italics his).

24. William Bartlet (d. 1682) was educated at New Inn Hall, Oxford and ministered to a congregation in Wapping, London during the 1640s. In 1649, he took up a lectureship at Bideford in Devon before being ejected in 1662.

25. Both these examples quoted by Nuttall in *Visible Saints 1640-60*, p.73

26. Owen, *True Nature of a Gospel Church*, XVI.29

27. Owen, *Eshcol*, XIII.62ff

28. Nuttall, *Visible Saints 1640-60*, p.131ff

29. Owen, *True Nature of a Gospel Church*, XVI.1ff.

30. Owen, *True Nature of a Gospel Church*, XVI.21(italics his).

31. Owen, *True Nature of a Gospel Church*, XVI.15f (italics his).

32. Owen, *True Nature of a Gospel Church*, XVI.18 (italics his).

33. Owen, *The Correspondence of John Owen*, p.136f

34. Owen, *Of Spiritual Gifts*, IV.477

35. Most notably in his works *Of Schism, A Review of the True Nature of Schism, An Answer to a Late Treatise About the Nature of Schism*

and *A Brief Vindication of the Nonconformists from the Charge of Schism*, all found in Volume XIII of his *Works*, p.90ff.

36. Owen, *True Nature of a Gospel Church*, XVI.21 (italics his).

37. Owen, *True Nature of a Gospel Church*, XVI.21f.

38. Owen, *Eshcol*, XIII.67f.

39. Owen, *Eshcol*, XIII.68. (italics his).

40. Baxter, *Rel. Baxt.*, app.IV.88

41. Owen, *Of Schism*, XIII.115

42. Nuttall, *Visible Saints 1640-60*, p.57f

43. Anonymous, *Two Captains, two Camps: Their Fatall and Finall Warres*, p.15f.

44. William Prynne (1600-69) was educated at Oriel College and Lincoln's Inn. He was a most prolific author, active in the Long Parliament and most scathing of Archbishop Laud. Prynne was a presbyterian who suffered imprisonment. After the Restoration, he was released and appointed Keeper of the Records in the Tower.

45. Prynne, *The Popish Royal Favourite*, 1643

46. Laud, *The Archbishop of Canterbury's Speech: or, His Funeral Sermon, preached by himself*, p.10f.

47. Prynne, *A looking-glasse for all lordly prelates*, 1636

48. Owen, *Eshcol*, XIII.69

49. Bartlet, *A Model of the Primitive Congregational Way*, p.48

50. Nuttall, *Visible Saints 1640-60*, p.53f.

51. Owen, *Eshcol*, XIII.69

52. A. Harold Wood, *Church Unity Without Uniformity* (London: Epworth Press, 1963), p.243

53. Owen, *The Correspondence of John Owen*, No.72, p.136

54. Owen, *The Correspondence of John Owen*, No.72, p.138

55. Baxter, *The Correspondence of John Owen*, No.73, p.142

56. On 10 May 1662, Baxter preached a sermon at St. Paul's Cathedral, thanking God for the peaceful restoration of the monarchy. On 22 July, he preached a sermon, *The Life of Faith*, before the King. G. Nuttall, *Richard Baxter* (London: Nelson, 1965), p.86

57. Nuttall suggests that '[Baxter's] contribution to the conference, as leader on his side, was second to none; and the "Reformed Liturgy" which he drew up for it was a remarkable achievement, even without regard to the fact that he composed it within a fortnight.' Nuttall, *Richard Baxter*, p.89

58. Nuttall, *Richard Baxter*, p.91

59. J.R. Jones ed., *The Restored Monarchy* (MacMillan: London, 1979), p.164

60. Owen, *Of Schism*, XIII.91ff

61. Owen, *Of Schism*, XIII.193

62. Jeremiah Burroughs (1599-1646) was educated at Emmanuel College, Cambridge, and was admitted pensioner in 1617. He left the university because of his nonconformity, and ministered with Edmund Calamy at Bury St. Edmunds. In 1631, he moved to Norfolk but was suspended five years later. In 1637, Burroughs moved to Rotterdam, returning to England in 1641. He was one of the Westminster divines in 1643.

63. Burroughs, *A Vindication*, p. 22 (1646)

64. Daniel Cawdry (1588-1664) was a presbyterian minister in Northamptonshire from 1625. Turning down a bishopric at the Restoration, he was ejected as a non-conformist in 1662. Cawdrey retired to Wellingborough, where he died.

65. Cawdrey, *Independencie A Great Schism*, p.189f

66. Owen, *An Inquiry into the Original*, XV.323 (italics his).

67. *The Works of John Owen*, IX.320ff. 3 November 1676 was a day of prayer and fasting.

68. Owen, *Perilous Times*, IX.329

69. Owen, *Perilous Times*, IX.330

70. A. Wood, *Athenae Oxonienses* (Oxford, 1813-18), Vol. IV, col. 98

71. Titus 2:14

72. Owen, *Perilous Times*, IX.330

73. Owen, *Perilous Times*, IX.331

74. Owen, *Perilous Times*, IX.326

75. Owen, *Perilous Times*, IX.327

76. Owen, *Perilous Times*, IX.327

77. For a brief treatment of the life of Arminius, see A. Harrison, *Arminianism* (London: Duckworth, 1937) also W. Robert Godfrey's article, 'Who was Arminius?' *Arminianism* May/June 1992 n.p. For a more in-depth biography, see C. Bangs, *Arminius – A Study in the Dutch Reformation* (Grand Rapids, Michigan: Francis Asbury Press, 1985).

78. The most comprehensive treatment of the influence of Arminianism during this period can be found in Tyacke's *Anti-Calvinists – The Rise of English Arminianism c.1590-1640*.

79. Tyacke, *Anti-Calvinists – The Rise of English Arminianism c.1590-1640*, p.20.

80. This comment is attributed to Menage in Goold's 'Prefatory Note' to *Vindiciae Evangelicae*, XII.4.

81. Gerard Vossius (1577-1649) was a Dutch scholar, appointed in 1600 as Rector of the school at Dort. In 1615, he took the same position

at the theological college in Leyden and was made a canon of Canterbury in 1629. He died in Amsterdam after having taken the Chair of History in 1632.

82. J. L'Evesque de Burigny, *The Life of the truly Eminent and Learned Hugo Grotius*, London, 1754

83. William Barrett (fl. 1595) was pensioner of Trinity College, Cambridge and fellow of Caius College. In 1595, he was ordered to recant of an anti-Calvinist sermon by the Cambridge heads of colleges. This he did, but in a most irreverent and ungracious manner. That was not the end of the matter, however, and Barrett was summoned to Lambeth to make a further recantation, which he did after much delay. In 1597, Barrett fled to the Continent and became a Roman Catholic. Eventually, he returned to England and lived out his days as a layman.

84. Lancelot Andrewes (1555-1626) was educated at Pembroke Hall, Cambridge. He was ordained in 1580 and was made Dean of Westminster in 1601. Andrewes held three bishoprics: Chichester (1605), Ely (1605) and Winchester (1619).

85. Laud, *The Archbishop of Canterbury's Speech*, 1644, p.14.

86. Prynne, *Canterburies Doome*, 1646, p.565

87. John Goodwin (1594?-1665) was educated at Queens' College, Cambridge, becoming a fellow in 1617. He was a popular preacher in East Anglia before moving to London in 1632. The Quaker Isaac Pennington was one of his parishioners. In 1645, he was ejected from his living for refusing to administer the sacraments to all parishioners. Goodwin was a passionate republican and supported the purging of Parliament. At the Restoration, Goodwin was arrested but soon returned to his congregation. He was a prolific author.

88. George Montaigne (1569-1628) was born into a humble farm home in Yorkshire. He was educated at Queens' College, Cambridge, becoming a fellow in 1592. After ordination, he became a private chaplain and only returned to Cambridge eight years later. In 1607, Montaigne was appointed professor of divinity at Gresham College, London and returned to a chaplaincy role. In 1609, he took a living in Cheam, Surrey and, a year later, was appointed dean at Westminster. Eight years later, he was appointed to the see of Lincoln and thereafter to Winchester in 1619. Three years later Montaigne was appointed Bishop of London. His appointment as Bishop of Durham in 1627 was a bitter blow to a man who had longed for the see of York. He only had to wait one year, however, for his dream to be fulfilled. Ironically, he died on the very day that he was enthroned as Archbishop of York.

89. John Howson (1557?-1632) was educated at Christ Church,

Oxford. In 1587, he was installed as prebendary of Hereford Cathedral. In 1592, he was installed at Exeter and made chaplain to the queen six years later. After numerous other livings, Howson became Vice-Chancellor of Christ Church but, unlike Owen in the future, did all he could to suppress Puritanism. In 1619, Howson was consecrated Bishop of Oxford from where he was translated to Durham in 1628. Three years later, he was buried in St. Paul's Cathedral.

90. John Buckeridge (1562?-1631) was a foundation fellow of St. John's College, Oxford and became President in 1605. He was tutor to William Laud and influenced him in anti-Calvinist doctrine. After a chaplaincy under Robert Devereux, earl of Essex, Buckeridge took a living in Leicestershire, only to be succeeded by Laud. He became royal chaplain, archdeacon of Northampton and, in 1604, was consecrated Bishop of Chichester. Thereafter, he was translated to Rochester. In 1628, he went to Ely and died three years later.

91. Richard Montague (1577-1641) was educated at King's College, Cambridge. After taking two livings – in Somerset and Essex – he was installed as dean of Hereford in 1616 and then archdeacon a year later. After twelve years as an able controversialist, Montague was consecrated Bishop of Chichester. He was always a controversial Bishop and handled polemical debate well in print. In 1638, he was translated to Norwich, where he died three years later.

92. Tyacke, 'Puritanism, Arminianism and Counter-Revolution' in *The Origins of the English Civil War*, ed. C. Russell (Basingstoke: MacMillan, 1973), p.132

93. John Cosin (1594-1672) was educated at Caius College, Cambridge. He was deprived of his benefice in 1641, ejected in 1644 and retired to Paris. He recovered his preferments at the Restoration and was involved in the final revision of the Book of Common Prayer.

94. William Chappell (1582-1649) was educated at Christ's Church, Cambridge where he excelled above all pupils and eventually became a tutor. In 1633, he was installed as dean at Cashel and, soon after, provost of Trinity College, Dublin. He was consecrated Bishop of Cork and Ross in 1638 and, later in the year, was translated to Dublin. In 1641, he returned to England where he was imprisoned the next year. Upon his release, he spent his time quietly in the Midlands until his death in Derby in 1649.

95. John Bramhall (1594-1663) was educated at Sidney Sussex College, Cambridge. After ordination, he took a living in Yorkshire and, thereafter, chaplain to the Archbishop of York. He went to Ireland in 1633 as Wentworth's chaplain. The following year, he was consecrated

as Bishop of Derry. Bramhall was impeached in 1641, accused of unconstitutional acts. Ussher saw to it that he was acquitted soon after. After the insurrection of 1641, Bramhall fled back to England and, seven years later, was in Brussels. He returned to Ireland late in 1648 and stayed until the Restoration. In 1661, he was translated to Armagh. He died in a courtroom from his third stroke.

96. D.D. Wallace, *Puritans and Predestination* (Chapel Hill: University of North Carolina, 1982), p.96

97. From 1626, at least five books were written in criticism of Montague. The chief protagonists were Henry Burton, John Yates, William Prynne, Daniel Featley and Anthony Wotton. For details of their printed attacks on Montague, see Tyacke *Anti-Calvinists - The Rise of English Arminianism c.1590-1640*, p.155-157.

98. Tyacke, *Anti-Calvinists - The Rise of English Arminianism c.1590-1640*, p.102f.

99. Prynne, *Canterburies Doome*, p.171

100. Published in London in 1645.

101. William Twisse (1578?-1646) was educated at New College, Oxford. After a short period as chaplain to the Queen of Bohemia, Twisse was given the living of Newton, Buckinghamshire. There, he devoted his energies to academic studies whilst pastoring his congregation. Twisse was a good controversialist, aware of subtleties of argument and, as such, opened the Westminster Assembly in 1643. In 1645, Twisse fainted in the pulpit and, thereafter, was often restricted to his bed until his death in Holborn the following year. Twisse was buried in Westminster Abbey but his remains were disinterred in 1661 and thrown into a common pit in St. Margaret's churchyard.

102. Goodwin, the Epistle Dedicatory, *Redemption Redeemed*, 1657

103. Francis Rous (1579-1659) was a Presbyterian member of the Long Parliament and the Westminster Assembly. He was made Provost of Eton in 1643 and was famed for his liturgical skills, especially his metrical version of the Psalms. Rous was, in his later years, appointed Speaker of the House during the Barebones Parliament.

104. Quoted by Harrison, *Arminianism*, p.140

105. Thomas Edwards (1599-1647) was opposed to both episcopacy and independency. He retired to Holland.

106. Edwards, *The First and Second Part of Gangraena*, p.74. Quoted by Wallace in *Puritans and Predestination*, p.109

107. Owen, Preface to William Twisse's *The Riches of God's Love*, Oxford, 1653.

108. John Stalham (d. 1681) was instituted as vicar of Terling, Essex

in 1632, succeeding Thomas Weld, who had been deprived by Laud. Stalham was a controversialist, most especially concerning infant baptism. In 1654, Stalham became assistant to the county commissioners for the removal of scandalous ministers. He wrote many polemical works against the Quakers before being ejected in 1662. He remained as pastor to a congregational church in Terling until his death.

109. Samuel Rutherford (c.1600-61) was a most devout Scottish pastor. His 1636 treatise, written against the Arminians, earned him a Chair of Divinity in Holland. Three years later, he was appointed Professor of Divinity at St. Andrew's. After the Restoration, the call for him to answer charges of high treason came too late; he was dying. The charges were subsequently dropped.

110. Owen, *A Display of Arminianism*, X.83f

111. Owen, *A Display of Arminianism*, X.84,85

112. Anthony Burgesse (fl. 1652) was educated at St. John's College, Cambridge and became a fellow of Emmanuel. He became vicar of Sutton Coldfield, Warwickshire but fled to Coventry during the Civil War. He was a member of the Westminster Assembly. Ejected after the Restoration, he retired to Tamworth, Staffordshire.

113. Burgesse, *The Doctrine of Original Sin Asserted and Vindicated*, 1658, p. A3f

114. Owen, *A Display of Arminianism*, X.84, 85

115. Owen, *A Display of Arminianism*, X.79

116. Owen, *Of Communion with God*, II.64.

117. 'Therefore as sin came into the world through one man and death through sin, and so death spread to all men because all men sinned – sin indeed was in the world before the law was given, but sin is not counted where there is no law. Yet death reigned from Adam to Moses, even over those whose sins were not like the transgression of Adam, who was a type of the one who was to come.' Romans 5:12-14 (RSV)

118. Owen, *A Display of Arminianism*, X.71

119. Owen, *Of Communion with God*, II.64

120. Owen, *Of Communion with God*, II.64f (italics his).

121. Owen, *A Display of Arminianism*, X.69

122. This view was taught, in embryonic form, by John Richardson, Regius Professor of Divinity at Emmanuel College, Cambridge, prior to 1610. In the manuscript *Lectiones D.D. Richardsoni de Praedestinatione*, he states that salvation is available 'to all men in general...[and to restrict] the grace of God to the elect removes any way for sinners to repent.' Quoted by Tyacke, *Anti-Calvinists – The Rise of English Arminiansim c.1590-1640*, p.38f..

123. Rem. Coll. Hag., fol. 76. Quoted by Owen, *A Display of Arminianism*, X.57

124. Owen, *A Display of Arminianism*, X.57

125. For biographical details, see T.M. Lindsay, *The History of the Reformation* Vol. 2 (Edinburgh: T & T Clark, 1908) and H. McLachlan, *Socinianism in Seventeenth-Century England* (London: OUP, 1951).

126. Lindsay, *The History of the Reformation*, Vol. 2, p.475f.

127. After receiving an Oxford education, John Bidle (1615-62) became Master of the Free School in Gloucester. His antitrinitarianism led to severe sufferings during the Commonwealth and, in 1655, he was banished to the Scilly Isles. Three years later, he was released but went straight back to London to preach. Four years of ministry ensued, after which he was imprisoned for non-payment of a £100 fine. He died in prison after five weeks.

128. McLachlan, *Socinianism in Seventeenth-Century England*, footnote, p.131

129. Francis Cheynell (1608-65) was educated at Merton College in 1623. He upset the authorities by denouncing episcopacy and ecclesiastical ceremonies but was presented a living near Banbury about 1632. His intellectual prowess was considerable and he was a member of the Westminster Assembly. Cheynell's house was plundered by royalist forces and he was forced to retire to Sussex. After having preached to Parliament on three occasions, he became a chaplain to the army of the Earl of Essex and was well respected as such. However, Cheynell was best remembered for his foul temper and bitter words which fell on those who opposed his views. He was deprived of his living prior to the Great Ejection and retired to Preston in Sussex.

130. Matthew Wren (1585-1667), educated at Pembroke Hall, was a protégé of Launcelot Andrewes. It was Andrewes who gave him the living of Teversham, near Cambridge, and by 1622 he had become chaplain to young Prince Charles. The next year, he was installed as Prebendary of Winchester. Two years later, he became master of Peterhouse, Cambridge before becoming dean of Windsor five years later. In 1634, he was given the see of Hereford. He only held that position for eight months before moving to Norwich and then again, in 1638, to Ely. In 1640, Wren was impeached and sent to the Tower. He was offered his freedom by Cromwell but refused to acknowledge his authority. He was discharged in 1659 but did not return to his palace until after the Restoration. He died at Ely House, Holborn.

131. Cheynell, *The Rise, Growth and Danger of Socinianisme*, 1643, p.1,7

132. Cheynell, *The Rise, Growth and Danger of Socinianisme*, 1643, p.24

133. Owen was commissioned in 1654 and the work was published a year later.

134. The full title of this work is as follows: *a Treatise of the Holy Ghost. In which the Godhead of the third Person of the Trinity is asserted against the subtleties of John Bidle.*

135. Full title: *The Blasphemer slaine With the Sword of the Spirit: Or a Plea for the Godhead of the Holy Ghost. Wherein the Deity of the Spirit of God is proved in the demonstration of the Spirit and vindicated from the Cavils of John Bidle.*

136. See *The Works of John Owen*, Vol. X and XII. e.g. Socinus himself X.506, 507, 522, 567, 569-583; XII. *passim*; Schlichting X.506; XII.412, 598, 599, 600; Smalcius X.506; XII.6, 28, 38, 40, 41, 59, 87, 117, 131, 154, 155, 180, 182, 268, 353, 354, 357, 377, 379, 412, 598, 600, 628, 629; and Crellius X.505, 506, 564-569, 593; XII.26, 27, 40, 50, 70, 88, 99, 108, 109, 117, 122, 126, 131, 155, 345, 402, 403, 412, 533, 598, 599, 601, 610, 625, 626, 627, 628, 629, 639.

137. Owen, *Vindiciæ Evangelicæ*, XII.146

138. McLachlan, *Socinianism in Seventeenth-Century England*, p.167

139. Owen, *Vindiciæ Evangelicæ*, XII.149

140. For short biographical accounts of the life of George Fox, see *The Dictionary of National Biography*, CD-Rom, Braithwaite, *The Beginnings of Quakerism*, and M. Davie, *British Quaker Theology Since 1895* (Lampeter: Edwin Meller Press, 1997).

141. Fox, *Concerning the Antiquity of the People of God called Quakers*, quoted by Hubbard, *Quaker by Convincement* (Harmondsworth: Penguin, 1974), p.32

142. Davie, *British Quaker Theology Since 1895*, p.13. See also Hill, *The World Turned Upside Down*, p.74, 79f.

143. M. Watts, *The Dissenters* Vol. 1, p.191f.

144. Owen, *On the Holy Spirit*, III.556

145. Owen, *On the Holy Spirit*, III.66

146. Owen, *A Defense of Scripture against Modern Fanatacism*, in Owen, *Biblical Theology* (Morgan: Soli Deo Gloria Publications, 1996), p.845

147. Owen, *A Defense of Scripture*, p.845

148. Owen, *A Defense of Scripture*, p.844

149. Owen, *A Defense of Scripture*, p.852

150. Owen, *A Defense of Scripture*, p.848

151. Owen, *A Defense of Scripture*, p. 839

152. Owen, *A Defense of Scripture*, p. 843

153. Owen, *A Defense of Scripture*, p. 851 (italics his).

154. T.L. Underwood, *Primitivism, Radicalism, and the Lamb's War* (Oxford: OUP, 1997), p.12f.

155. Owen, *The Shaking and Translating*, VII.263 cf. *A Vision of Unchangeable, Free Mercy*, VIII.24

156. John Whitgift (c.1530-1604) was educated at Queen's College, Cambridge. He was ordained in 1560 and translated to the see of Worcester in 1577. Having been consecrated as Archbishop of Canterbury in 1583, Whitgift crowned James I. He held very strong Calvinist opinions.

157. William Whitaker (1548-95) was educated at Cambridge before becoming Canon of Norwich Cathedral in 1578. He was regius professor of divinity two years later and chancellor of St. Paul's the same year. After having become master of St. John's College in 1586, he was made canon of Canterbury in the year of his death. Whitaker was renowned for the strength of his Calvinism and the profundity of his polemical writings.

158. Nuttall, *Visible Saints 1640-1660*, p.56f.

159. For details, see Michael B. Young, *Charles I* (London: MacMillan, 1997), p.122.

160. Young, *Charles I*, p.122.

161. Owen, *A Vision of Unchangeable, Free Mercy*, VIII.28

162. Owen, *A Vision of Unchangeable, Free Mercy*, VIII.30

163. Owen, *The Shaking and Translating*, VIII.274

164. Owen, *The Chamber of Imagery in the Church of Rome Laid Open; or, An Antidote Against Popery*, VIII.549(italics his).

165. Owen, *The Chamber of Imagery*, VIII.551

166. Owen, *The Chamber of Imagery*, VIII.550

167. Owen, *The Chamber of Imagery*, VIII.552

168. Owen, *The Chamber of Imagery*, VIII.552

169. Owen, *The Chamber of Imagery*, VIII.554

170. Owen, The Epistle Dedicatory to *Of the Divine Original*, XVI.285

171. Owen, The Epistle Dedicatory to *Of the Divine Original*, XVI.283

172. Owen, Preface to *Of the Mortification of Sin in Believers; the Necessity, Nature and Means of it*, VI.3

173. Owen, *The Reason of Faith*, IV.67

174. Owen, *The Chamber of Imagery*, VIII.554

175. Owen, *The Chamber of Imagery*, VIII.558 (italics his).

176. Owen, *Seasonable Words for English Protestants*, 1681, IX.3f (italics his).

177. Owen, *Seasonable Words for English Protestants*, IX.4

178. Owen, *Perilous Times*, IX.331

179. See Rev. Dr. Stephen Mayor, 'The Teaching of John Owen Concerning the Lord's Supper' *Scottish Journal of Theology*, 1965: 170-181.

180. Owen, *The Chamber of Imagery*, VIII.563

181. Owen, *The Chamber of Imagery*, VIII.564 (italics his).

182. Owen, *The Chamber of Imagery*, VIII.559

183. Owen, *The Chamber of Imagery*, VIII.567 (italics his).

184. Owen, *The Chamber of Imagery*, VIII.574 (italics his).

185. Owen, *The Chamber of Imagery*, VIII.579

186. William Lloyd (1627-1717) was educated at Oriel and Jesus College, Oxford. He became a royal chaplain in 1666 and Bishop of St. Asaph in 1680. He took up two further Bishoprics - Lichfield and Coventry in 1692 and Worcester in 1700. A staunch opponent to Romanism, Lloyd was imprisoned in the Tower of London in 1688 but later acquitted. He assisted at the crowning of William and Mary.

187. Lloyd, *A Seasonable Discourse Shewing the Necessity of Maintaining the Established Religion, In opposition to Popery*, p.7

188. Henry Care (1646-88) was a political writer and journalist who studied medicine and astrology. He was responsible for a controversial paper called the 'Weekly Pacquet of Advice from Rome,' which resulted in his prosecution in 1680. Little is known of Care but Anthony Wood described him as 'a little despicable wretch...a poor snivelling fellow'.

189. Quoted by J. Miller, *Popery and Politics in England 1660-1688* (Cambridge: CUP, 1973), p.75

190. Robert Wild (1609-79) was educated at St. John's College, Cambridge before taking a living in Aynoe, Northamptonshire in 1646. Wild was a Presbyterian with Royalist leanings, especially gifted in song, poetry and prose. He was ejected in 1662 and moved to Oundle, Northamptonshire. He died of a fit of apoplexy.

191. Wild, *Oliver Cromwells Ghost: or Old Noll Newly Revived*, 1679

192. Owen, *The Chamber of Imagery*, VIII.591 (italics his).

193. Owen, *A Brief and Impartial Account of the Nature of the Protestant Religion*, XIV.547

Chapter Five: Sin and the Need for Holiness

1. Owen, *Two Short Catechisms*, I.464ff

2. Owen, *The Duty of Pastors and People Distinguished*, XIII.2ff, and *Eshcol*, XIII.52ff

3. Toon, *God's Statesman*, p.17. See also P. Lewis, *All Saints Church,*

Fordham – A Guide (Fordham, 1984 n.p.), p.24

4. Owen, Preface to *Two Short Catechisms*, I.465

5. The parish of All Saints, Fordham stands within this tradition to this day.

6. Parish Records for All Saints, Fordham 1643-1646. See also Lewis, *All Saints Church, Fordham – A Guide*, p.13

7. Toon, *God's Statesman*, p.26

8. Sir Charles Lucas (1613-48) was admitted fellow-commoner of Christ's College, Cambridge in 1628. John Alsop, late Rector of Fordham, was his chaplain. He commanded a troop of horse in the king's army during the second Scottish war, and was knighted in 1639. Lucas served in the armies throughout the civil war, seeing action at Powick Bridge, Cirencester, Nottingham, Lincoln and York. He was taken prisoner at Marston Moor. He was released in late 1644 and was involved in further action before Colchester.

9. John Lucas was created Lord Lucas in 1645.

10. Information about this incident has come from the Essex County Archives in Chelmsford.

11. A letter prefacing his sermon, *A Memorial of the Deliverance of Essex County, And Committee*, VIII.74. Owen became chaplain to Fairfax by dint of the fact that Coggeshall was used as army headquarters for the duration of the siege.

12. Owen was elected to the temporary Board of Visitors in April 1652 and thereafter became a member of the permanent Board in January 1655. Toon, *God's Statesman*, p.65, 67

13. Owen, *The Correspondence of John Owen*, No. 14, p.63

14. *The Correspondence of John Owen*, p.47

15. Henry Cromwell (1628-74) was the fourth son of Oliver Cromwell. By 1650, he was a colonel and served on the Irish expedition. In 1654, he entered Gray's Inn after having served in the Barebones Parliament. After the Restoration, Cromwell lived in obscurity.

16. Owen, *The Correspondence of John Owen*, No. 52, p.100f

17. John Conant (1608-94) was a childhood genius from Bicton in Devonshire. He was particularly gifted in linguistic studies. After spending time at Oxford, he moved to Somerset during the Civil War. He moved to St. Botolph's in London before becoming a domestic chaplain at Harefield. Conant became rector of Exeter College in 1649 and undertook to reform the place until, consequently, it flourished. Replacing Owen, Conant remained Vice-chancellor at Oxford until August 1660, by which time he had reversed much of Owen's work. He was an advocate of the Restoration and enjoyed a living at Northampton

before becoming archdeacon of Norwich in 1681. Sadly, he became totally blind in 1686.

18. The Commissioners in Ireland, *The Correspondence of John Owen*, No. 1, p.50f

19. Fraser gives excellent detail of the Drogheda siege in *Cromwell Our Chief of Men*, p.332ff. It is important to stress that, as bloody as the massacre was, Cromwell never gave an order to kill civilians. It was an uncontrollable element within the Army ranks which perpetrated the cruel execution of more than one thousand people in the streets of the town. The image of Cromwell himself as a barbarous murderer, which is still common in Ireland today, is mythological and has no basis in fact.

20. The history of rebellions in Ireland is a complex issue, dating back at least to 1641. The threat that German troops would use Ireland to launch an English invasion was very real. So was the threat of the return of Charles II to England via that country. For these reasons, among others, Cromwell recognised the need to deal swiftly with the Irish problem. Hill deals with this issue with great objectivity in his book, *God's Englishman*, p.106f.

21. For details on the formation of this Parliament - and Cromwell's high expectations of it - see Fraser, *Cromwell Our Chief of Men*, p.431f.

22. For the Fifth Monarchists' part in the Barebones Assembly, see Fraser, *Cromwell Our Chief of Men*, p.432, 439, 445f.

23. Owen, Nye, Goodwin and Simpson, *The Correspondence of John Owen*, No. 18, p.67

24. Owen, *The Correspondence of John Owen*, No.10, p.59f

25. An anonymous letter sent under the pseudonym Thomas Truthsbye, *The Correspondence of John Owen*, No.64 p.116f

26. Owen, *God's Presence with a People the Spring of their Prosperity*, VIII.431 (italics his).

27. Owen, *God's Work in Founding Zion and His People's Duty Thereupon*, VIII.401ff

28. Owen, *God's Presence with a People*, VIII.452

29. Toon, *God's Statesman*, p.93

30. Edward Pococke (1604-91) was born at Oxford. He lived and died there too. He was professor of Arabic from 1630-36 and spent three years in Constantinople before taking a living in Childrey, Berkshire in 1642. Despite a tumultuous career, he retained the professorship of Hebrew at Christ Church as well as two lectureships at the time of his death. Pococke was recognised as a leading Orientalist of his day.

31. Owen, *Of Temptation*, VI.112 (italics his).

32. In 1664, Owen was prosecuted for holding meetings in Stadham.

In 1669, it was reported that he had a conventicle meeting in the City of London, near Moorfields. By 1682, Owen had taken over the leadership of Joseph Caryl's congregation in Leadenhall Street, London. Toon, *God's Statesman*, p.130, 131, 149.

33. Toon, *God's Statesman*, p.166

34. '*That after God hath, by so many ways and so many means, declared unto us his displeasure against our sin, having declared the sentence in his word, yet he hath visibly granted an arrest of judgment.* "The sentence shall not be put in execution," saith God, "while I give this people a time, a space, and a season of repentance and reformation."' Owen, *Seasonable Words*, IX.14 (italics his).

35. 'He *hath reserved a remnant among us that do make use of this space and season to apply themselves unto the throne of grace, and to cry mightily for mercy*...there are yet among us precious souls who do lift up prayers to God night and day...for this poor land of our nativity, that, if it were the will of God, [he] would pity, and spare, and have mercy upon it.' Owen, *Seasonable Words*, IX.15 (italics his).

36. 'But yet evident it is that [Catholic practices] are all of them contrary unto the common sense, reason, and experience of all Christians, all that believe the gospel, as well as directly contradictory unto the Scripture and example of the primitive church. It is therefore left unto the judgment of all sober persons, such as are not yet made drunk with the cup of their abominations, to determine whether any thing but either profound ignorance and spiritual darkness, or love of sin, with a desire to live securely therein...can prevail with men to make an entire, absolute resignation of their souls, and all their eternal concernments, unto the conduct of this pretended guide.' Owen, *The Church of Rome No Safe Guide*, XIV.507f.

37. 'So is it here with this miserable and distressed church and people of God; – all is lost and gone, and yet faith cries, "Doubtless thou art our Father." And if, in the matters of this day, God would help us to maintain and not let go our interest in him as our Father, by faith, we should have a bottom and foundation to stand upon.' Owen, in *God's Withdrawing His Presence, The Correction of His Church*, a sermon preached in March 1675, IX.296f.

38. 'We are always to carry about the dying of Jesus Christ in *our thoughts and meditations*. O that our thoughts were much fixed upon it! I verily believe that the life of faith doth answer in proportion to our thoughts about the dying Jesus.... Let us carry about us always thoughts hereof, for his sake who loved us, and who died for us. Meditate more on these things.' Owen, *Discourse XXIV*, delivered in September 1677,

IX.619 (italics his).

39. 'Would you have another object of your meditation in this matter? – let it be *the infinite wisdom and the infinite love of God, that found out this way of glorifying his holiness and justice*, and dealing with sin according to its demerit...Bring forth your faith.... Here is a glorious object for it to work upon, – to consider the infinite wisdom and love that found out this way. It was out of love unsearchable. And now, what may not my poor, sinful soul expect from this love? what difficulties can I be entangled in, but this wisdom can disentangle me? and what distempers can I be under, but this love may heal and recover? "There is hope, then," saith the soul, in preparation for these things.' Owen, *Discourse VI*, IX.559f. (italics his).

40. Owen, *The Person of Christ*, I.168ff

41. Owen, *The Person of Christ*, I.171f

42. Owen, *The Person of Christ*, I.174f

43. Owen, *The Person of Christ*, I.184

44. Owen, *The Person of Christ*, I.184

45. Owen, Preface to *Grace and Duty*, VII.263. There is no record of the illness that Owen was suffering, although within two years he was to die with gallstones. It is likely that Owen wrote this treatise at the Wooburn house of Philip Lord Wharton. He sent a letter to his congregation in Leadenhall Street from there during this period, stating that 'The continuance of my painfull infirmities and the increase of my weaknesses will not allow me at present to [be with you].' Owen, *The Correspondence of John Owen*, No. 94, p.170

46. Owen, *Grace and Duty*, VII.273

47. Owen, *Grace and Duty*, VII.275

48. Owen, *Grace and Duty*, VII.280f

49. Owen, *Discourse XIV*, IX.404

50. Owen, *On Mortification*, VI.1f

51. Owen, *On the Holy Spirit*, III.1f

52. Owen, *On Mortification*, VI.14

53. Owen, Preface to *On Mortification*, VI.3

54. Gleason, *John Calvin and John Owen on Mortification*, p.153.

55. Owen, Preface to *On Mortification*, VI.3

56. Owen, *On Mortification*, VI.79 (italics his).

57. Owen, *On Mortification*, VI.58 (italics his).

58. Brooks, *The Crown and Glory of Christianity*, in *Works*, IV.392

59. Owen, *On Mortification*, VI.85

60. Owen, *On Mortification*, VI.33

61. Owen, *On Mortification*, VI.35

62. Owen, *On Mortification*, VI.5f (italics his).

63. Calvin, *Commentary on the Epistle to the Romans* (Grand Rapids, Michigan: Eerdmans, 1961), p.167

64. Calvin, *Institutes*, 3.7.1, p.7

65. Gleason's published work is taken from his ThD. thesis for Dallas Theological seminary, 1992.

66. Calvin, *Institutes*, 3.7.1, p.7

67. Calvin, *Institutes*, 3.7.8, p.13

68. Owen, *On Mortification*, VI.24f

69. Phil.3:12, 21; Col.2:10

70. Owen, *On Mortification*, VI.25

71. Owen, *On Mortification*, VI.26

72. Owen, *On Mortification*, VI.26

73. Owen, *On Mortification*, VI.28 (italics his).

74. Owen, *On Mortification*, VI.30 (italics his).

75. Owen, *On Mortification*, VI.30 (italics his).

76. Owen, *On Mortification*, VI.31

77. Owen, *On Mortification*, VI.50 (italics his).

78. Owen, *On Mortification*, VI.63 (italics his).

79. Owen, *On Mortification*, VI.56 (italics his).

80. Owen, *On Mortification*, VI.60 (italics his).

81. Owen, *On Mortification*, VI.70

82. Owen, *On Mortification*, VI.31 (italics his).

83. Owen, *On Mortification*, VI.31f

84. Owen, *On Mortification*, VI.32

85. 1 Corinthians 9:27

86. Owen, *On Mortification*, VI.61

87. Owen, *On Mortification*, VI.61

88. Owen, *On Mortification*, VI.59

89. Owen, *On Mortification*, VI.70 (italics his).

90. Owen, *On Mortification*, VI.77f

91. Owen, *On Mortification*, VI.32

92. Owen, *On the Holy Spirit*, III.548

93. Owen, *On the Holy Spirit*, III.482

94. Owen, *The Person of Christ*, I.183 (italics his).

95. Owen, *On the Holy Spirit*, III.548

96. Owen, *On the Holy Spirit*, III.219 (italics his).

97. Owen, *On the Holy Spirit*, III.316,317 (italics his).

98. Owen, *On the Holy Spirit*, III.317

99. Owen, *On the Holy Spirit*, III.468f (italics his).

100. Calvin, *Institutes*, 3.1.1, p.463

101. Clarkson, *Works*, III.166, quoted by R. Tudur Jones in his article 'Union with Christ: The Existential Nerve of Puritan Piety,' *Tyndale Bulletin*, 41 (Nov. 1990) 186-208.

102. Matthew Barker (1619-98) was educated at Trinity College, Cambridge and thereafter taught at a school in Banbury, Oxfordshire. In 1641, he moved to London and took up ministry at Garlick Hill. In the mid-1640s, he moved to Mortlake in Surrey as lecturer. Barker became parliamentary preacher in 1648 and, two years later, took a living in Eastcheap, London. He was ejected in 1662 but continued with a congregation in Miles Lane.

103. Barker, *A Continuation of Morning-Exercise* (1683) Sermon xix.1022. Quoted by Tudur Jones.

104. Baxter, *Directions and Persuasions to a Sound Conversion*, in *Works*, VIII.138

105. Goodwin, *Commentary on Ephesians*, II.242ff

106. Goodwin, *Commentary on Ephesians*, II.246

107. Tudur Jones, *Tyndale Bulletin* 41.2 (1990), 186-208

108. Owen, *The Epistle to the Hebrews*, XXI.151, 236f

109. This is a parable that would have appealed greatly to Owen – and not just because of its biblical importance. Judging by the contents of his library, Owen was a keen gardener! The books auctioned at his death included the following titles: Dr. Monardus' *Vertue of Herbs, Trees, Oyls, Stones &c.* (America, 1577); R.C.'s *Manner of Planting, Preserving, Sowing, Measuring &c.* (London, 1612); R. Austin's *Treatise of Fruit-trees, with the Art of Planting* (Oxford, 1653); Joseph Evelyn's *Sylva, or a Discourse of Forest Trees* (London, 1679); Nehemiah Grew's *Catalogue and Description of the Rarities in Gresham Colledge* [sic] (London, 1681) and his *Anatomy of Plants, with Figures* (London, 1682); Meager's *English Gardener* (1682). Incidentally, it seems Owen was also a discerning ale drinker, given the inclusion of *A Treatise of Warm Beer* (Cambridge 1641)!

110. Owen, *On the Holy Spirit*, III.414, cf. *The Epistle to the Hebrews*, XXI.150

111. Owen, *Doctrine of the Saints' Perseverance*, XI.340

112. Calvin, *Institutes*, 3.1.3, p.465

113. Owen, *Of Communion with God*, II.56

114. Tudur Jones, *Union with Christ: The Existential Nerve of Puritan Piety*, p.199

115. Quoted by Tudur Jones from *The Letters and Life of...Samuel Rutherford*, C. Thompson, I.324

116. Owen, *The Person of Christ*, I.170 (italics his).

117. Owen, *Doctrine of the Saints' Perseverance*, XI.337

118. Owen, *Doctrine of the Saints' Perseverance*, XI.336 (italics his).

119. Owen, *The Duty of Pastors*, XIII.23 (italics his).

120. Owen, *The Epistle to the Hebrews*, XXI.150

121. Owen, 'Epistle to the Reader', *Biblical Theology*, p.xxxiiif

122. Owen, *Of Communion with God*, II.86. 'O poor, trembling, wandering soul, into what places of darkness and defilement art thou going? Pale, stiff and naked.' This is a poem, recited on Hadrian's death-bed, which Owen also alludes to in *On the Glory of Christ*, I.280 and *A Vindication of the Animadversions on "Fiat Lux"*, XIV.202

123. Owen, *A Vindication of the Animadversions*, XIV.431, 434

124. Owen, *On Communion with God*, II.94

125. Owen, *On Communion with God*, II.82

126. Owen, *On Communion with God*, II.56, 84, 87, 88, 93, 95, 105 and *Doctrine of the Saints' Perseverance*, XI.338

127. Owen, *On Communion with God*, II.113

128. Owen, *On Communion with God*, II.113 (italics his).

129. Owen, *On Communion with God*, II.99

130. Owen, *The Correspondence of John Owen*, No. 69, p.130f

131. Owen, *The Correspondence of John Owen*, No. 76, p.148

132. Owen, *The Correspondence of John Owen*, No. 82, p.156f, No. 84, p.158f, No. 87, p.160f and No. 94, p.170f

133. King, *The Correspondence of John Owen*, No. 97, p.173f

134. Asty, *Memoirs of the Life of Dr. Owen*, p. xxxii

135. Quoted by Goold in his *Life of Dr. Owen*, I.CIII

136. Owen, *The Correspondence of John Owen*, No. 95, p.172

137. The content of this treatise has been largely treated in Chapters One and Two.

138. These are found in Volume IX of his Works.

Conclusion

1. Clarkson, *A Funeral Sermon on Dr. John Owen*, quoted in *A Complete Collection of the Sermons of the Reverand and Learned John Owen, D.D.*, p.lvii

2. Introduction, p.7

3. Introduction, p.7f.

4. Introduction, p.8f.

5. Owen, *A Dissertation on Divine Justice*, X.619

6. Owen, *Biblical Theology*, p.603

7. Owen, *Biblical Theology*, p.668

8. Owen, *Biblical Theology*, p.618

9. Owen, *Causes, Ways, and Means*, IV.144

10. Ferguson, *John Owen on the Christian Life*, p.92

11. Owen, *Of Communion with God*, II.227 (italics his).

12. Gleason, *John Calvin and John Owen on Mortification*, p.7f.

13. Gleason, *John Calvin and John Owen on Mortification*, p.147f.

14. Barth, *Church Dogmatics*, IV.2, p.809

15. Clifford, *Atonement and Justification*, p.ix

16. G.C. Berkouwer, *Faith and Justification* (Grand Rapids, Michigan: Eerdmans, 1954), p.148 (italics his).

17. Owen, *Of the Death of Christ*, X.449

18. Berkouwer, *Faith and Justification*, p.149

19. Owen, *Of the Death of Christ*, X.450

20. Owen, *The Doctrine of Justification by Faith*, V.208 (italics his).

21. *Westminster Confession*, XI.IV

22. M. Walzer, *The Revolution of the Saints* (New York: Atheneum, 1972), p.3 (italics his).

23. Many authors have written about Calvin's work in Geneva. Two good sources are H. Hopfl, *The Christian Polity of John Calvin* (Cambridge: Cambridge University Press, 1982), p.128ff. and F. Wendel, *Calvin* (London: Collins, 1963), p.46ff.

24. Cited by F.J. Bremer, *The Puritan Experiment* (Hanover and London: University Press of New England, 1995), p.44

25. Capp, *The Fifth Monarchy Men*, p.39

26. S. Baskerville, *Not Peace But a Sword* (London: Routledge, 1993), p.8

27. Owen, Preface to *On Indwelling Sin*, VI.155

28. Baird Tipson, 'A Dark Side of Seventeenth-Century English Protestantism: The Sin Against the Holy Spirit' (*Harvard Theological Review*, 77:3-4 (1984) 301-30), p.301.

29. G. Wakefield, *Bunyan the Christian* (London: Harper Collins, 1992), p.29.

30. Baird Tipson, 'A Dark Side of Seventeenth-Century English Protestantism: The Sin Against the Holy Spirit,' p.302. Sadly, the conscientious efforts of these ministers do not seem to have brought a strengthening of Christian charity within the Drake family. According to the records of their local church, St. Mary's, Walton (where the astrologer William Lilly was buried), Richard Drake and his successors had held the lease on the Rectory since 1584. By 1705, the Vicar's salary had not increased beyond the paltry sum of £12 per annum and he survived on marriage, burial and christening fees. The wealthy Drake

family were unwilling to provide any further funds and the parishioners were forced to buy another, more manageable vicarage. (M.E. Blackman, *Walton & Weybridge Local History Society Paper no.28 – A Short History of Walton-On-Thames*, n.d., n.p.). Incidentally, the Drakes have been immortalised by the naming of a road in their memory: Drake's Close, Esher.

31. Baird Tipson, 'A Dark Side of Seventeenth-Century English Protestantism: The Sin Against the Holy Spirit,' p.318.

32. Packer, *Among God's Giants*, p.251.

33. Owen, *On Indwelling Sin*, VI.201.

34. Owen introduced his *Two Short Catechisms* to the congregation at Fordham thus: 'Brethren, My heart's desire and request unto God for you is, that you may be saved.... I have great heaviness, and continual sorrow in my heart, for them amongst you who, as yet, walk disorderly, and not as beseemeth the Gospel, little labouring to acquaint themselves with the mystery of godliness.' Preface to *Two Short Catechisms*, I.465.

35. After the fall of Colchester, and again at Romford on September 28, 1648 (not Rumford, as Goold has it in *The Works of John Owen*, VIII.72), Owen preached to the army from Habakkuk 3:1-9. He concluded his sermons by saying, 'You that have received so great mercy, we that have seen it, and all who have heard the doctrine confirmed, let us learn to live by faith. Live above all things that are seen; subject them to the cross of Christ. Measure your condition by your interest in God's all-sufficiency. Do not in distress calculate what such and such things can effect; but what God hath promised.... Let this possess your thoughts, let this fill your souls, – let this be your haven from all former storms.' *Ebenezer*, VIII.126.

36. In September 1657, Owen wrote to Henry Cromwell, in the face of opposition, concerning the statutes of the University: 'I am glad to heare of your indeavour to dispose of that university to the interest of piety and learninge; and am bold to informe your Lordship, that out Statutes, as those also of the other university, beinge framed to the Spirit and road of studys in former days, will scarsly upon consideration, be found to be the best expediente for the promotion of the good ends of Godlinesse and solid literature which are in your ayme.' *The Correspondence of John Owen*, No.52, p.100.

37. An example of this is Owen's introduction to the printed version of his Parliamentary sermon of March 8, 1649: 'That you might be prevailed on to give glory to God, by steadfastness in believing, committing all your ways to him, with patience in well-doing, to the contempt of the most varnished appearance of carnal policy, was my

peculiar aim in this ensuing sermon.' *The Steadfastness of the Promises*, VIII.209.

38. Towards the end of his life, possibly in 1681, Owen's illnesses kept him from his congregation in Leadenhall Street, London so he wrote them a pastoral letter. In that correspondence, Owen stated that 'although I am absent from you in body, I am in mind, affection and spirit present with you, and in your assemblies; for I hope you will be found my crown and rejoicing in the day of the Lord: and my prayer for you night and day is, that you may stand fast in the whole will of God, and maintain the beginning of your confidence without wavering, firm unto the end.' *The Correspondence of John Owen*, No.94, p.170.

39. Owen, *On Indwelling Sin*, VI.200.

40. Owen, *On Indwelling Sin*, VI.200f.

41. Owen, Preface to *On Indwelling Sin*, VI.156.

42. Thompson, *Life of Dr. Owen*, I.cx.

Subject Index

Affections 49, 51, 53, 58, 59

Antinomians 71, 72-4, 231, 262

Arminian(ism/ists) 9, 39, 64, 145, 146, 147, 164-74, 181, 183, 184, 194, 196, 204, 210, 229, 251, 283, 287

Calvinist/ism 9, 10-12, 63, 64, 73, 146, 165, 166, 167, 168, 169, 170, 180, 181, 227, 229, 230, 233, 251, 263, 284, 285, 290

Cambridge 10, 166, 252, 259, 262, 263, 264, 272, 277, 278, 283, 284, 285, 286, 287, 288, 290, 291, 292, 297

Cambridge Platonists 62-4, 71, 229, 259, 260, 278, 284

Clarendon Code 132

Coggleshall 8, 96, 151196, 197, 226, 234, 292

Congregational(ist/ism) 8, 145, 150, 151, 153, 154, 155, 157, 158, 159, 161, 232, 287

Covenant 18, 19, 20-9, 30, 39, 45, 54, 55, 58, 60, 66, 90, 93, 146-52, 172, 173, 181, 209, 216, 219, 220

Diggers 97, 267-8

Drogheda massacre 96, 200, 267, 293

Dublin, Univ of 199-200, 275, 285

(Trinity College)

Election 99, 136, 145, 146-52, 154, 155, 160, 164, 168, 171, 173, 174, 193, 194

Experience, (Christian) 18, 49, 185, 186, 188, 190, 193, 205, 206

Faith 61, 62, 79, 85, 87, 99, 107, 146, 147, 150, 151, 160, 163, 175, 176, 185, 186, 187,189, 190, 193, 196, 202, 205, 206, 216, 219, 220, 225, 230, 294, 295, 300

Fall, The 12, 26, 30, 32, 53, 59, 64, 65, 66, 80, 87, 90, 91, 92, 93, 171, 172, 175, 177, 181, 182, 206, 228

Federal theology 18-29, 54, 55, 145, 172-3, 219, 254

Fire of London 111, 138-9, 164

Fordham 151, 196, 197, 226, 234, 292, 300

Glory 34, 42, 43, 92, 93, 112, 114, 116, 119, 121, 128, 151, 160, 162, 177, 179, 182, 188, 189, 190, 191,191, 205, 212, 221, 225, 226, 28, 235, 301

Gospel 19, 59, 57, 67-8, 70, 87, 88, 105, 106, 109, 114, 115, 123, 126, 147, 152, 153, 155, 157, 170, 177, 188, 193, 200, 201, 203, 210, 222, 225, 267, 294

Grace 21, 22-3, 25, 26, 27, 30, 38, 40, 42, 44, 48, 53, 67-8, 73, 76, 79, 81, 86, 91, 105, 112, 115, 122, 129, 139, 140, 146, 148, 149, 160, 164, 168, 169, 170, 176, 181, 182, 193, 200, 203, 206, 209, 216, 217, 218, 219221, 222, 229, 231, 233, 235, 288

Holiness 9, 13, 14, 23, 25, 34, 40, 41, 42, 43, 60, 63, 67, 76, 80, 84, 87, 139.146, 147, 152,

Holiness, cont., 154,155, 160,
  162, 174, 184, 190, 194, 195-
  26, 197, 198, 199, 200, 203,
  204, 206, 207, 210, 211, 215,
  218, 220, 226, 228, 233, 235,
  295
Image of God 14, 18, 29-44, 55,
  58, 60, 62, 80, 86-90, 93, 130,
  171, 172, 178, 193, 195, 206,
  207, 208, 216
Jews 112, 116-, 161, 211, 274
Justification 72, 73, 74, 76, 146,
  164, 176, 219, 230-2, 262
Levellers 94-8, 101, 103, 267-8
Lollards 99
Mercantilism 101-2 .
Millen(ium)arianism 108-116,
  117, 119, 120, 121, 129, 156,
  195, 202, 271, 273, 274
Mind 49, 51, 53, 58, 59-78, 81,
  82, 83, 84, 85, 87, 89, 92, 93,
  178, 188, 193, 213, 218
Monarchy 97, 98, 103-8, 113,
  121, 124, 125, 126, 127, 128,
  129-30, 131, 135-6, 143, 168,
  204, 282
Monarchy(ists), Fifth 131, 200-
  1, 233, 278, 279, 293
Mortification 11, 50, 79, 142,
  180, 207, 209-18, 229
Muggletonians 131, 278
Nationalism 100-3, 109
Obedience 24, 25, 27, 28, 33,
  34, 40, 41, 45, 46-9, 60, 69, 74,
  84, 89, 106, 147, 150,151, 172,
  174, 181, 189, 204, 206, 216,
  220, 221
Oxford 7, 8, 119, 162, 166, 197,
  198, 199, 204, 209, 234, 249,

  262, 263, 266, 268, 269, 270,
  275, 276, 277, 278, 279, 281,
  285, 286, 288, 291, 293
Parliament(ary) 95, 96, 104,
  105, 109, 112, 115, 116, 119,
  122-3, 124, 125, 126, 127,
  128, 142, 198, 201, 202, 250,
  251, 262, 266, 269, 270, 272,
  275, 276, 282, 286, 288, 292,
  293
Pastor(al) 13, 44, 49, 51, 53, 74,
  96, 142, 195, 196, 197, 203,
  204, 226, 227, 233, 234, 235,
  236, 301
Plague 110-1, 138, 164, 279
Platon(ic)ist 45, 64, 89, 173
Predestination 14, 99, 136, 147,
  167, 168, 170, 174, 175, 176,
  180
Presbyterian 10, 153, 154, 155,
  156, 158, 159, 160, 161, 201,
  251, 252, 270, 271, 272, 276,
  282, 283, 286, 291
Protestant 10, 11, 133, 156, 167,
  176, 184, 204, 232, 233, 251
Providence 131, 136-41, 143,
  226, 267
Puritan 7, 9-10, 19, 20, 70, 73,
  74, 103, 108, 134, 167, 168,
  184, 196, 197, 201, 204, 205,
  218, 219, 221, 232, 251, 271,
  285
Quakers 71-2, 131, 132, 145,
  178-84, 194, 199, 203, 210,
  229, 261, 278, 279, 284, 287
Reason 60-5, 80, 83, 88, 99,
  175
Redemption 26, 29, 54, 55, 129,
  136, 219, 221

Reformed 7, 9, 10, 11, 12, 14, 18, 20, 21, 22, 31, 34, 53, 55, 57, 59, 73, 74, 81, 87, 88, 89,105, 145, 146, 165, 166, 169, 173, 176, 183, 189, 191, 194, 196, 203, 211, 218, 224, 229, 232, 233, 282

Regeneration 65, 146, 176, 182, 217, 218

Republican(ism) 97, 101, 103, 108, 113, 121-30, 142, 262, 266, 268, 276, 284

Restoration 8, 122, 130-5, 205, 250, 259, 263, 266, 267, 268, 271, 272, 275, 276, 278, 279, 282, 283, 284, 285, 286, 287, 289, 292, 293

Righteousness 23, 24, 25, 29, 30, 34, 39, 40, 41, 60, 63, 73, 84, 87, 96, 105, 111, 115, 123, 152, 164,197, 206, 207, 231

Roman Catholic(ism) 103, 112, 117, 145, 155-7, 165, 166, 184-93, 194, 210, 215, 258, 291 (Church of Rome)

Royalist 103-4, 159, 197, 262, 263, 269, 275, 276, 277, 278, 288, 291

Sacraments 58, 147, 284

Salvation 21, 26, 66, 79, 109, 139, 146, 154, 155, 159, 161, 170, 174, 175, 180, 181, 182, 220, 225, 229, 230, 232, 288

Sanctification 29-30, 44, 65, 73, 79, 90, 146, 174, 218, 219, 221, 262

Savoy Assembly/Declaration of Faith 8, 112, 160, 266, 267

Seekers 179-80

Separatist/separation 153-64, 202, 232

Society 95-100, 101, 103, 141, 142, 143, 147-8, 161, 184, 194, 233

Socinian(ism) 28, 29, 145, 165, 166, 174-8, 183, 184, 194, 203, 217

Trinity 26, 35-7, 38, 54, 175, 176, 180, 210, 229, 231, 254

Truth 64, 81, 113, 139, 147, 164, 179, 185, 193, 203, 228, 229, 232

Uniformity, Act of 131, 135, 278

Wars, Civil 105, 114, 138, 232-3, 269, 270, 276, 279, 287, 292

Westminster Assembly 219, 250, 262, 266, 277, 283, 286, 287, 288

Westminster Confession 22-4, 27, 28, 55, 231

Will 51, 52, 53, 54, 58, 59, 60, 65, 66, 79, 82-6, 87, 92, 93, 100, 169, 170, 175, 176, 187, 212, 213, 218, 264

Worship 34, 69, 107, 135, 147-8, 149, 155, 157, 158, 160, 161, 179, 180, 183, 186, 188, 189

Persons Index

Abbot, Archbishop 73
Allsop, V. 237
Alsop, John 196, 292
Alsted, Johannes 109, 271
Andrewes, Lancelot 166, 284, 288
Annesley, A. 73, 132, 262
Aquinas, Thomas 11, 30, 34, 37-8, 44, 45, 55, 60-1, 229, 256, 259
Aristotle 13, 31-3, 60, 80-1, 83, 171, 223, 224, 229, 237, 256, 259
Arminius, Jacobus 164-5, 237, 283
Arrian 224
Ashe, John 275
Ashley, M. 252
Asty, J. 121, 132, 225, 279, 298
Augustine 11, 13, 30, 34-7, 38, 44, 45-9, 52, 55, 61, 65, 83, 229, 254, 257, 258, 259, 273
Austin, R. 297
Baker, 21
Ball, B.W. 251, 270
Ball, John 18, 108, 253
Bangs, C. 283
Barker, Matthew 218, 297
Barrett, William 166, 284
Barth Karl 23, 29, 54 , 230, 232, 241, 254, 255, 258
Bartlet, William 151, 158, 281, 282
Baskerville, 233, 299
Baxter, Richard 13, 23-4, 25, 58, 153, 155, 158-60, 196, 219, 230, 237, 254, 258, 264, 282, 297

Benn, William 31, 255-6, 265
Berkeley, Lord 132
Berkouwer, G.C. 231, 299
Beza 63, 165
Bidle, John 175-6, 177-8, 288
Bierma 21, 25, 253, 254
Blackman, M.E. 300
Boncle, John 118
Boughton, Lynne C. 254
Boyle, Pierre 253
Bradford, Captain 124
Brailsford, H.N. 98, 268, 269
Braithwaite, William 71, 262, 289
Bramhall, John 168, 286
Brauer, J.C. 251
Bremner, F.J. 299
Brightman, Thomas 112, 113, 272
Broghill, Lord 124, 275
Brooks, Thomas 138, 211, 279, 296
Bruggink, D.J. 254
Buckeridge, John 167, 285
Buckingham, Duke of 99
Bullinger 21
Bunyan, John 234
Burgesse, A 171, 263, 287
Burroughs, Jeremiah 161, 283
Burton, Henry 286
Busby, Mr. 199
Calvin, John 11-12, 13, 21, 22, 24, 25, 27, 3034, 38, 39-40, 43, 44, 55, 59, 62, 65, 83, 87-8, 89, 212, 213, 218, 220, 227, 229, 230, 232, 233, 254, 256, 257, 259, 260, 264, 265, 296, 297, 299
Camfield, Benjamin 134, 279

Capp, B.S. 273, 299
Care, Henry 191, 291
Caryl, Joseph 8, 119, 142, 250, 294
Cawdrey, Daniel 161, 283
Chamberlayne, Edward 138, 279
Chappell, William 168, 285
Charles I 98, 103, 104, 105, 106-7, 110, 115, 121, 126, 129, 137, 142, 157, 167, 168, 198, 200, 238, 250, 262, 264, 275, 276
Charles II 127, 130, 131, 137, 138, 159, 191, 238, 250, 263, 268, 270, 276, 278, 279, 293
Chewney, Nicholas 176
Cheynell, Francis 176, 288, 289
Child, John 234
Cicero 224
Clare, Sir Ralph 160
Clarendon, Lord 8, 250
Clarkson, David 9, 218, 227, 250, 297, 298
Claypole 124
Clifford, A. 230, 249, 299
Clinton, Sir Gervase 268
Cocceius, Johannes 28, 29, 54, 255
Cole, Thomas 269
Collinson, P. 10, 251, 252
Conant, Dr John 199, 292-3
Constantine 223
Copleston, F. 260
Corvinus 171
Cosin, John 167, 285
Cotton, John 63, 266, 277
Cotton, Robert 196
Cragg, G.R. 99, 252, 253, 260, 268
Crellius 289

Crofton, Z. 271
Cromwell, Richard 8, 121, 199
Cromwell, Henry 199, 292, 300
Cromwell, Oliver 8, 95-6, 98, 99, 102, 117-9, 121, 123, 124-5, 126, 128, 129, 138, 142, 192, 198, 200, 201, 204, 234, 267, 268, 269, 271, 275, 276, 277, 289, 293
Cudworth, Ralph 62, 259, 260
Culverwell, Nathaniel 62, 63, 260
Cumming, G.J. 251
Davenant, J. 238
Davie, M. 289
Dent, Arthur 113
Desborough 12, 125, 202, 276
Desborough, Jane 276
Devonshire, Earl of 268
Dewsbury, William 71, 261
Digges, Dudley 104, 269
Dod, John 234
Dodd 63
Doran, S. 253
Downing, George 275
Drake, Joan 234
Drake, Richard 300
Driver 269
Duffield, G.E. 252
Durston, C. 253
Dyke, D. 259
Eaton, John 72-3, 262
Edward I 117
Edwards, Thomas 170, 287
Elizabeth, Queen 102
Elwood, T. 238
Endecott, John 250
Essex, Earl of 275, 285, 288
Estwick, Nicholas 176, 177

Evans, G.R. 48-9, 52, 258, 273
Evelyn, Joseph 297
Fairfax, General 123, 128, 198, 275, 276, 292
Fawkes, Guy 264
Featley, Daniel 286
Fenner, William 79, 259, 263
Ferguson, S. 26-7, 30, 77-8, 147, 228-9, 249, 254, 255, 263, 267, 281, 299
Fleetwood, Charles 124, 275, 277, 279
Fox, George 178-9, 289
Gataker, Thomas 74, 262
Gilbert, T. 250
Gilson, E. 45, 257
Glanville, Joseph 130, 278
Gleason, R.C. 11, 210, 213, 229, 249, 295, 296, 299
Godfrey, W. Robert 283
Gomarus, Franz 22-3, 254
Good, Rev W. 267
Goodwin, John 167, 169, 284, 286,
Goodwin, Thomas 95, 119, 142, 200, 219, 266-7, 297
Goold 106-8, 270, 284, 298, 300
Greenhough, G.H. 21, 253
Gregory of Nyssa 219
Grew, Nehemiah 297
Grotius, Hugo 166, 253
Gunter, Peter 72
Hadrian, Emperor 223, 298
Hall, Basil 12
Haller 109, 270
Harrington, J. 100-1, 125, 268, 269

Harrison, A. 283, 286
Hartlib, Samuel 110-1, 271
Hayes, C.J.H. 102, 269
Helm, P. 252
Hermondszoon, Jakob see under Arminius, Jacob
Hieron 224
Hill, Christopher 98, 99, 108, 112, 251, 252, 253, 258, 267, 268, 270, 271, 272, 273, 275, 276, 278, 293
Hoare, Dr Leonard 250
Hobbes, T. 99, 100-1, 268, 269,
Hoekema, A. 254
Homer 224
Hooker, Thomas 234
Hopfl, H. 299
Horrocks, J.W. 269
Hoskin, Prof. 267
Hoult, Mr 199
Howson, John 167, 285
Hubbard, G. 289
Hus 117
James (II), Duke of York 191
James I (VI) 167, 290
Jenkins, D. 239
Jones, J.R. 283
Jones, R. Tudur 219, 221, 278-9, 297
Katz, D.S. 271, 274
Kendall, R.T. 12, 252
Kevan, E.F. 251, 252, 262
King, Dr Edmund 224, 298
Knappen, M.M. 10, 251
Kyle, R. 273
Kynaston, Mary 249
Kynaston, Roger 249
L'Evesque de Burigny, Jean 166, 284

Lactantius 224
Lambert, John 124, 202, 276
Lane, Samuel 169
Laud, Archbishop 9, 106, 157, 166-7, 168, 196, 251, 264, 270, 282, 287
Laud, W. 282, 284, 285
Lawrence, Henry 119, 274
Lewis, P. 292
Lilburne, John 98
Lilly, William 110, 271-2, 300
Lindsay, T.M. 288
Lloyd, William 191, 291
Locke, John 100-1, 268-9
Lombard 224
Love, Christopher 104-5, 270, 277
Lucas, Sir Charles 197, 198, 292
Lucas, Sir John 198, 292
Ludlow, Edmund 125, 276
Luther, Martin 21, 73, 184
MacPherson, C.B. 100, 268
Manning, B. 267, 269
Marshall, Stephen 232-3, 239, 277
Martiall, Master 105
Matthews, A. 111-2, 129, 274, 278
Mayor, Rev Dr Stephen 291
McLachlan, H. 176, 178, 288, 289
Meager 297
Mede, Joseph 113
Menage 284
Menasseh ben Israel 117-8
Mercurus 224
Merton, R.K. 267
Miller, J. 291
Milton, John 271

Mitchell, A.F. 252
Montague, Richard 167-8, 275, 286
Montaigne, George 167, 284
Moore, Thomas 170
More, Henry 62, 63, 259, 260, 278
Morton, Thomas 81-2, 258-9, 263, 264
Muller, R.A. 20, 253
Murray, I.H. 271
Musculus 21
Napier, John 110, 113, 114, 271
Neale 167
Needham, Marchamont 128, 277
Nichols, Mr 224
Norton, John 232
Nuttal, G.F. 13, 150, 152, 156, 184, 281, 282
Nye, Philip 95, 119, 128, 142, 200, 201, 266, 293
Olevianus 21
Orrey, Earl of 132
Overton Richard 99
Owen, Elizabeth 7, 249
Owen, Elizah 7, 249
Owen, Henry 269
Owen, John 7, 249
Owen, Judith 7, 249
Owen, Mary 7, 249
Owen, Mathew 7, 249
Owen, Philemon 96
Owen, Thomas 7, 249
Owen, William 203
Packe, Sir Christopher 275
Packer, J.I. 11, 12, 79, 234, 249, 254, 262, 263, 300
Packington, Sir John 160
Paul, R.S. 275

Payne, William 225
Pennington, Isaac 284
Perkins, William 10, 21, 57, 63, 252, 258
Peter, Hugh 95, 118, 198, 266, 267
Pierce, Thomas 81, 260, 263-4, 265
Plato 224, 257
Pococke, Edward 103, 293
Poole, Matthew 176, 177
Porter, Edmund 176
Porter, H.C. 10, 251
Potter, John 196
Powicke, F.J. 260
Preston, John 234
Pride, Col. Thomas 125, 276
Prynne, William 157, 167, 282, 284, 286
Reeve, Thomas 130, 278
Reid, W. Stanford 12
Richardson, John 288
Rist 264
Roberts, Dr Michael 119
Rogers, John 151
Rooke, Miss Mary 7
Rous, Francis 169, 286
Rowe, J. 266
Russell, William 177
Rutherford, Samuel 170, 221, 287
Schlichting 289
Sibbes, R. 63
Simon, Richard 253
Smalcius 189
Smith, A.G.R. 252, 267, 274
Smith, C.R. 270
Smith, John 62, 259, 260
Socinus (Sozzini, Fausto) 174, 289

Socrates 224
Solt, L.F. 268
Spinoza 99, 253
Stalham, John 170, 287
Sterry, Peter 109-10, 118, 260, 271
Stone, L. 252
Teate, Faithful 91, 266
Thomas, K. 267, 268
Thompson ? 301
Thornton, John 130
Tillotson, John 230, 251
Tipson, Baird 233, 299, 300
Tomkins, T. 279
Toon, P. 12-13, 108, 121-2, 130-1, 199, 203, 204, 250, 252, 267, 269, 270, 272, 274, 275, 276, 277, 278, 279, 292, 293, 294
Trevor, Sir John 132
Trinterud, L.J. 10, 21, 251, 252, 253
Trueman, C. 12, 20-1, 253
Tuckney, A. 129, 260, 277, 278
Twisse, William 113, 169, 170, 286
Tyacke, N. 167, 251, 283-4, 285, 286
Tyndale, Wiliam 20-1, 253
Underwood, T.L. 290
Ursinus 21, 22-3
Ussher, James 104, 184, 234, 269, 286
Vane, Sir Henry 125, 276-7
Venning, R. 240
Virgil 224
Vossius, Gerard 166, 284
Wakefield, G. 234, 299
Wallace, D.D. 286, 287

Walzer, M. 232, 299
Warwick, Earl of 263
Watts, M. 275, 279, 281, 289
Webster, John 98
Weld, Thomas 287
Wendel, F. 299
Wentworth 286
Wesley 230
Wharton, Lord 132, 195
Whichcote 62-3, 259, 260, 277
Whitaker, Thomas 225
Whitaker, William 184, 290
Whitefeild 27, 255
Whitgift, John 184, 290
Wilburn, P. 251
Wild, Robert 192, 291

Willoughby, Lord 132
Wilmot, John (Earl of Rochester) 99-100
Wink, Walter 266
Wood, Anthony 158, 162, 278, 282, 283, 291
Wood, H.G. 251
Wotton, Anthony 286
Wren, Matthew 176, 288-9
Wycliff 117
Xenophanes 224
Yates, John 286
Young, Michael B. 290
Young, Samuel 73, 88-9, 262, 265
Zwingli 21

Christian Focus Publications publishes biblically-accurate books for adults and children. The books in the adult range are published in three imprints.

Christian Heritage contains classic writings from the past.

Christian Focus contains popular works including biographies, commentaries, doctrine, and Christian living.

Mentor focuses on books written at a level suitable for Bible College and seminary students, pastors, and others; the imprint includes commentaries, doctrinal studies, examination of current issues, and church history.

For a free catalogue of all our titles, please write to
Christian Focus Publications,
Geanies House, Fearn,
Ross-shire, IV20 1TW, Great Britain

For details of our titles visit us on our web site
http://www.christianfocus.com

Steve Griffiths is an Anglican minister, serving an inner city congregation in the East End of London. He is also Advisor to the Bishop of Barking on Youth Issues. Steve is the author of a number of articles on historical theology and youth ministry and is Chief Editor of 'The Journal of Youth and Theology'. He serves on the Executive for the International Association for the Study of Youth Ministry and lectures regularly in both London and Oxford. Steve is married to Clare and they have one daughter, Rebekah.